Prai

The WISEST O

"Read, be surprised and become wiser."

—*Scientific American*

"Those with a keen interest in human behavior will devour this insightful look into our minds that also teaches how to apply these lessons to our own experiences."

—*Library Journal*

"The wisest ones in the room are, in fact, Tom Gilovich and Lee Ross. This is a powerful book that brings the best of psychology to bear on the way we live our lives."

—Malcolm Gladwell, bestselling author of *The Tipping Point,* *Blink, Outliers,* and most recently *David and Goliath*

"Two of the world's most brilliant social psychologists have distilled the field's wisdom into a few essential lessons for understanding the fabric of our everyday lives. This is the essential lecture that you never heard in college. Don't miss it a second time."

—Daniel Gilbert, professor of psychology at Harvard University and bestselling author of *Stumbling on Happiness*

"In *The Wisest One in the Room,* Gilovich and Ross weave social science, history, and anecdotes in a compelling way to help us understand human nature, where we make mistakes and how we might be able to live to our full potential."

—Dan Ariely, professor of psychology and behavioral economics at Duke University and bestselling author of, most recently, *Irrationally Yours*

"With deep insight about theory and research and compelling real-world stories, two great social psychologists explore human triumphs and shortcomings—from heroism and happiness to racism and human conflict. Gilovich and Ross will help you to be more persuasive and less subject to the wiles of marketers, and also better informed about the psychological dimensions of challenges we face as a society. If you want to be wiser, happier, and more successful (and who doesn't), this book is a must-read."

—Sonja Lyubomirsky, professor of psychology at
the University of California, Riverside, and
bestselling author of *The How of Happiness.*

"If you want to dramatically improve your 'insight quotient,' decision-making and understanding of your fellow humans—this is the book for you. It's a profound book, of immense personal utility, from two of the world's greatest social psychologists."

—Claude Steele, executive vice chancellor and provost
at the University of California, Berkeley

"This fine volume is essential reading if you want a deeper understanding of why people (you included) think, feel, and act, as they do . . . I came away from this remarkable work feeling wiser not only about my day-to-day life, but also about an issue to which I have devoted much of my career—escalating climate disruption and our continuing collective failure to address it."

—Paul R. Ehrlich, professor of population studies at
Stanford University and award-winning author of,
most recently, *Betrayal of Science and Reason*

The WISEST ONE in the ROOM

HOW YOU CAN BENEFIT FROM SOCIAL PSYCHOLOGY'S MOST POWERFUL INSIGHTS

THOMAS GILOVICH
and LEE ROSS

FREE PRESS

New York London Toronto Sydney New Delhi

*f*P

FREE PRESS
An Imprint of Simon & Schuster
1230 Avenue of the Americas
New York, NY 10020

First Free Press trade paperback edition December 2016

FREE PRESS and colophon are registered trademarks of
Simon & Schuster, Inc.

For information about special discounts for bulk purchases,
please contact Simon & Schuster Special Sales at 1-866-506-1949 or
business@simonandschuster.com.

The Simon & Schuster Speakers Bureau can bring authors to your
live event. For more information or to book an event contact the
Simon & Schuster Speakers Bureau at 1-866-248-3049 or
visit our website at www.simonspeakers.com.

1 3 5 7 9 10 8 6 4 2

The Library of Congress has cataloged the hardcover edition as follows:

Gilovich, Thomas
The wisest one in the room : how you can benefit from social psychology's
most powerful insights / Thomas Gilovich and Lee Ross.
pages cm
1. Insight. 2. Human behavior. 3. Social psychology. I. Ross, Lee. II. Title.
BF449.5.G55 2015
302—dc23   2015018053

ISBN 978-1-4516-7754-6
ISBN 978-1-4516-7755-3 (pbk)
ISBN 978-1-4516-7756-0 (ebook)

For Richard Nisbett

CONTENTS

CONTENTS

PREFACE

In late spring 1944, Allied forces were making final preparations for the momentous events of D-Day, the landing of troops on the five beaches of Normandy, code-named Utah, Omaha, Gold, Juno, and Sword. The invasion would take place in two phases: an assault by twenty-four thousand British, American, and Canadian airmen shortly after midnight and a massive amphibious landing of Allied infantry and armored divisions at 6:30 a.m. The British commander, General Bernard Montgomery, gave the officers who would lead the assault their final briefing—a tour de force performance, thorough in its content and impeccable in its delivery.

The Supreme Allied commander, General Dwight D. Eisenhower, known to all as "Ike," had assigned this task to "Monty" and did not do much talking himself in the final hours before the invasion. He did not reiterate details about the operation. Nor did he offer his own perspective on the larger significance of the operation or of the long struggle ahead—a struggle that would culminate in the defeat of the Third Reich. He simply walked around the room shaking hands with each and every man who would lead the assault, mindful, as they were, that many would not survive.

He recognized that their thoughts would be focused on the challenge that each of them would face in the next twenty-four hours, on the fates of their comrades-in-arms, and on the well-being of their families. He gave no hint that he was contemplating his own fate or future reputation. His wordless handshakes communicated to each

1

officer that he understood what *they* were thinking and feeling, and that he honored them for what they were about to risk and what they were about to experience. He was the wisest one in the room.[1]

Words of wisdom are easy to find. They are offered in books of quotations, desktop calendars, daily planners, and even bumper stickers. Advice is given to us, often unsolicited, by friends, relatives, and colleagues. We can look to sages for counsel about how to manage our personal finances (*Neither a borrower nor a lender be.* —William Shakespeare) or how to proceed in our careers (*Be nice to those on the way up; they're the same folks you'll meet on the way down.* —Walter Winchell). People who aspire to power can seek guidance from a Renaissance Italian diplomat (*It is wise to flatter important people.* —Niccolò Machiavelli), and those who have the more modest goal of "winning friends and influencing people" can find similar advice from a bestselling twentieth-century author (*Be lavish in praise.* —Dale Carnegie) or a U.S. National Medal of Freedom winner (*People will forget what you said, people will forget what you did, but people will never forget how you made them feel.* —Maya Angelou).

We're given guidance about how to achieve our goals (*The best way to get what you want is to deserve what you want.* —Charles Munger) and, from the Sufi poets of old, advice about how to deal with difficult times (*This too shall pass*). We can even find all-encompassing prescriptions for the meaning of life and the path to personal fulfillment (*The* meaning *of life is to find your gift; the* purpose *of life is to give it* away) from sages whose names have been lost to us.

Insight and skill in dealing with human conflict have long been seen as particularly important elements of wisdom. We see this in the Old Testament tale of King Solomon resolving a custody battle and in the success of Nelson Mandela, two and a half millennia later, in achieving a bloodless end to apartheid.

There are many different kinds of wisdom, as these quotations attest. Some people are Buddha wise, others Bubba wise, and still others Buffett wise. It is telling that Webster's dictionary distinguishes three types of wisdom: (1) *knowledge*, or accumulated philosophic or scientific learning; (2) *insight*, or the ability to discern inner qualities and relationships; and (3) *judgment*, or good sense.

This emphasis on discernment and good sense highlights the fact that being wise is not the same thing as being smart. By "the wisest one in the room" we do not mean the person with the highest IQ or the greatest command of facts and figures. The smartest one in the room may lack insight about human affairs and display poor judgment in both day-to-day interactions and the larger pursuit of a rewarding and meaningful life. Indeed, *The Smartest Guys in the Room** is an account of the people at the top of Enron, the failed energy corporation, who by all accounts were extremely smart and very sophisticated in their financial manipulations. But their arrogance, greed, and shortsightedness got the better of them (as well as their company's employees and shareholders), making it clear that they were anything but wise. What they lacked was not just a moral compass, but wisdom about what goals are truly worth pursuing and the means by which they are best pursued.

A critical difference between wisdom and intelligence is that wisdom demands some insight and effectiveness around people. Intelligence does not. A person can be "smart" without being smart about people, but it makes no sense to say someone is wise if the person has no feel for people or no understanding of their hopes, fears, passions, and drives. You can be a savvy investor or an accurate weather forecaster even if you aren't particularly savvy about people, but you can't be a wise *person* if you aren't wise about people. Montgomery's preinvasion briefing may have been more intelligently crafted and more skillfully delivered than any that Eisenhower ever gave. But it was Ike's understanding of the needs of his officers, and his deftness in attending to those needs, that testify to his wisdom.

---

*McLean, Bethany, and Elkind, Peter. (2003). *The Smartest Guys in the Room: The Amazing Rise and Scandalous Fall of Enron*. New York: Penguin.

Any analysis of wisdom must reflect the fact that the most important things in life involve other people. That is true for the executive trying to run a Fortune 500 company, the candidate seeking public office, the artist trying to create work that will speak to the ages, or the single mother trying to get her child through the tumultuous adolescent years. It's true even for the software engineer who merely wants to be left alone to write code for most of the day or the poker player who just wants to feel the rush that comes from using her wits with money on the line. Our exploration of what makes someone the wisest one in the room therefore focuses on human psychology—on *social* psychology in particular. Wisdom requires understanding the most common and most powerful influences on people's behavior. It also requires knowing when and why people get off track and end up making faulty judgments, erroneous predictions, and poor decisions. To be wise, one must be *psych*-wise.

Wisdom also requires perspective, something that runs through all three components of Webster's definition: knowledge, insight, and judgment. A wise person is able to put individual events in perspective and take a broader view of the issue at hand. Eisenhower was able to get beyond his concern with the overall scope and success of the mission and connect with his men on what was at the forefront of their minds—their safety, their families, and what the first hours of the invasion might be like.

In this respect as well, the difference between wisdom and intelligence is noteworthy. Intelligence involves taking the information available and processing it effectively—thinking about it logically and drawing sound conclusions. That is certainly an important component of wisdom. But a wise person does something else—a wise person goes *beyond* the information that is immediately available. Wisdom involves knowing when the information available is insufficient for the problem at hand. It involves the recognition that how things are right now might seem very different down the road.

We became convinced that this is the right time for a book like this because of the tremendous progress that's been made in two fields that deal with these two critically important components of wisdom—the field of social psychology and that of judgment and decision making. It has been our privilege to have worked in these two fields for a combined eighty years, and an honor to have contributed to them along the way. Of all the scientific disciplines, it is social psychology that focuses most directly on understanding the thoughts, feelings, choices, and actions of the average person. Important findings have poured out of social psychologists' research labs over the past forty years, providing insights into human behavior that anyone seeking to become wiser should know.

The field of judgment and decision making, meanwhile, has illuminated how and why people are quick to draw conclusions when they would be better served by stepping back and looking at things from a broader perspective. This field has undergone a revolution over the past forty years, a revolution that has made it clear that judgment and decision making have a lot in common with perception. Like perception, they are subject to illusions. Anyone aspiring to greater wisdom needs to know when to be on the lookout for these illusions and how to steer clear of them.

The aim of this book is to help you be wiser so that you can deal more effectively with your employees and coworkers, have an easier time getting your children to realize their potential, or resist the temptations crafted by slick advertisements and clever marketers.

But the book has a higher aim as well. Aristotle maintained that wisdom entails an understanding of causes, of why things are the way they are. To him, a knowledgeable person knows a lot about *what* and *how*, but a wise person understands *why*. Although we trust that you will gain a great deal of practical wisdom from reading this book, we also hope to give you a deeper appreciation of the broader principles that provide the foundation for that practical advice. In so doing, we hope you will gain a better appreciation of why people act the way they do and why we all have such a hard time getting beyond our narrow perspectives. In the end, you should have a better sense of which pithy quotations are worth attending to and which are best ignored, and a deeper understanding of the advice offered by the sages and leaders we most revere.

The Wisest One in the Room is not a textbook. Many excellent textbooks in psychology are available for anyone who wants to explore the breadth and depth of psychological science. If you've read one of those textbooks or taken a course in psychology, you will recognize how much we omit or mention only briefly here. We have chosen instead to discuss a small number of specific insights that we believe are especially important components of wisdom. They are the ones that should give you the deepest understanding of *why* the things happening around you unfold the way they do. They are also the insights that should be the most useful in understanding and influencing the people in your life, dealing with the conflicts that inevitably come with living and working with other people, and making better decisions about your time, money, health, and relationships.

Our promise to explore important insights about why people behave as they do raises an obvious question: Haven't human beings evolved over countless millennia to deal effectively with each other? Don't people therefore already know most of what there is to be known about people's motives and inclinations, and about what can be done to channel behavior in the most productive direction? Haven't wise observers of the human condition already passed down the insights about human frailties that we most need to know?

To be sure, human beings, like all other animals, already know a great deal about human behavior—their own and that of those around them. We all know that behavior is purposeful and goal driven and that people generally try to maximize pleasure and minimize pain. We also know a lot about the effects of specific drives and emotions such as hunger, thirst, sex, and fear, as well as subtler ones such as the need to feel good about ourselves and the desire to be liked and respected.

Indeed, we all know quite a bit of lay social psychology. We know about the discomfort people feel when their opinions and tastes deviate from the norms of their group. We know about the importance of good parenting and good role models and the advantages of good education. We are aware of some of the ways in which judgments and decisions (at least the judgments and decisions of other people) can be distorted by self-interest, previous experience and expectations, and religious teachings and ideological indoctrination. Without such knowledge, social life would be chaotic and unmanageable.

Our own immersion in both academic and applied psychology, and our continuing reflections on our own misjudgments and unwise decisions over the years, have convinced us that some of the most important insights about human behavior are by no means obvious. This conviction stems from provocative research findings that contradict our everyday assumptions—findings that force us to recalibrate our impressions about what is likely to matter a lot or only a little in determining how people behave, and what is likely to be effective or ineffective in trying to solve particular types of problems.

Other insights that we will discuss are not exactly new. They involve things that we recognize in some particular contexts, without fully appreciating the breadth of their applicability. Still others involve patterns that we recognize in others, but not in ourselves or those who share our views. Ultimately you will have to judge the usefulness of the insights and research that we'll describe. But to give you a sense of what's to come, we preview a few examples of the kinds of phenomena and research findings that can make anyone who knows about them—and the psychological principles underlying them— notably wiser.

Do you believe that we, the authors of this book, can discern your political views?

We begin chapter 1 with just such a demonstration, one that we think you will find convincing. When you understand the psychology behind our accomplishment, you will have a better understanding of interpersonal and intergroup conflict, a topic we pick up again in chapter 7.

In Denmark (as in the United States), motorists can make their organs available for transplantation in the event of premature death by signing the back of their driver's license. Only about 4 percent of Danes do so. In Sweden, drivers are told that their organs will be made available for donation unless they indicate on the back of their license that they do not want to do so. What percentage of Swedes would you estimate make their organs available for medical use by not putting their signature on that line?

If your estimate was somewhere in the neighborhood of 4 percent or even 40 percent, you are way off. You will find the answer in chapter 2, where we discuss the impact of default options. Then, in chapter 3, you will learn more about why this and other seemingly small differences in the way choices are offered can have such big effects.

Everyone knows that rewards and punishments "work." But do big rewards and punishments work better than small ones? The answer—if your goal is to change not just immediate overt behavior but sustained motivation and underlying feelings about the activities in question—is no. When it comes to rewards and punishments, often less is more.

In chapter 4, you will read about the classic studies that elaborate on this important insight and learn more about the primacy of behavior—and why attitude change frequently follows behavior change rather than vice versa.

Research participants were given data about the number of times tennis players worked out strenuously the day before a match and then won their subsequent matches, the number of times they did so and lost, the number of times they did not work out strenuously and nonetheless won, and the number of times they failed to work out strenuously and lost. One group was asked to determine on the basis of that information whether working out strenuously made players more likely to win; another group was asked whether working out strenuously made them more likely to lose. Both groups, strangely, said yes.

Understanding this paradoxical result involves an appreciation of what one psychologist called the "mother of all biases." Chapter 5 gives you some insight into the ways this and other biases can narrow the way you evaluate information, distort your judgment, and undermine your decisions.

If given a choice, should you add a brief, somewhat unpleasant experience to a very unpleasant one? How much would doubling the length of a pleasant vacation add to your long-term feelings about how enjoyable it was?

The answers to these questions in chapter 6 (yes to the first; virtually nothing to the second), will give you some useful pointers about steps you can take to maximize your own happiness.

Jewish Israeli students took part in a negotiation exercise with an Israeli Arab about the disbursement of funds for a project that would benefit both sides of the ongoing Israeli-Palestinian conflict. After some time, they received a final offer from their negotiation counterpart who, unbeknownst to them, was an experimental confederate who made the same offer in each negotiation. A statement that the researchers sometimes added and sometimes omitted at the outset of the negotiation raised the likelihood that the offer would be accepted from 35 to 85 percent. What statement, which did not involve any change in the terms being proposed or the costs of not reaching an agreement, had that much impact?

The answer to this question is provided in chapter 7, where we focus on the problem of intractable conflict. What psychological processes create barriers to mutually beneficial agreements, and what can be done to overcome them?

Several recent studies show that the academic performance of black and Hispanic students (and female students in science and engineering programs) can be improved through simple and inexpensive psych-wise interventions involving mere words. What are those interventions, what barriers do they address, and why do they have so much impact?

You will find the surprising answers to these questions in chapter 8. There we discuss the tough problem of reducing academic underachievement—and then move on in chapter 9 to the even tougher global problem of dealing with global climate change.

Our book is organized in two parts. Each of the first five chapters deals with a general principle of human behavior that can add to your understanding of a wide range of events and make you more psychwise in dealing with ordinary and not-so-ordinary challenges. They are followed by four chapters that use these principles to shed light on particularly important concerns we face as individuals and as a society: the pursuit of happiness, overcoming barriers to intractable conflict, the challenge of educating disadvantaged and underperforming students, and the even greater challenges posed by the threat of catastrophic climate change. We are convinced that reading about the research and insights contained in these nine chapters will help you to be wiser in the way you understand the people and events you encounter, and wiser in the way you deal with the challenges that are sure to come your way—perhaps even help you to become the wisest in the room.

—Thomas Gilovich and Lee Ross

Part 1

PILLARS OF WISDOM

1

The Objectivity Illusion

In the early decades of the twentieth century, Albert Einstein dramatically challenged our understanding of the world in which we live. His revolutionary theories of special and general relativity suggested that time and space are linked in a manner best comprehended not through our subjective experience but through mathematical formulas and imaginative thought experiments. He tried to imagine, for example, what would happen if we were in a vehicle that was moving at nearly the speed of light. His famous $E = mc^2$ formula alerted us to the amount of energy that could be produced from the conversion of matter; but the same formula, when rearranged, suggested that matter itself could be seen as condensed energy. Indeed, in one of his many frequently quoted statements, Einstein went as far as to maintain that "reality is an illusion."

Scholars have debated exactly what he meant by that assertion. Most agree that he was alerting us to the ways in which experience is dictated by the perspective and circumstances of the perceiver. But for our purposes, the quotation serves as a reminder that what we experience in our everyday perceptions is not just a simple registering

of what is "out there." Rather, it is the product of an interaction between the strange and complex stuff that resulted from the "big bang"
(the latest theory being that the stuff in question consists of vibrating
strings of unimaginably tiny particles that somehow acquire mass as
they interact with fields of energy) and the same stuff of which we
ourselves are made. It is that interaction that produces our subjective
experience of a world containing the solid three-dimensional objects
we touch, the sounds we hear, the wide palette of colors we see, and
the broad range of odors we detect.

Another twentieth-century genius, the comedian George Carlin,
once asked his audience: "Have you ever noticed that anybody driving slower than you is an idiot, and anyone going faster than you is a
maniac?" About two decades ago, the two of us began to consider the
connection between Einstein's message about reality and Carlin's wry
question. That connection, we believe, takes us to the very heart of
human psychology and much of human folly. We human beings not
only reflexively assume that our perceptions bear a one-to-one corre-
spondence to reality; we often go a step further and presume that our
own personal perceptions are especially accurate and objective.

To help you appreciate the nature of this objectivity illusion, let us
engage in some political mind reading.

Specifically, let us show you that we can discern your political
views from the mere fact that you are reading this book. We can con-
fidently predict that:

> You see yourself as being about as politically liberal as it is
> reasonable to be. On most issues, you see people who are to
> the left of you as a bit naïve, as more idealistic than realistic,
> and overly inclined to political correctness. At the same time,
> you see those who are to the right of you as rather selfish and
> uncaring, as somewhat narrow-minded and not fully in touch
> with the lives that many people live and the problems they face
> in today's world.

Does this description capture the way you see yourself politically? We are confident that it does. The trick is that the political portrait we painted *must* apply not only to you and other readers of this book but to virtually anyone else. For if you felt that the people to the left of you were more attuned to reality than you are, you would have already moved in their direction. The same is true about people on your right.

In short, you (and everyone else) see your own political beliefs and leanings as the most *realistic* response to the specific times in which we live and the particular problems we face. You also see your views and positions as attuned to the realities of human nature. What's more, given that you believe your political views are the ones most grounded in reality, it follows that those who do not share your views—especially those far removed from you on the political spectrum—are necessarily less realistic than you are. They lack your objectivity. They are more prone to seeing political matters through the prism of their ideology, self-interest, upbringing, or some other distorting influence.

Remember Carlin's observation about your views of your fellow motorists. Your first response was likely to be, "As a matter of fact, I *have* noticed that about other drivers." But after a moment's reflection, you grasp Carlin's point: Since you adjust your speed to what you consider appropriate to the prevailing road conditions, anyone driving more slowly *must* be driving *too* slowly, and anyone driving faster *must* be driving *too* quickly. The conviction that you see things as they truly are and those who see things differently are therefore getting something wrong is inevitable—at least as an initial reflexive response.

Everyday experience offers many examples of the same basic phenomenon. When your spouse says, "It's freezing in here," and turns up the thermostat, even though you feel quite comfortable, you wonder what is making your spouse feel so cold when the temperature is just fine. Conversely, when you are freezing and your spouse or someone else says the temperature is just fine, you wonder why they are so oblivious to the *actual* temperature. You don't immediately consider the possibility that *you* are the one being overly sensitive, or insensitive, and that the other person is the one responding appropriately to the "real" room temperature.

Similarly, when you say the music is "too soft," or "too loud," you believe that you're making a statement about the music and not about yourself—or, rather, not about the complex interaction between the sound output, your auditory receptors, and whatever experiences have shaped your tastes and preferences. When you claim that the food is "too spicy" or "too bland," you believe you are noting something about the food rather than your taste buds or the cuisine of your childhood and culture. And when others disagree—when they say the music *you* enjoy is a lot of noise and not up to the standards of *their* youth, or when they question how anyone could like *that* food (or *that* art, or *that* style of clothing), you wonder what's responsible for the oddity of their tastes.

To be sure, you can probably think of counterexamples: times when you conclude (typically after some reflection) that you are the one who's anomalous. You conclude that you're particularly sensitive to the cold because you grew up in Costa Rica. Or you think your aversion to meatloaf might have its origin in the dry and tasteless recipe you were forced to eat on your frequent visits to your grandmother. Fair enough. These exceptions are real and important, but they are just that—exceptions. They result from the tendency we all have, especially when young, to ruminate when we feel or think differently from our peers about matters of taste in things like art or music or enjoyment of particular leisure activities. As adolescents we might have even wondered, "Why can't I be like everyone else?" As we grow older, such ruminations tend to shift from what is wrong or unique about *me* to what's wrong with *them*.

But ruminations aside, our phenomenological experience is that we perceive things as they are—that the room really is cold and that Grandma's concoction really is awful. In the remainder of this chapter, we examine how the tendency to treat our sense of what's out there as a matter of objective perception rather than subjective interpretation lies at the root of many types of human folly.

Psychologists, following the lead of Lee and his colleagues, refer to the seductive and compelling sense that one sees the world the way it is, and not as a subjective take on the world, as *naïve realism*. Recognizing that you and everyone else is a naïve realist is a vital step in becoming a wiser person. It will make you wiser about all sorts of experiences you will encounter in your daily life. It can help you deal more effectively with disagreements with friends, family members, and coworkers. It will also make you wiser about political and social issues of great significance at a time when our nation and our troubled world are beset with disagreements and conflicts. But to fully understand how an appreciation of naïve realism can promote the type of wisdom we have in mind, we must back up and ask a more basic question. What gives rise to the conviction that there is a one-to-one relationship between what we experience and what is "out there"?

Stealth Workers

One of the main jobs of the three pounds of neural circuitry we carry around in our skulls is to make sense of the world around us. That circuitry determines, effortlessly and with dispatch, whether a surface affords walking, an object is benign or threatening, a movement was intentional or random, or a face is novel or familiar. Most of this sense making is done through mental processes that operate without our awareness, leaving us with the *sense* but no awareness of the *making*. A host of stealthy mental processes works away without our knowledge or guidance, rendering sensible the barrage of conflicting and confounding information that confronts us. This lack of conscious access to our sense-making machinery leads to confusion between what

Immanuel Kant called "the thing as it is" (*das Ding an sich*) and "the thing as we know it" (*das Ding für uns*).

When we see a toaster, smell a delicious aroma, or detect a threatening gesture, it feels as if we're experiencing the stimulus as it is, not as we've constructed it. Our own role in the construction of our sensory experiences is perhaps easiest to appreciate when it comes to color vision. It appears to us that the apples we see are red, the oceans blue, and the tall arches near fast food establishments yellow. But the colors we see are not simply "out there" in the objects we perceive; they are the product of the interaction between what's out there and the functioning of our sensory systems. Our experience of color is the result of the activation of particular photoreceptors that are differentially sensitive to various wavelengths of light striking the retina, as well as further processing of the complex pattern of activation that reverberates higher up in the brain.

It is a telling fact about how thoroughly the brain creates this illusion of red apples, blue oceans, and yellow arches that we commonly say that dogs are color blind (actually they do see colors, but the colors they see are neither as rich nor as varied as we humans see them), yet we never say that we are "odor blind." We don't acknowledge that the world really is smellier than it seems, but that we, because of the limitations of our olfactory organs and brains, are able to detect and distinguish only a tiny fraction of the odors that dogs (and almost all other mammals) readily perceive.

Educated adults are aware of the basic facts of color vision, but that awareness in no way alters the perception that color inheres in objects. Nor does it stop us from talking about orange sunsets, blue eyes, and auburn tresses. And when it comes to more complex cognitive events, we are even less aware of our own contribution to our experience. We effortlessly fill in gaps in the sensory signals available to us, without any awareness that there are gaps to be filled—or that we did the filling.

Remarkably, the filling-in can be driven not just by prior information and expectations, but also by information we receive only after the fact. In one telling study, research participants heard sentences with the first part of a key word omitted (which we indicate by "*"), and with different endings of the sentence presented to different participants. Thus, some participants heard "The *eel was on the *axle*," and others heard "The *eel was on the *orange*." In both cases, the participants reported hearing a coherent sentence—"The *wh*eel was on the *axle*" in the first case and "The *p*eel was on the *orange*" in the second—without ever consciously registering the gap. Nor did it register that they themselves had provided the *wh* or *p* they "heard" in order to make sense of the sentence.[1]

Confusing our mental models of the things out there in the world with the things themselves is not of great consequence when everyone else has the same mental model, as they tend to do for apples, the sky, or McDonald's arches. Nor is it a problem when we all manage to edit out the same speech disfluencies. But this confusion can have less benign consequences when dealing with social problems and policies. This is particularly true when two parties bring very different experiences, priorities, and beliefs to the task of sense making. In such cases, perceptions of what is fair, what is sacred, or who is responsible for the woes of the world are bound to vary. Disagreements are likely to lead to accusations of bad faith or bad character, making those disagreements even harder to resolve. It is in these circumstances that the wisest in the room recognize that their take on "reality" is just that—a *take*, and not an objective assessment of what "just is."

They Saw a Protest

You're driving down the road and see a group of police officers trying to break up a protest in front of a reproductive health clinic. Does it seem that the police are overreacting, curtailing the protesters' right of assembly? Or is the protest getting out of hand, requiring deft intervention by the police? A remarkable study by Yale Law professor

Dan Kahan and his colleagues shows just how much your answers to these questions are likely to be influenced by your political views. Mind you, it is not simply that your political leanings are likely to influence your *opinions* of the actions of the police or the protestors. They also influence what you *see* the police and protesters doing.

Kahan and colleagues showed participants segments of an actual conflict between protesters and police that took place in Cambridge, Massachusetts, in 2009.[2] Half of the participants were told that the demonstrators were protesting the availability of abortion in front of a reproductive health center; the other half were told they were protesting the military's "don't ask, don't tell" policy in front of a campus military recruitment center. The participants had earlier filled out a survey of their political attitudes and values, and so the investigators had a good sense of whether they were likely to be sympathetic or opposed to a protest against abortion rights or a protest against the don't ask, don't tell policy.

The participants with different political outlooks "saw" very different actions on the part of the protesters and police. Three-quarters of the supporters of women's reproductive rights saw the protesters blocking access to the health center; only a quarter of those from the opposite side of the political spectrum saw them doing so. When participants were told the action took place in front of a military recruitment center, these judgments were reversed: Three-quarters of the more conservative respondents saw the protesters blocking access to the center, compared to only 40 percent of those from the other side of the spectrum. A similar disparity in perceptions was observed when participants were asked whether the protesters had screamed in the faces of those trying to enter the health center vs. the recruitment center.*

---

* Kahan and colleagues' paper, and the title of this section of the chapter, allude to an earlier study by Albert Hastorf and Hadley Cantril ("They Saw a Game") that found similarly divergent perceptions of the actions on the field during a Princeton-Dartmouth football game on the part of those rooting for Princeton vs. Dartmouth.[3]

The investigators did not ask their participants to discuss the case. We wish they had. It would have been interesting—and informative—to see how they would have dealt with their very different assessments of what they had "seen." We are all used to dealing with people who have different values and opinions than we do, and while discussions about those differences are not particularly enjoyable, they are usually civilized and we generally make some effort to understand our differences. But when we are challenged about what we consider "the facts," the discussion heats up and civility often goes out the window.

Biased Perceptions of Consensus

At the end of *Star Trek III: The Search for Spock*, after the heroes from the *Starship Enterprise* have spent more than ninety minutes trying to retrieve their Vulcan friend Spock's body for proper burial on his home planet, a resurrected Spock gratefully says, "You came back for me." James Kirk, the captain of the *Enterprise*, thereupon modestly dismisses any assumed heroism with the assertion "You would have done the same for me."

Here on earth, this "you would have done the same" conviction is remarkably common. We witness it whenever a person-on-the-street who has administered CPR, saved a drowning child, or run into a burning building to rescue an elderly resident is interviewed. "Anyone would have done the same thing" is the usual reply. We also see it on the other side of the moral spectrum, when those guilty of wrongdoing defend their actions. During the 2005 congressional inquiry into the doping scandals in Major League Baseball, for example, admitted steroid user Mark McGwire said, "Anybody who was in my shoes that had those scenarios set out in front of them would have done the same exact thing."[4] The assumption is so common that it serves as the title of a track from the hip-hop trio Naughty by Nature, "Would've Done the Same for Me."

But is the assumption valid? Or does naïve realism lead us to overestimate the degree to which others share our views and behavioral choices? It does indeed. Because people have the conviction that they see things as they are—that their beliefs, preferences, and responses follow from an essentially unmediated perception of objects, events, and issues—it follows that other rational, reasonable people should reach the same conclusions, provided they have been exposed to the same information. This seemingly reasonable leap gives rise to a phenomenon that Lee and his colleagues dubbed the *false consensus effect*: People tend to think that their beliefs, opinions, and actions enjoy greater consensus than is really the case. More precisely, people who have a given opinion or preference tend to think that it is more common than do those with the opposite opinion or preference.[5]

People who prefer Italian to French cinema think their preference is more common than French film enthusiasts do.[6] People who are guilty of particular misdeeds think that those deeds are more common than people who wouldn't dream of such transgressions.[7] Liberals think that there is more support for their candidates, and their views on contentious social and political issues, than conservatives do, and vice versa.[8] And voters from both sides of the political spectrum think that nonvoters would have voted for their candidate if they had only cast their ballots.*[9]

In a vivid illustration of this phenomenon, Lee and his colleagues asked student volunteers to walk around campus wearing a large

---

* The false consensus effect does not imply that people always believe they are in the majority. Snake owners and skydivers do not believe that their preferences are shared by most other people. But they do tend to believe that more people like snakes and jumping out of perfectly functioning airplanes than do people who'd rather own a dog or people who choose to spend their leisure time golfing.

sandwich-board sign bearing a message (e.g., "Eat at Joe's") and to note the reaction of people they encountered. The students, however, were given the opportunity to decline the invitation to participate if they wished (and return for a later study instead). Immediately after agreeing or refusing to participate, the students were asked to estimate the frequency of agreement on the part of other participants and to make inferences about the personal attributes of someone who would accept the experimenter's invitation and someone who would refuse it.

As predicted, the consensus estimates and trait inferences were very different for the two types of participants. Those who agreed to wear the sign estimated agreement to be more common than refusal and less revealing of the person's personal attributes. Those who refused to wear it thought that refusal would be more common than agreement and assumed that agreeing to wear the sign said more about a person's personality.

It is easy to appreciate the role that naïve realism played here. Those who imagined wearing the sign in benign terms—walking relatively unnoticed, explaining to acquaintances that one is taking part in a psychology experiment (and being complimented for being a "good sport")—would be inclined to agree to the experimenters' request and to think that most other "normal" students would also agree. For such individuals, the refusal to undertake this task and have such experiences would seem to reflect uncooperativeness, uptightness, or some other departure from normality.

By contrast, those who imagined what it would be like in less positive terms (e.g., walking through throngs of giggling, finger-pointing students; seeing acquaintances shake their heads and avert their gazes as they wordlessly hurry off) would be likely to refuse the experimenters' request and expect others to refuse. For them, agreeing to wear the sign would seem more reflective of something atypical or negative (e.g., submissiveness or inclination to show off and make a fool of oneself).

The essential dynamic here was recognized long ago by the ground-breaking social psychologist Solomon Asch, who stressed the importance of distinguishing between different "judgments of the object" and different "objects of judgment."[10] When sizing up the responses of their peers, people often fail to take into account the possibility that their peers may be responding to a very different set of "facts" and "circumstances."

Evidence for this dynamic was offered in a series of studies that Tom conducted.[11] If the false consensus effect arises from the failure to recognize that other people may be responding to very different "objects of judgment," the effect should be greatest when the issue at hand offers the most latitude for different interpretations and for fleshing out details and resolving ambiguities. To test this idea, a panel of judges was asked to rate the items used in Lee's previous research on the false consensus effect in terms of their ambiguity and latitude for different interpretations. As anticipated, items that offered the most room for different interpretations ("Are you competitive?" "What percentage of your peers are competitive?") yielded much larger false consensus effects than those for which there was little room for different interpretation ("Are you a first-born or later-born child?" "What percentage of your peers are first-born children?").

Tom went on to conduct a study inspired by the intense arguments music fans can get into over the relative merits of different eras of popular music. Participants in this study were first asked whether they preferred 1960s or 1980s music and then were asked to estimate the percentage of their peers who would have each preference. As predicted, those who preferred 1960s music thought that more people would share that preference than did those who preferred 1980s music. Conversely, those who preferred the 1980s music thought that more people would share their preference than did those who preferred 1960s music.

The study then zeroed in on the source of these different assessments by asking the participants what particular examples of music they had in mind when they offered their assessments. Those who preferred the music of the 1960s and expected most of their peers to do likewise offered examples of music from the 1960s that independent judges rated highly (the Beatles, the Rolling Stones) and music from the 1980s that independent judges did not like as much (Judas Priest, John Mellencamp). Those who preferred 1980s music listed vastly different examples (Herman's Hermits and the Ventures as 1960s music and Bruce Springsteen and Michael Jackson as 1980s music). Participants' preferences, in other words, were certainly a reflection of different musical tastes. But they were also a reflection of the particular examples they happened to generate when answering the question they were asked, and they failed to recognize their own role in fleshing out the two categories when estimating the likely responses of their peers.

This same dynamic plays out in the domain of political discourse. Issues and events that are the object of social, political, or ethical controversy are bound to be construed differently by different individuals. This was illustrated by the study of what people on different sides of the political spectrum saw in a clash between protesters and police. It is also illustrated by the different reactions on the part of the political Left and Right when it comes to the abortion issue, the use of lethal force by the police, and ongoing debates about the treatment of prisoners at Guantánamo Bay.

When Fox News anchors proclaim that the United States should use enhanced interrogation techniques and that those who say otherwise are putting the country at risk, they have in mind harsh physical treatment of those who are indeed determined to kill as many innocent civilians as possible. But when the talking heads at MSNBC take their very different stance, they have in mind the torture of minor al-Qaeda functionaries or innocent individuals who were accused of misdeeds by someone with a personal score to settle.

To be sure, those on the Left and Right would likely disagree about the use of specific interrogation techniques even when an individual's exact links to a terrorist network are known with certainty. When Dick Cheney says, for example, "I'm more concerned with the bad guys who got out and released [from Guantánamo] than I am with the few that, in fact, were innocent,"[12] he is articulating a set of values that few on the Left would endorse. But disagreements on this issue are heightened, and attributions about those on the other side become more malignant, when, in Asch's memorable language, the participants in the debate are responding to "different objects of judgment."

This failure to recognize that those with different views may be responding to very different objects of judgment can thus fuel misunderstanding and prolong conflict. It leads disputants to make unwarranted, highly negative inferences about each other's values, beliefs, compassion, or sincerity—inferences that can serve only to intensify the conflict at hand. Individuals and groups involved in conflict are often urged to walk in one another's shoes and try to see things through one another's glasses. Such footwear and eyewear exhortations are easy to offer but difficult to follow. But the wisest ones in the room can at least try to distinguish disagreements about facts and interpretations from disagreements about values and preferences.

Biased Perceptions of Objectivity and Bias

Many Americans went to bed on November 7, 2000, thinking that Al Gore had just been elected president. But when they awoke the next morning, they learned that George W. Bush had inched ahead of Gore in the crucial state of Florida with its twenty-five electoral votes, giving him enough votes to stake a claim to the presidency.

Because Bush's margin of victory in Florida was so small (less than half a percent of the votes cast), a vigorous legal battle ensued between the rival campaigns, leading the Florida Supreme Court to order a manual recount of all ballots in the state. The very next day, however, the U.S. Supreme Court granted a stay of the enforcement of the Florida court's decision. And a few days after that, the U.S. Supreme Court blocked the recount altogether, with the majority arguing that allowing the vote to go forward would violate the equal protection clause of the Fourteenth Amendment.

Democrats were quick to criticize the decision and claim bias on the part of the prevailing justices in the 5–4 decision that split perfectly along liberal-conservative lines. As one legal scholar observed, "I do not know a single person who believes that if the parties were reversed, if Gore were challenging a recount ordered by a Republican Florida Supreme Court ... [the majority] ... would have reached for a startling and innovative principle of constitutional law to hand Gore the victory."[13] What seemed to many to be especially suspicious was that the conservative majority on the Court was suddenly willing to insert federal authority in this case despite their frequently expressed reservations about judicial activism and their advocacy of states' rights and a narrow interpretation of the equal protection clause.

While most Democrats thought the majority's decision was tainted by ideological and motivational bias, the five justices who wrote the opinion didn't see it that way. They insisted that they were applying the law in an even-handed fashion. Shortly after the decision, for example, Justice Clarence Thomas told a group of students in Washington, D.C., that the decision was not in any way influenced by partisanship.[14] Justice Antonin Scalia has been even more dismissive of any such claim, telling an audience at Wesleyan University to "get over it."[15]

Research has shown that the five majority justices in *Bush v. Gore* are hardly exceptional in this regard. Lee and one of his former stu-

dents, Emily Pronin, asked people about how susceptible they were
to a host of biases that plague human judgment. Their respondents
were told, for example, "People show a 'self-serving' tendency in the
way they view their academic or job performance. That is, they tend
to take credit for success but deny responsibility for failure; they see
their successes as the result of personal qualities, like drive or ability,
but their failures as the result of external factors, like unreasonable
work requirements or inadequate instruction." They then rated how
prone they and their peers were to this and seventeen other common
failings of judgment.

You can probably anticipate their responses. Just as the average
person (especially the average liberal) harbors doubts about the objectivity of the conservative majority in the Florida recount case, the
respondents in this study thought that their peers were decidedly
more susceptible to bias than they themselves were.[16] Bias, in short,
is much easier to recognize in others than in oneself. Or, as noted
in Matthew 7:3 of the King James Bible, "Why beholdest thou the
mote that is in thy brother's eye but considerest not the beam that is
in thine own eye?"

An important first step in achieving wisdom, then, is recognizing
that bias is not something that afflicts only the eyes of others. It can
distort our own views as well. It's not simply that we're blind to our
own biases because we're defensive or want to think well of ourselves.
Those motives exist, as we discuss further in chapter 3. But they are
not the whole story. The deeper problem is that when we introspect,
we find no phenomenological trace of self-interested bias in the way
we've considered the pertinent facts and arguments. We end up convinced that although our conclusions are in accord with our self-
interest or the best interests of our group, those considerations played
little, if any, role in how we evaluated the evidence. We insist that it
just happens that the most objective conclusion is one that serves us
(and people like us) best.

Naïve realism has the most impact when the gap between our

own views and those of someone who disagrees with us is most pronounced. This was clearly demonstrated in a simple study the two of
us conducted with Emily Pronin. We asked a large sample of participants to fill out a survey indicating their positions on various issues
such as affirmative action, capital punishment, and abortion rights
and how much they approved of various prominent political figures
and media sources.

We then collected these surveys and redistributed them at random
to other participants. Next, we asked the participants to rate how similar the views of the person whose questionnaire they had received
were to their own views. Finally, we asked them to assess the extent
to which they felt that that person's views, as well as their own views,
reflected various "considerations." Some of the considerations listed
were ones that are generally regarded as reasonable and valid, such as
"attention to fact," "concern with justice," and appropriate attention
to "long-term consequences." Others specified particular biases such
as "desire for peer approval," "wishful thinking," and "political cor-
rectness."

The results, depicted in figure 1.1, were clear and dramatic. They
also provide some perspective when we see liberals bitterly complain-
ing about the views expressed on Fox News, or conservatives about
what they see and hear on liberal media outlets. The more the other
person's views differed from the respondents', the more the other's
views were chalked up to bias rather than rational considerations (the
shaded bars in the figure).[17]

Tellingly, the level of disagreement did not exert much influence
on the degree to which participants felt their own views reflected
valid considerations rather than bias (the unshaded bars in the figure). Nor did marked disagreement make them particularly open to
the possibility that they had been less than objective. On the contrary,
when the disagreement was greatest, participants not only tended to
be especially harsh in their assessment of the other individual's views,
they also tended to be especially generous in how they assessed the

rationality of their own views. In all, it is hard to imagine more direct support for Benjamin Franklin's observation that "most men ... think themselves in possession of all truth, and that wherever others differ from them, it is so far error."[18]

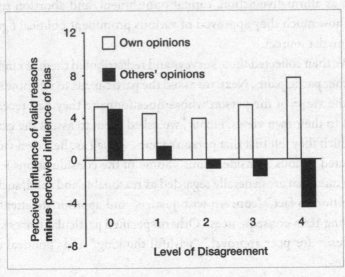

Figure 1.1. The shaded bars depict respondents' assessments of how much others' opinions are influenced by valid, rational considerations *minus* how much they're influenced by various sources of bias. The unshaded bars depict the corresponding assessments of how much their own opinions are influenced by rational considerations versus bias. (From Pronin, Gilovich, & Ross, 2004.)

How convenient, you might say, and how self-serving. Convenient, yes, and self-serving perhaps. But this pattern of ratings follows directly from the fact that most of the mental processes that allow us to make sense of the world operate automatically and without our awareness. Again, naïve realism gives us the impression that we see things the way they are, not as filtered or constructed in light of our expectations, preferences, or overarching ideology. It is then a short step to seeing alternative views as the product of hearts and minds that are somehow defective.

As the distinguished British philosopher Isaiah Berlin wrote as he reflected on the bitter lessons of the twentieth century, "Few things have done more harm than the belief on the part of individuals or groups (or tribes or states or nations or churches) that he or she or they are in sole possession of the truth, especially about how to live, what to be and do—that those who differ from them are not merely mistaken, but wicked or mad: and need restraining or suppressing. It is terrible and dangerous arrogance to believe that you alone are right, have a magical eye which sees the truth, and that others cannot be right if they disagree."[19]

Precisely because it's so easy to detect the stain of bias in other people's judgments, it can be hard to believe that they don't see it as well. That's why those with whom we disagree don't seem "merely mistaken, but wicked or mad." At best they are seen as misguided and lacking in objectivity. Both liberals who applaud former vice president Dick Cheney's uncharacteristically tolerant views about gay rights and conservatives who decry it are likely to feel that his views on the subject would be less broad-minded if his daughter were not a lesbian. Conservatives tend to assume that his views would be less wrong-headed if they were not influenced by the sexual orientation of his daughter, and they wonder why he is not able to recognize this "obvious" source of bias. Liberals wonder why his tolerance on this issue doesn't extend to other groups that suffer discrimination.

By the same token, liberals doubt that Nancy Reagan would have been such an outspoken advocate of government support for stem cell research if her husband hadn't suffered from Alzheimer's disease. Why doesn't she see, they wonder, that her stance is at odds with her husband's oft-repeated jibe that "the nine most terrifying words in the English language are, 'I'm from the government and I'm here to help.'" Liberals also find it odd that Sarah Palin would campaign on a platform that emphasized reduced government spending while championing increased federal spending on programs for disabled children—until they realize that she herself has a disabled child. The same could be said of the views of the conservative who has spent a night in prison or the leftist who has been mugged or been harassed by the board of health inspectors when trying to open a restaurant.

Are we saying that such individuals are unaware that their own personal experiences have influenced their judgment? No, or at least not always. The influence of naïve realism is more nuanced. People are sometimes quite willing to acknowledge that their personal experiences have influenced their judgment. But they insist that far from being a source of bias, *their* particular experiences are a source of enlightenment.

Thus, one hears that "You can't truly understand the importance of stem cell research unless you've seen up close the ravaging effects of Alzheimer's"; "You can't appreciate the need to fight homophobia until you've seen the burden it places on a gay friend or family member"; "You would understand why we need affirmative action if you had experienced the subtle and not-so-subtle types of racism I have encountered in my career"; or "You wouldn't be so dismissive of conservative concerns about governmental regulation of commerce if you were trying to run a small business."

To probe this sort of thinking, the two of us, along with one of our former students, Joyce Ehrlinger, told a sample of Cornell students that the university was in the process of reviewing its affirmative action policies and, as part of that review, had assembled a student committee to provide input on any proposed changes.[20] Each respondent was then asked to evaluate the extent to which a Caucasian or minority student's input to the committee would likely be biased versus enlightened by his or her ethnicity. They did so by checking the appropriate point on a continuum between "student's ethnicity likely to detract from his or her ability to see the issues clearly" and "student's ethnicity likely to enhance his or her ability to see the issues clearly."

The results were straightforward and telling. Both minority and Caucasian respondents thought that the other group's race would get in the way of their ability to see the issues clearly. But neither group thought that their own racial heritage would bias their judgment, and the minority students thought that theirs gave them rare and important insight into the issues at hand.

This same pattern of responses was found when we queried varsity and intramural athletes about a less emotionally charged issue: whether a new workout facility should be available to varsity athletes only or to the entire campus community. Both groups insisted that the other group's views were more biased by self-interest than their own, and that their own status (as a varsity athlete or not) gave them a more enlightened and reasonable perspective on the issue.

So it is not just that people tend to think they are less influenced by bias than others (especially those on the other side of a contentious issue). They also tend to think that the very things that cloud other people's judgment are sources of enlightenment for themselves. A wise person, in contrast, recognizes that there are two sides of every coin: A vantage point that makes some things easy to see can obscure considerations that would be obvious from another perspective.

What Happened to Fair and Balanced?

During the 2012 National League Championship Series between the defending World Series Champion, the St. Louis Cardinals, and the soon-to-be World Series Champion, the San Francisco Giants, Giants fans complained loudly that one of the announcers calling the game for Fox Sports, Joe Buck, was biased against their team. It's easy to see why: Buck had earlier served as the Cardinals' play-by-play announcer for sixteen years. And his dad, the legendary Jack Buck, broadcast Cardinals games for nearly half a century. In defending himself against complaints about partisanship, Buck said, "If it makes people feel any better, I get the same thing in St. Louis. People say I'm against the Cardinals."[21] He added, "I'm accused of being biased no matter who's playing in the World Series. Over the years

I've been accused of rooting for Anaheim, Philadelphia, Boston, and New York. And I've also been accused of rooting against Anaheim, Philadelphia, Boston and New York. That's the way it goes."[22]

Of course, accusations of partisan bias go beyond the world of sports. If you follow politics at all, you probably have had the following experience: During a presidential debate, you watch your candidate make one compelling point after another while his or her opponent stumbles badly, evades question after question, and offers flimsy responses to those questions that aren't ducked. You anticipate that the talking heads who weigh in afterward will acknowledge how well your candidate has done. Or maybe you've had a different, less satisfying experience: Your candidate hasn't done as well as you'd hoped. He has failed to respond forcefully enough to the distortions, glib one-liners, and outright lies put forth by his opponent. You hope that the postdebate pundits—or at least those without an ideological ax to grind—will set things straight and alert viewers to what "really" went on in the debate.

In either case, we suspect that what you ended up hearing left you more than a little frustrated and disappointed. The commentators seemed to go out of their way to maintain some kind of superficial balance, not fully crediting your candidate's strong points and rejoinders, and ignoring the other side's evasiveness on critical issues. Indeed, the pundits seemed to grant the opponent's highly questionable claims the same status as your candidate's more reasonable assertions. In short, they failed to call things the way they were.

This experience is not restricted to debates. If you are like most people, you probably think the media generally are overly critical of the party and candidates you favor, and insufficiently critical of the party and candidates you oppose. You find media coverage of political and social issues frustrating because those on your side seem to be "telling it like it is," while the other side's contributions consist of little more than a series of lies, distortions, and half-truths.

We trust that you recognize how this experience follows from naïve realism. If our sense-making machinery gives us a clear picture of how things are, any analysis that offers a different picture will seem off the mark. If things appear all black to one side and all white to the other, both will be chagrined by a third party who claims to see lots of gray.

To probe this phenomenon in detail, Lee and his colleagues Robert Vallone and Mark Lepper conducted a study in the immediate aftermath of a particularly horrific event in the long and tragic history of Israeli-Palestinian conflict: the 1982 massacre of civilians in refugee camps on the outskirts of Beirut by Christian Falangist gunmen.[23] The question was how fair the media coverage of the massacre seemed to different constituents—in particular, how fair the discussion was of a possible role in the massacre of the Israeli government, which had some ties with the Falangists (who were vying for power against various Muslim groups). The participants were Stanford University students, some pro-Israeli and some pro-Palestinian in their sentiments. Both partisan groups were shown the same samples of coverage by the major news networks and then asked about what they had seen.

As predicted, both groups saw the coverage as decidedly biased in favor of the other side. In fact, there was no overlap at all in their responses! Not a single one of the sixty-eight pro-Israeli participants thought the coverage was as favorable to Israel as any of the twenty-seven pro-Palestinian participants. Moreover, both groups came away convinced that nonpartisan viewers would become more favorable to the other side as a result of what they saw.

Because people tend to think of their own take on events not as a "take" but as a veridical assessment of what is taking place, anyone who tries to offer an even-handed account of events will tend to be seen as biased and hostile to the perceiver's interests. This is one reason that the fourth estate is held in such low regard by the public. Right wingers in the United States curse the "lamestream" media, while those on the left complain that the major news outlets maintain a mindless neutrality by giving extreme right-wing perspectives the same coverage and treatment as much more centrist positions offered by those on their side of the political spectrum. And both groups regard the networks' "pandering" to the other side as blatantly dishonest, whereas they see the network that shares their perspective as a source of refreshingly clear thinking.

This hostility toward third parties extends beyond politics to influence how disputants react to the efforts of conflict mediators, whether they be well-meaning friends trying to help dampen a domestic quarrel, professional mediators called in to settle a legal dispute, or high-level diplomats trying to avert or lessen an international conflict. The wisest in the room is bound to share such frustrations, especially in the heat of the moment. But he or she will be the one, after a bit of reflection, to recognize and point out that those on the other side are likely to have similar feelings and convictions—not because they are dishonest but because they too are naïve realists.

Dealing with Disagreement, and a Problem with the Golden Rule

People often carry a kind of scorecard in their heads on which they keep track of how often, at least in their own minds, they have "won" versus "lost" arguments. On that scorecard the first number is likely to be large and the second small. Viewing an argument, whether personal or political, through the lens of naïve realism produces much the same result as witnessing a debate between "our" candidate and "their" candidate. We think our points are valid and those of the other person invalid, or that we were sincere and the other person stonewalled or tried to score debating points rather than engage in an honest interchange.

Naïve realism also encourages the belief that we'll be able to convince reasonable individuals who disagree with us if only they would sit down and talk (or, rather, sit down and listen). It's easy to feel that only *un*reasonable people will fail to see the light once the facts are laid out. Even people of goodwill who genuinely want to reach an accommodation with those on the other side do so with that optimistic presumption. They do not seriously consider the possibility that such a discussion will lead them to change *their own* views. And they rarely discover otherwise.

An understanding of naïve realism also suggests that some conventional wisdom about tolerance and goodwill must be turned on its head. It may not be so wise, for example, to obey the golden rule and "do unto others as you would want them to do unto you." As the great playwright and renowned wit George Bernard Shaw noted, the risk of mindlessly applying that rule is that "their tastes may not be the same."[24] An awareness of the power and pervasiveness of naïve realism encourages a more modest, negatively framed version, one articulated by the Jewish sage Hillel: "What is hateful to you do not do to your neighbor: That is the whole Torah; the rest is commentary." It should come as no surprise that Confucius, the philosopher who is so often stereotyped as the embodiment of wisdom, similarly advised us to "never impose on others what you would not choose for yourself."

Recognizing When Two Heads Really Are Better Than One

The various prediction markets that have arisen in the past several decades, such as Intrade, the Iowa Electronic Markets, and the Hollywood Stock Exchange, attest to the value of aggregating opinions to predict how the stock market will move, who will win the Academy Awards, or who will be the next president. These markets developed on the heels of research showing that averaging the estimates of a large number of people concerning almost any uncertain variable—the temperature of a room, the number of jelly beans in a jar, or the likely winner of the Nobel Peace Prize—results in a value that is almost always more accurate than the overwhelming majority of individual estimates.[25] When it comes to making predictions or estimates, or assessing costs, risks, and benefits, seeking others' opinions is a good idea.

What many people don't realize, however, is that the input of even a single other person can lead to markedly better estimates and predictions. But do people take advantage of this benefit of aggregation? Before we share the results of research on this topic, consider the following: Suppose someone asks you and a friend to estimate the length of the Golden Gate Bridge, the price of a house that is about to go on the market, or the number of soldiers who will die in a military campaign. How much weight would you give your partner's estimate—especially if it were very different from your own? Would you simply average your two guesses? Or would you consider which estimate was more likely to be correct (presumably your own) and give it more weight?

If your two estimates are relatively close, chances are that both are either higher or lower than the correct answer. In that case, averaging your estimates would produce an error that is exactly the same as the average error of each of your estimates. But if your two estimates are far apart, odds are that they lie on opposite sides of the true value. In that case, averaging them would produce a smaller error than the average error of your separate estimates. It's a mathematical certainty. If the two of you were about equally off the mark in opposite directions, you would both gain accuracy. But even if one of you had initially been close and the other far off, so that the one who was close would become somewhat less accurate and the one who was far off would become much more accurate, the average of your two errors would still be reduced. (Of course, if you could agree on which estimate was better informed, you could both gain in accuracy by giving that estimate more weight. But naïve realism makes such agreement difficult to achieve.)

What happens when pairs of individuals are called on to make these sorts of estimates? We trust that our discussion of naïve realism allows you to anticipate the answer. Both are likely to think that their own assessments are less subject to bias and error than the other person's. That in turn should make them reluctant to give the other person's estimates much weight—especially when the other's estimates diverge substantially from their own. But of course that is precisely when averaging is most likely to improve accuracy!

To test this prediction and highlight its consequences, Lee and his colleagues Varda Liberman, Julia Minson, and Chris Bryan conducted a series of experiments in which pairs of participants were asked to estimate a variety of unknown values.[26] Some of the studies were conducted in Israel and involved estimates of political opinions (the percentage of their classmates who believed Israel should give up the Golan Heights in a peace treaty with Syria) or demographic facts (the Druze population of Israel). Others were conducted in the United States and involved people with some expertise (ballroom dancers estimating the scores they would receive from judges, or lawyers and law students estimating the awards to plaintiffs in tort cases).

In each study, participants first made their own individual estimates. Then, after learning each other's estimates, they made a second set of estimates, giving the input of their partners as much or as little weight as they wished. In a third round, the two partners were required to offer a joint estimate on which both agreed. Financial rewards for accuracy were offered in each round of estimates.

No one, of course, knew the right answers. In some cases, one participant might have had good reason to assume that her own estimates were more accurate and in other cases that her partner would be more accurate. Most often, however, there was no reason for participants to believe that one estimate was any better than the other. Nevertheless, participants usually gave their own initial estimates much more weight than those of their partners. In fact, more than a third of the time they gave their partner's estimates no weight at all. And they paid a heavy cost for doing so. They consistently did less well than they could have done if they had simply averaged their own estimate and that of their partner (something they did only about 10 percent of the time). Furthermore, when the partners were forced to agree on a single estimate, they consistently became more accurate.

The lesson should be clear: We pay a price for assuming that our own assessments are better than those of other people with similar information and expertise. The wisest in the room tries to reduce that price by reasoning together to narrow disagreements and, when in doubt, finding a middle ground.

Beyond Naïve Realism

What would it look like to escape the adverse consequences of naïve realism? It would not involve somehow ceasing to see things through the prism of one's own expectations, needs, and experiences. That's not possible. What is possible is to acknowledge that one's own perspective may be no more valid than someone else's. Indeed, it may be less valid. History provides a remarkable example of such acknowledgment in the context of one of the most momentous events in American history. Ten years after the end of the Civil War, at the dedication of the Freedom Memorial Monument honoring Abraham Lincoln, Frederick Douglass offered this assessment of the martyred president:

> Viewed from the genuine abolition ground, Mr. Lincoln seemed tardy, cold, dull, and indifferent.

This assessment was understandable in light of Douglass's longstanding impatience with the pace of the president's steps toward the abolition of slavery. But he then showed a remarkable capacity to get beyond his own perspective by adding:

> Measuring him by the sentiment of his country, a sentiment he was bound as a statesman to consult, he was swift, zealous, radical, and determined.... Taking him all in all, measuring the

tremendous magnitude of the work before him, considering the necessary means to ends, and surveying the end from the beginning, infinite wisdom has seldom sent any man into the world better fitted for his mission than Abraham Lincoln.

What Douglass did that spring day is something we must all strive to do if we are to understand the world around us more clearly: We must recognize that our view of the world is just that—a view that has been shaped by our own vantage point, history, and idiosyncratic knowledge. The man Douglass was eulogizing had a similar capacity for open-mindedness. Regarding a political opponent, Lincoln famously remarked, "I don't like the man, I must get to know him better." This charitable reaction conveys an important truth: Often when we get to know someone whose words and deeds were off-putting, once we get a better sense of how that person is understanding events, our dislike dissipates.

Of course, to better understand another person it is important to appreciate not only how that person sees the world, but also the actual situational influences and constraints confronting that person. That is especially true when the person's actions seem surprising or unreasonable. We take up that issue in the next chapter.

2

The Push and Pull of Situations

I magine that a nice young man knocks on your door and asks if you would be willing to have a sign installed on your front lawn, bearing the message: "DRIVE SAFELY." From the picture he shows you, the sign is crudely lettered and would completely obscure your front door and much of the front of your house. He tells you that the sign would stay there for a week. How would you respond?

Amazingly, in one condition of a 1966 experiment, 76 percent of the homemakers in a middle-class enclave in Northern California agreed to just such a request.[1] How did the researchers conducting the study achieve such an extraordinary rate of agreement? Did they offer lavish payments? Make impassioned arguments? Make some ominous threat? None of the above. Instead, they used a variant of the foot-in-the-door technique.*

---

* The term *foot-in-the-door* refers to the tactic employed by the door-to-door salesmen of yore. To get into a home or to see a buyer, they would ask a small favor (e.g., asking for a glass of water or a chair because "I feel a little faint") in the belief that a small first act of compliance on the part of the resident or receptionist would create a personal connection that would make it easier to go through one's spiel and make a sale. The technique in the study we've described differs from the classic one in that the initial small request and the later much larger request were made by different individuals.

A week or so earlier, a different member of the research team had simply asked these same homeowners if they would put a four-by-four inch sticker in the window of their house or car bearing the message "BE A SAFE DRIVER." Virtually everyone agreed with this trivial request, and in so doing they made themselves vulnerable to the much larger request to come.*

Social psychologists have a long tradition of showing that people can be induced to do surprising things without being offered much in the way of incentives, threats, or compelling arguments—that seemingly minor variations in the situation confronting people can have sizable effects on the way they behave. The message we can take from virtually thousands of studies is that people are more suscepti-ble to subtle situational influences than most of us realize. A corollary message from both the research laboratory and the observation of real-world events is that good people, or at least people who would behave admirably in many contexts, can find themselves in a situation that leads them to behave badly.

Consider, for example, the responses of Princeton divinity stu-dents who encountered a shabbily dressed man slumped in a doorway calling for help as they walked from one building to another, where they would soon be giving a sermon on the parable of the Good Sa-maritan. What percentage of these future clergy and professors of religious studies offered assistance? What determined whether they responded charitably, as the Good Samaritan in the parable had done, or hurried on like the priest and the Levite? It depended a great deal

---

* In the control condition of this study, where no prior small request was made, only 17 percent agreed to put up the big, ugly sign—actually quite a high percentage, but still only a fraction of the compliance rate in the foot-in-the-door condition. The high compliance rate even here probably reflects the fact that people have difficulty saying no to a novel request—that is, one that is not for money or time or the loan of some valued possession. Most people are practiced at declining those sorts of requests but wouldn't have a ready script available for declining the unusual request in this study, especially because the cause was so obviously one that everyone would endorse.

on whether they had been told by the person who had asked them to prepare the sermon that they had ample time to get to the lecture site or that they were running late and would have to hurry. Whereas nearly 67 percent of those with time on their hands stopped to offer assistance, only 10 percent of those in a hurry did so.[2]

Both of these studies highlight the fact that people are more malleable than we might think. But a note of caution is in order before jumping to the wrong conclusion about how easy it is to influence people. It takes a lot of skill and attention to detail to design experiments that yield such dramatic results—even if you have a general understanding of the psychological principles they illustrate.

Both the surprising results of these studies and the skill and attention to detail required to get them to work illustrate the same general point—that people are highly sensitive to specific aspects of the situations they face. As a result, they often act in dramatically different ways in situations that seem on the surface to be very similar. And ordinary men and women can be led by seemingly insignificant features of the surrounding context to do things, both positive and negative, that would surprise you—and surprise their friends, family members, and neighbors as well. How often have you heard, in the aftermath of a homicide, a terrorist attack, or a financial scandal, those closest to the perpetrator expressing surprise that he (almost always a *he*) could do such a thing?

Because it is so easy to overlook the subtleties of situational influence, the natural response when informed of the results of the two studies we have described is to assume that the people involved were unusual in some way. Homeowners must have been more compliant fifty years ago. Students, even seminary students, are too preoccupied with getting good grades in their narrow, ivy-splashed world to look after those around them. Besides, many of them are hypocrites who aren't really interested in people in need. Appreciation of the power of the situational context should lead us to hesitate before jumping to conclusions about someone who has done something surprising.

The wisest one in the room reserves judgment until the details of the situational pressures facing that person have been given due consideration (and a wise person will even do a little detective work to find out more about those details).

Lessons about the surprising power of situational influence come not just from cunningly designed social psychology experiments. They come as well from a number of natural experiments that resulted from changes in policy or circumstances or from differences between practices in different locales. Anyone who wants to become wiser about people and about the way they make decisions can learn from the results of these natural experiments.

Lending Money to Uncle Sam

As World War II dragged on, the U.S. government offered war bonds to Americans who wanted to do their part to support the war effort and earn a small return on their investment in the process. (A typical bond cost $75 and paid $100 at the bond's maturity date ten years later.) The percentage of American workers who bought war bonds increased dramatically over four successive offerings between April 1943 and June 1944. Estimates based on interviews of more than one thousand people tell us that the percentage went from about 20 percent on the first of these offerings to 47 percent for the last. What caused this dramatic increase? Was there a surge in patriotism as ever greater numbers of young Americans enlisted and news from the battlefield became more positive? Did workers have more money in their pockets from working overtime to meet the demands of the military?

Each of these factors may have played a role. But something else proved to be especially important: a simple shift in marketing strategy. The first drive had relied mainly on patriotic appeals presented on billboards, in newspapers, on radio, and in movie theaters. Subsequent bond drives, in contrast, increasingly emphasized face-to-face solicitation in the workplace, with a coworker asking for a commitment to purchase a bond then and there. Whereas only 25 percent of those surveyed in the first sales drive received these face-to-face appeals, 58 percent received them in the fourth drive.

This change in strategy paid immediate dividends, and the effectiveness of the face-to-face "sign-up-here-and-now" appeals was evident over the course of the four drives. In the April 1943 drive, 47 percent of those directly solicited bought one or more bonds versus only 12 percent of those not directly solicited. These figures increased to: 59 percent versus 18 percent in the September 1943 drive, 63 percent versus 25 percent in the January 1944 drive, and 66 percent versus 22 percent in the June 1944 drive.[3]

It is worth noting that the percentage of workers purchasing bonds went up in successive drives even among those who did not receive a face-to-face request. It seems that as more and more face-to-face solicitations yielded more and more purchases, norms about what was commonplace and expected shifted accordingly. As people heard about more friends, neighbors, and coworkers buying bonds, they felt more inclined to do so as well.

Opt In versus Opt Out: Why Swedes Say Yes to Organ Donation and Danes Say No

Another natural experiment shows even more dramatically that people's willingness to behave admirably may depend on exactly how the opportunity to do so is presented to them. This study examined organ donation rates in European countries with different donation "default" policies.[4] Like the United States, many European countries have opt-in policies: To be a potential donor, a person must take some action—generally just signing the back of his or her driver's license. Without that signature, the person's organs cannot be used for someone in need. In other European countries, the default is reversed: Individuals are assumed to be willing donors but have the option to indicate, often with a simple signature on their driver's license, that they are *un*willing to do so. In other words, they have to opt out of the donation program.

As shown in figure 2.1, the participation rates in the opt-in and opt-out countries differ more dramatically than you would guess. Although public opinion polls reveal comparable enthusiasm for organ donation across these different countries, the participation rates are close to 100 percent in nearly all the opt-out countries but average only 15 percent in the opt-in countries. The lowest participation rate among opt-out countries was more than 85 percent (in Sweden), whereas the highest participation rate among opt-in countries was under 30 percent (in the Netherlands).

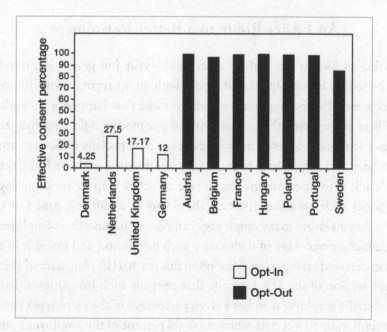

Figure 2.1. Consent rates by country

Are these dramatic differences just a matter of people doing what is easy? Making the desired behavior easier is certainly a big part of the story, and the wisest one in the room will start there. If people already want to do something (like donate their organs), it's not wise to spend a lot of time, energy, or money trying to increase their motivation. Just make the behavior easier to perform. Make the path from good intentions to effective action clearer. By the same token, make the behavior you want to discourage a bit harder. But there is more to it than that. When seemingly small differences have such big effects, it is generally because those seemingly small differences involve something quite big from the standpoint of human psychology. As we'll see in chapter 3, one of the big things that default options change is the meaning that people assign to the choices they face.

An Easier Route to a Better Retirement

We'd all like to live well in retirement—visit the grandkids, travel the world, or simply relax at home without worrying about future expenses. But putting money aside to make that happen is difficult. There are so many things that demand our money right now that it's easy to ignore our retirement needs. It can be especially difficult to put money aside if you have to make an active decision to do so. But if the default is to *save* and one has to take an active step to *avoid* putting money aside, amassing a nest egg should not be as difficult. And it isn't.

As you know, many employees can choose to have their employer deduct a percentage of their salary each pay period and invest it in a tax-deferred savings plan. Most often this is a 401(k) plan, named after the section of the U.S. tax code that controls such investments, and often the employer matches a given percentage of the employee's contribution up to a certain amount (say, 6 percent of the employee's salary). Historically, participation in these plans required an active step on the part of the employee. If he or she did not actively enroll, the default was nonparticipation. The implicit assumption was that most people would want to save and therefore enroll in the plan. But that second assumption proved to be wrong, as publication after publication has documented the woeful savings rate in the United States.

Are people too shortsighted to recognize the advantage of enrolling? Are they simply too lazy to enroll? Not necessarily. While it may be easy to click the "enroll" button on a website to complete the process, it is far from easy to sort through all the investment options available. How much of one's savings should be in the U.S. stock market? How much should be in stocks of foreign companies? In real estate? In money market funds? These decisions are hard, and rather than make them, many employees say to themselves, "I can't do this now; I'll decide later." The problem is that the "later" they have in mind never comes.

In one study, only a little more than 50 percent of the employees in a company with such an opt-in participation plan chose to enroll within the first six months of their employment. The likelihood of participation went up the longer the employee was with the company, but even after two years on the job more than one in five employees had still not gotten around to enrolling (and getting the "free money" offered by their employers). To encourage greater rates of participation, the company switched to an opt-out enrollment program.* New employees were then automatically enrolled in a simple savings plan and had to take an active step to have some or all of the money earmarked for savings go to their paycheck instead. Some had 3 percent of their salary automatically put into the 401(k) plan; others had 6 percent automatically saved.

---

*In this company, the default allocation was to a money market fund, but employees had seven investment options from which to choose. Different companies have chosen different default allocations, with many choosing 50 percent in a money market fund and 50 percent in a stock fund.

The percentage allocated to saving turned out not to matter much. But changing the default mattered a lot. The participation rate in both opt-out programs was substantially higher than among employees hired under the earlier opt-in program—35 percent higher after three months on the job and 25 percent higher two years down the line.[5] The lesson isn't a subtle one: If you are looking for a way to increase savings, make it easier. This realization, and the opt-out savings plans it has inspired, are what Nobel Prize winner Daniel Kahneman has called the signature triumph of behavioral economics.

Barriers and Channels

Many regard Kurt Lewin as the father of American social psychology. He certainly was the source of many of the most important ideas and insights we share in this book. Lewin was born in Prussia in 1890, and his life as a young man was similar to that of a great many other German Jewish scientists of that era. He fought in World War I, and after being wounded in combat, he returned to Berlin to complete his PhD. When Hitler came to power in 1933, Lewin was clear-eyed about what the future held for people like him and left Germany.

After spending the summer of 1935 as a visiting professor at Stanford and considering options to pursue his career in various countries, including Japan and the Soviet Union, he made another wise choice by immigrating permanently to the United States. He held academic positions first at Cornell, then at the University of Iowa, and finally at MIT, where he organized the Research Center for Group Dynamics. He died in 1947, just as he was about to move to the University of Michigan and assume leadership at the newly founded Institute for Social Research.* In his relatively short time in the United States,

---

* The Institute for Social Research at the University of Michigan continues today to carry on the Lewinian tradition of combining theory development with efforts to address important social issues and pressing contemporary problems.

Lewin, whose famous aphorism was "There is nothing as practical as a good theory," worked ceaselessly to show how useful social psychological principles could be in addressing the pressing problems of the day. His efforts led to theories and research methods that reshaped that academic discipline and still prove useful today.[6]

One of Lewin's many contributions to psychology was a simple change of focus. He noted that when people try to change someone's behavior, they typically try to give the person a push in the desired direction: They promise rewards or issue threats. They hire motivational speakers to get their employees to take more initiative; they offer their kids money to get better grades; they give impassioned speeches about the importance of eating right, avoiding wasteful spending, or practicing safer sex. When it is their own behavior they are seeking to change, they try to psych themselves up by promising themselves rewards for success or focusing on the high costs of failure. They look for inspiring role models, or simply vow to try harder—to get more exercise, make more sales calls, lower their credit card balance, or put down mystery novels and use their reading time to improve their minds.

Sometimes this works. When motivation is the problem, finding ways to increase it can be the ticket to success. But more often than not, motivation is not the real problem. Most people are already highly motivated to become healthier, wealthier, and more productive in their jobs. Young women are highly motivated to prevent unwanted pregnancies, and workers anticipating retirement are highly motivated to make sure they save enough so that their retirement years are free of financial strain. In such cases, trying to amp up motivation is unlikely to do much good. A more fruitful strategy, Lewin suggested, is to identify, and then eliminate, the obstacles standing in the way of the desired behavior.

Lewin's insight applies broadly. To produce change, smooth the path or open a clear channel that links good intentions to effective action. Having difficulty saving money? Set up an automatic deduction plan. Having trouble losing weight? Empty your cupboard of tempting foods. Want your son to spend less time playing computer games and more time reading? Start him out with graphic novels and comic books rather than Bellow, Baldwin, or Barth.

The same principle applies to changing the practices of particular groups or whole societies. To improve the educational performance of disadvantaged students, address the problem of potentially disastrous climate change, or help forge agreements to end conflicts, we must go beyond exhorting, threatening, or offering rewards. As we discuss in the last three chapters of this book, a more psych-wise strategy is to figure out what is preventing the desired changes from taking place and then implementing strategies to remove the relevant barriers.

Consider how people in recent times have dramatically increased the amount of waste they recycle across much of the United States. In most communities, people now dutifully recycle cans, bottles, and paper. The secret to this success was not the introduction of any rewards or punishments. Nor was it accomplished with media blitzes featuring pictures of overflowing garbage dumps or persuasive messages about benefits to the environment. What did the trick was the introduction of specially colored receptacles to be put out alongside one's garbage cans for curbside pickup.

When one had to store and sort recyclable materials and then drive them to the nearest recycling center, many saw the practice of recycling as something for hippies, tree huggers, and liberals. Eliminating the need to do these things removed a barrier, making it easier to recycle. Even more important, perhaps, putting recyclable materials in the appropriate container has come to be seen as something that ordinary good citizens just do, a message reinforced any time one walks down the street or drives through the neighborhood on trash collection day. Nudges change norms and, in the process, change the very meaning of the behavior in question.

Saint, Sucker, or Good Citizen?

As we were finishing this book, Europe was experiencing a prolonged period of economic malaise—a downturn that started with the discovery that Greece was more deeply in debt than had been recognized and that it might default on its obligations to its creditors. This discovery quickly spread to questions about the solvency of Ireland, Italy, Portugal, and Spain—and in turn led to a climate of doubt that affected financial markets around the world and slowed economic growth nearly everywhere.

Sympathy for Greece was not enhanced when it was learned that a big part of its budget problems was a Greek tradition of tax evasion. Economic analyses indicated that fully a third of Greece's budget problems could be fixed instantly if Greek citizens would simply pay the taxes they owe.[7] In Greece, however, avoiding taxes is seen as a normal, indeed normative, practice. It is something that everyone believes everyone else does, so that *not* hiding income or inflating expenses is something only "suckers" would do.

As it happens, a reluctance to pay taxes is by no means unique to Greece. Nor is it restricted to countries with very high tax rates, lax enforcement policies, or long histories of government corruption and inefficiency. It is estimated that the U.S. Treasury is shortchanged by $200 billion a year by individuals underreporting income or fraudulently reporting deductions.[8] Many taxpayers succumb to the temptation to underreport income or overreport deductions and then rationalize their misdeeds ("Everyone does it"; "Multimillionaires, with their Swiss bank accounts and high-priced tax consultants, pay a lower percentage of their income in taxes than middle-class folks like me"). What can be done? Is there a way to encourage more honest reporting without threatening stiffer penalties or hiring armies of accountants to increase the number of audited returns?

A recent study suggests one possibility. Students worked on a series of math puzzles and were asked to report how successful they had been, and hence how much money they were due. The students believed that the experimenter would not know how well they had done, but in fact their performance was covertly monitored. The experimental manipulation was very simple. Half the participants were asked to sign an "honesty statement" at the end of the form on which they reported how well they had done, just as Americans are required to do on the last page of their income tax forms. The other participants were asked to sign the honesty statement at the beginning of the form—*before* they indicated how successful they had been at the task. The result of having the honesty statement up front was a dramatic reduction in overreporting—from 79 percent to 37 percent.[9]

In a follow-up study, the investigators examined the odometer readings motorists reported to a prominent insurance company—readings that determined their premiums. They found that having the motorists attest to the accuracy of their reports before indicating their odometer readings rather than afterward led to a 10 percent increase in reported mileage.* When it comes to morality (as opposed to comedy), timing may not be everything, but it clearly matters. Wise observers of human frailty recognize the broader message—that honesty or dishonesty may depend not only on the character of the person, but on the specifics of the situation that make dishonesty more or less tempting—and the norm of honesty more or less salient.

It is not that we are passive puppets who can be manipulated simply by pulling the right string. We are more like the CEO of a small company trying to manage multiple objectives simultaneously: keeping customers, employees, and shareholders happy; keeping an eye on competitors, shifts in the marketplace, and changes in federal regulations; and attending to the company's good reputation in the community. Change

---

*Higher mileage results in higher premiums because of the extra risk associated with more time on the road.

one element in the complex web of influences and the effects reverberate broadly. What the wisest person in the room bears in mind in the face of such complexity is the Lewinian recipe: Make the actions you want to encourage easier, akin to moving downhill; make the actions you want to discourage more difficult, akin to moving uphill.

Resisting the Lure of Sugar, Salt, and Fat— Without a Lot of Willpower

Where can a channels-and-barriers approach be best employed in everyday life? One target is overeating. We've all read or heard the statistics. More than a third of the U.S. population is obese, including nearly one in five children. Another third of the population is overweight. Excess poundage is the leading medical cause of potential recruits being rejected for military service.[10] The problem is not a lack of motivation to be slimmer. Four in ten Americans are on a diet at any one time, fueling a $70 billion weight loss industry. But the sad fact is that the overwhelming majority of dieters fail to achieve their goals.[11]

From a situationist perspective, none of this is surprising. Temptations to consume foods rich in fat, salt, and sugar—in other words, foods we all enjoy—are everywhere. And smooth channels designed by clever marketers to make the path from temptation to purchase to consumption are all too easy to traverse. We are bombarded with advertisements for tempting snacks and fast-food meals. Grocery stores are stocked to the rafters with offerings doctored by food scientists to appeal to our deepest biologically based cravings. The foods that are worst for us (but most profitable for the sellers) are often the ones most prominently displayed and most conveniently situated.

It's hard to fill up the car with gasoline without confronting a display urging us to down a giant candy bar, eat a gourmet ice cream bar, or slurp an oversized soda. University libraries no less than shopping centers now house coffee bars that offer delicious blended coffee drinks with nearly the same caloric content as a milkshake. To eat moderately requires a near constant exercise of willpower—or perhaps we should say *won't*-power.

Fortunately, researchers have progressed beyond exhorting us to resist temptation. They have given us some tools to help us eat right. Psychologist Brian Wansink has been conducting experiments for the past twenty years to see how the eating environment might be altered to give dieters a fighting chance.[12] "Mindful" dieting, he cautions, is too hard to sustain. The caloric reduction necessary to achieve noticeable results creates hunger pangs that overwhelm our resolve—especially once weight loss slows down, as it inevitably does. Dieting sends the body into something akin to starvation mode in which it uses energy more efficiently, furthering the difficulty of losing weight. Rather than trying to fight these biological forces through the exercise of will or any of the latest fad diets, Wansink offers some specific situationist strategies to help you "mindlessly" reduce the amount you eat.

In one notable study, Wansink and colleagues gave moviegoers either a giant tub or a more modest-sized box of popcorn on their way in to see a film. Although one was much larger than the other, both contained more popcorn than a person could normally eat. The notable finding was that those given the bigger container ate 50 percent more popcorn, a result made even more notable by the fact that the popcorn was several days old and had roughly the texture of packing nuggets.

This finding caught the attention of the media, and when a segment on Wansink's findings was to be aired on television, he invited his colleagues in Cornell's nutrition department to watch the program. To make the event more festive, he served everyone ice cream. Unbeknownst to his colleagues, half were given large bowls and a large scooper to dole out whatever quantity they wished and half were given smaller bowls and a smaller scooper. Bear in mind that these viewers were nutrition scientists, folks who are probably as conscious about what they eat—and as informed about what they *should* eat—as anyone on the planet. Nevertheless, those given the larger bowls ate half again as much as those given the smaller bowls.

The message from these studies is clear: Much of our eating is mindless. Promoting healthy eating therefore calls out for a channels-and-barriers analysis. We can all benefit by making the path to healthy foods and reduced consumption easier and the path to unhealthy foods and mindless consumption more difficult. That's exactly what former New York City mayor Michael Bloomberg tried to do with his controversial proposal to essentially outlaw supersized soda offerings in restaurants. The inevitable result was a flood of angry charges on one side about the specter of an overreaching "nanny state" and countercharges about the willingness of profiteers to put children at risk in the pursuit of profit. But regardless of one's views about the government's role in people's lives, there is no question that reducing the cup size at soda fountains would reduce consumption of sugary drinks—even when "mindfully" getting a refill remains an option.

There are lots of ways to alter the context surrounding food to elicit healthier eating. People tend to eat what's on their plates, so if you want to eat less or get those at your table to eat less, use smaller plates and serve smaller portions. (The average plate size has increased substantially over the past fifty years, no doubt contributing to the increase in average waist size during this time.)[13] When it comes to candy, don't store it in a transparent container; cover it up. Put tempting foods at the back of the refrigerator or cupboard, or don't keep them in the house at all. If you have to have candy bars or cookies around, don't buy an assortment of different kinds. Buy just one kind because we tend to sample the variety of goodies available to us and eat more when an assortment is available. In short, rather than making resolutions and chastising yourself when your resolve proves unequal to the challenge, be psych-wise: Control the channels that lead to more or less eating and you'll be on your way to a healthier diet.

Beware of Slippery Slopes—Unless You Want to Get the Ball Rolling

Stanley Milgram's studies of obedience to authority are among the most famous (some would say infamous) experiments in the history of psychology.[14] Milgram found that two-thirds of the people he recruited for his study in New Haven, Connecticut, obeyed an experimenter's instructions to administer dangerous levels of electric shock to someone they believed to be a fellow participant in a study of learning. At the experimenter's urging, they continued administering shocks even after the "learner"—in reality, an accomplice of Milgram who was out of sight but in voice contact from an adjacent room—had cried out in pain and voiced a great deal of distress. Indeed, they continued to do so even after the learner had said he refused to go on, had ceased to give answers in the supposed learning task, and had fallen ominously silent.*

Milgram's studies continue to provoke controversy more than a half-century later. Although the learner in the study did not actually receive any shocks, the participants thought he did and had to live with the knowledge of what they had done. The question we are left to consider is what the actions of these participants say about human behavior. Were their actions a reflection of blind obedience to authority? Indifference to the suffering of others? Some hidden reservoir of sadism in seemingly ordinary people? Why else would so many people be willing to obey the instructions of an experimenter they had never met before and knew next to nothing about, even to the point of administering what they believed were more than four hundred volts of electricity to another human being?

---

* Milgram's participants were first asked to administer fifteen volts of electricity to the learner, something nearly everyone would agree to do. Then, after each error by the learner, they were asked to deliver fifteen more volts. Rather quickly the shock levels became quite high and the feedback from the learner quite ominous.

Image 2.1. Stanley Milgram with the shock machine he commanded his volunteer participants to use in order to (supposedly) deliver an electric shock whenever the learner failed to respond correctly.

Image 2.2. The learner being strapped into the shock-delivery apparatus.

To answer these questions, it is essential to do what many who have written about these studies have not done: that is, examine the details of Milgram's procedure more carefully. He did *not* simply ask his participants to administer four hundred and fifty volts of electricity to the learner. Not at first. Instead, participants were first asked to administer fifteen volts, then thirty, then forty-five (this last a shock level Milgram had shrewdly given each of his subjects prior to the "learning" phase of the experiment so they would know something of what the learner was experiencing and also so they would believe the shocks were real). Who wouldn't be willing to provide such "feedback"? The learner had agreed to be in the study, and the roles had been determined by a (rigged) flip of a coin and seemingly could just as easily have been reversed. Milgram's participants had no idea, at least initially, that they were being led down a step-by-step path to ever more egregious actions. Nor could they anticipate how difficult it would be to get off that path.

Milgram's experiments were in fact a demonstration of the potency of a particular type of behavioral channel—a slippery slope that took them one step at a time from unexceptional to exceptional behavior. Very few people would be willing to administer four hundred and fifty volts of electricity out of the blue to a fellow research participant. But doing so after delivering a long series of prior shocks in fifteen-volt increments is much easier—just one further step at a time. Whatever rationale (or, rather, whatever rationalization) allowed the participants to justify the previous steps allowed them, indeed, compelled them, to justify the next step.

Participants could not have anticipated how difficult it would be to get off the path that led from unexceptional compliance with the experimenter's instructions to harmful obedience. Even if participants decided that they wanted to get off the path they were on, it wasn't at all clear how to do so. There was no clear exit out of the (traumatic) situation in which they found themselves. Any reservations they might express, any polite suggestions that the experimenter check on the condition of the learner, and any offers to forgo their participation fee in exchange for stopping the study were met by the experimenter's calm insistence that the participant proceed and that "the responsibility is mine."

Even when participants got up from their chairs, as many did, and announced that they weren't going any further, the experimenter insisted that "the experiment requires that you continue." Unless the participant took the truly extraordinary step of directly challenging the experimenter by saying, "I don't care what you say or who you are or what you think of me, I quit and you can't force me to continue," the only option was to continue and hope against hope that the ordeal would soon end.

The experimenter's implacable insistence served as a powerful barrier to the action most participants wanted to take, which was to end the experiment and the learner's suffering. Moreover, there were no clear channels around that barrier. Imagine how different the results would have been with a small change in the situation facing the participants. Imagine if right next to the shock machine there had been a button labeled "University Research Ethics Board: Press if you'd like to stop the experiment and discuss the study with University administration officials." How many participants would continue to administer ever-increasing levels of shock when given this easy way out?

We can't be sure, but the situationist message that lies at the heart of social psychology gives us every reason to believe that far fewer participants would have continued. The results of Milgram's study would have been less shocking to the generations of students who learn about his research in their introductory psychology classes, and they would not have provided the same lesson about the power of the (skillfully engineered) social situation.

We have described Milgram's experimental procedure in so much detail because we want you to recognize how slippery-slope and no-easy-exit situations can give rise to extreme behavior. Sometimes the result is a tale of depressing inhumanity, greed, or folly; but sometimes it is one that inspires. Heroic actions and lifelong commitments to noble causes often start with small acts in particular circumstances that the individual happens to confront. A child volunteers to walk dogs at the local SPCA because she likes pets. She then responds favorably to a request to donate to the SPCA. Soon she's soliciting signatures to preserve the habitat for a local species of owl and then joins the ranks of Greenpeace activists.

The long process that culminated in the legalization of gay marriage in many states and the acceptance of gays in the military began with small steps. In the case of the armed forces, first a few brave servicemen and servicewomen "came out," earning them a tacit acceptance by fellow soldiers who knew these barrier-breakers as individuals and valued their professional contributions and admired their courage. This made possible the temporizing policy of "don't ask, don't tell," and, finally, the more generalized acceptance we see today.

Effective action is often best accomplished by capitalizing on behavioral momentum and harnessing the power of step-by-step progression. Writing a long paper (or a book!) can be difficult, but it's easier once the writing threshold is crossed. Rather than waiting for inspiration or a surge of motivation, it is often best to plunge in and write a few sentences or paragraphs—perhaps indicating (roughly) what you want to say, as if in a letter to a friend.

A depressed individual can find the challenges and chores of everyday life overwhelming, but those difficulties can seem less onerous after getting up from the chair and doing something far removed from the source of the depression, even if it is only taking a short walk or a shower. A messy teenager might find a request to clean her room too intimidating, but might view picking things up off the floor as more manageable—creating momentum toward more thorough efforts.

Once a person gets going in the desired direction, it's easier to keep going. The notion that a journey of a thousand miles begins with a single step is fully supported by a channels-and-barriers analysis and by empirical research. The wisest in the room understands that the secret to getting big things done is to get the ball rolling, take additional smallish steps one at a time, block whatever channels make it easy to get sidetracked, and then count on the boost in motivation that comes when the end is in sight.

The Fundamental Attribution Error

Imagine that while touring a university campus with your teenager, you are given the opportunity to sit in on a psychology experiment. You watch as the experimenter explains to the two participants that the study will involve a test of general knowledge. One participant, chosen by a coin flip, is to devise challenging trivia questions for the other to answer, with the proviso that he must know the answer himself. After a few moments of preparation, the test begins, and the first participant fires off such questions as, "Who played the role of E. K. Hornbeck, a cinematic stand-in for H. L. Mencken, in the film version of *Inherit the Wind*?"; "Who are the three coinventors of the transistor?"; and "What Shakespearean play contains the soliloquy that begins, "If music be the food of love, play on?"*

The second participant, the contestant in this quiz show reenactment, is generally stumped and answers correctly only two or three of the ten questions posed. And you fare no better as you silently (thank goodness) try to come up with the right answers yourself. The experimenter then asks the two research participants and, to your surprise, you as well, to estimate how much general knowledge each of the participants possesses.

What would you conclude? If you are like the participants in this study, which was run more than three decades ago by Lee and two of his students, both you and the beleaguered contestant would likely conclude that the first participant has an unusual aptitude for trivia and a broad base of factual knowledge.[15] You're also likely to come away a bit shaken about your own general knowledge. Given the esoteric knowledge the questioner displayed—so much more than you or the contestant seemed to possess—what else could you (or the contestant) conclude?

To draw a different conclusion, you and the contestant would have to focus less on the comparative display of knowledge and more on the obvious (once you think of it) situational advantage enjoyed by the questioner. The questioner only asked questions about the particular bits of trivia he happened to have at his fingertips. He didn't

---

*The answers are (1) Gene Kelly; (2) Bardeen, Brattain, and Shockley; and (3) *Twelfth Night*.

display his *lack* of knowledge about countless other topics, and even when he happened to know a particular fact about a particular subject, it didn't necessarily mean he knew much else about that subject. Indeed, the questioner could have simply relied on what he remembered from an old movie he watched on television the night before, what he read in an obituary for the founder of a local company, or the play he was dragged by his parents to see when he was a teenager (from which he probably garbled the quotation anyway).

But precious few participants in that study were wise enough to recognize the way in which the questioner's role-conferred advantage resulted in his seemingly impressive display of knowledge. Instead, they succumbed to what social psychologists (following Lee, who coined the term) call the *fundamental attribution error* (FAE). We commit that error whenever we overestimate the extent to which people's actions, especially their successes and failures and their displays of apparent virtue or vice, are reflections of the kind of people they are—and underestimate the extent to which they are the product of situational influences.

The whole history of social psychological research suggests that we are all highly susceptible to this error. Hearing that a research participant was willing to administer four hundred and fifty volts of electricity to another person, we assume he is uncaring, or perhaps a bit sadistic. Seeing someone display a bit of esoteric knowledge, we assume she knows a lot about the topic in question and perhaps is deeply knowledgeable about other domains as well. Observing solar panels on a neighbor's roof, we assume the neighbor to be an environmentalist and probably liberal on a variety of social issues as well. And learning that a neighbor agreed to erect an ugly sign promoting auto safety on her front lawn, we assume she is especially concerned about the issue, or perhaps that she had suffered the loss of a loved one because of an unsafe driver (never dreaming that she has succumbed to the wiles of a clever social psychologist conducting a foot-in-the-door study).

The FAE is hard to overcome and applies beyond our understanding of the actions of other people. Aristotle and those who followed in his footsteps for nearly two thousand years claimed that objects behaved as they did—rocks fell, logs floated, and the moon rose—because of their *essence*. It was only with the contributions of Copernicus, Galileo, and especially Newton, and later those of Faraday, Maxwell, and a host of twentieth-century physicists, that scientists (and philosophers as well) at last fully recognized that to understand how some entity behaves, it is necessary to look at the surrounding field of forces at play. This slow progress from an essentialist to a field perspective on the physical world is paralleled in how people are inclined to interpret human behavior.[16] It is natural—reflexive even[17]—to see the causes of human action in the character and dispositions of those doing the acting. But as George Eliot noted at the end of *Middlemarch*, "There is no creature whose inward being is so strong that it is not greatly determined by what lies outside it." Thus, a truly wise person is a field theorist, withholding judgment until the nature of the surrounding situation is known and given careful consideration.

I Am Not Spock

The FAE is apparent when the roles people occupy call for certain behavior that is then taken as a reflection of their personalities. Thus, copy editors are seen as persnickety, nurses as caring, police officers as tough, and firefighters and soldiers as self-sacrificing. Some of them are, certainly, and that's why they chose those professions. But not all copy editors are fussy in other parts of their lives, not all nurses are warm to their spouses and children, and some soldiers enlisted just to get away from home. The tendency to confuse the person with the role is so strong that it even applies to professional actors. That is why Robert Young, TV's *Marcus Welby*, could get away with stating in a well-known ad campaign, "I am not a doctor, but I play one on TV."

And it is why Leonard Nimoy, who played the ultrarational Mr. Spock in the enduringly popular *Star Trek* TV series, felt compelled to title his biography, *I Am Not Spock.**

The consequences of the fundamental attribution error are sometimes far less benign. When Hurricane Katrina devastated the city of New Orleans in 2005, people across the United States and around the world were puzzled by the thousands of residents who stayed in the city rather than evacuate—costing the lives of nearly fifteen hundred of them and leading to a harrowing several days for many more. Viewers were puzzled because they saw staying behind as a *choice* to stay. As Secretary of Homeland Security Michael Chertoff put it, "Officials called for a mandatory evacuation. Some people chose not to obey that order. That was a mistake on their part." Michael Brown, who ended up losing his job as head of the Federal Emergency Management Agency as a result of his handling of the federal response to the hurricane, echoed the same sentiment when he stated that "a lot of people . . . chose not to leave."

But how many really "chose" to stay? Those who stayed behind were poorer, were much less likely to own a car, had less access to news, and had smaller social networks than those who evacuated. If you don't have a car to get out of the city, don't have the money to pay for lodging wherever you flee, and are less likely to get the word about the gravity of the threat from friends, family, or the media, you might very well end up, as they did, staying put and riding out the hurricane. Yet when relief workers from around the country (doctors, counselors, firefighters, police officers) were asked to provide three words to describe those who evacuated in advance of the hurricane and those who stayed behind, their responses were telling. Those who fled were most often described as "intelligent," "respon-

---

* Indeed, the fundamental attribution error is so powerful and pervasive that Nimoy eventually gave up, titling the second of his autobiographies, *I Am Spock.*

sible," and "self-reliant," whereas those who stayed behind were described as "foolish," "stubborn," and "lazy." Getting suckered into the FAE is easy to do here because we can see that some people left and some stayed, and that those who left ended up better off than those who stayed behind. What's harder to see are all the background influences that made it so much easier for some people to evacuate than others.[18]

In their important book *Scarcity*, Sendhil Mulainathan and Eldar Shafir note that there are parallels in the problems faced by the poor, including how they are viewed by much of the general population.[19] Their basic thesis is that scarcity reduces attentional "bandwidth" and other cognitive resources. Some of these scarcity effects are adaptive—they help people deal with immediate crises and challenges— but many are maladaptive. These include heightened impulsivity (making unwise purchases they can ill afford), neglect of long-term consequences (taking out payday loans at usurious rates), and poorer performance on a variety of judgment and decision-making tasks.

These ideas are not entirely new. Earlier investigators had documented similar effects of chronic high stress and provided evidence that willpower is an exhaustible resource that, when taxed too long or too hard, similarly leads to impulsive, maladaptive, and unwise behavior. But when considering the humane portrait that Mulainathan and Shafir have painted of the everyday lives of economically disadvantaged members of our society, it is noteworthy how those individuals are further victimized by the FAE. The *consequences* of their poverty in terms of nonoptimal judgment and decision making are seen as the *cause* of their failure to escape their condition and used as a justification for doing little to ease their difficulties.

Among history's most pernicious examples of the fundamental attribution error was the tendency of slave owners to view their slaves as incapable of functioning on their own. What they didn't see was how the very conditions of slavery robbed their slaves of the chance to demonstrate their full capabilities. Even an intellect as formidable as Thomas Jefferson's provides no safeguard against this.

You can sense Jefferson struggling mightily against the FAE in his *Notes on the State of Virginia* when he cautions that in making any comparisons between whites and blacks, "It will be right to make great allowances for the difference of condition, of education, of conversation, of the sphere in which they move." Nevertheless, he concludes that "in memory they are equal to the whites; in reason much inferior, as I think one [black] could scarcely be found capable of tracing and comprehending the investigations of Euclid; and that in imagination they are dull, tasteless, and anomalous." On another occasion, when trying to convince his friend Edward Coles not to free his slaves, he argued that blacks were "as incapable as children of taking care of themselves."[20] We would surely regard Jefferson as wiser, and consider his place in U.S. history even more laudable, if he had resisted such dispositional and, in this case, racist inferences and fully recognized and acknowledged the impact of living in slavery.

The Broader Message

Differences in traits, abilities, and character exist, of course. You are not wrong to believe that some people are more likely than others to donate their time or money to good causes, persevere in the face of failure, reliably perform the tasks they undertake, make wise financial choices, or prove an agreeable companion during a backpacking trip.

But the ability to make such predictions does not depend solely on assessing individual differences in traits, character, or ability. Instead, in everyday circumstances, actors and situations come in a package—psychologists would say they are confounded. We observe people who occupy particular roles or have made particular commitments (and will fare badly if they do not honor them). In addition, many of these people have told us something about their priorities, preferences, values, and intentions, and we know something of their current life circumstances and the incentive structures under which they operate.

We can be confident that the newscaster on CNN will offer more liberal views than the one on FOX and less liberal views than the one on MSNBC. We can safely assume that while we are away for the weekend, our neighbor will take in our morning newspapers as she promised, the guitarist in our favorite bistro will play sad love songs, and the Southern televangelist will hold forth about the evils of pre-marital sex, recreational drugs, and probably rap music as well. However, if we happen to encounter those same individuals in different situations from the ones in which we are accustomed to seeing them, we may very well get a big surprise.

The research we have reviewed in this chapter can make you wiser about particular situational factors that generations of social psychologists have shown to be so instrumental—so *surprisingly* instrumental—in channeling people's behavior. And a fuller appreciation of the power of the situation and the fundamental attribution error can spare you from making unwarranted or premature judgments. Such an appreciation will prevent you from jumping to the conclusion that the child who is currently failing in school is intellectually deficient, that the employees at an underperforming automobile assembly plant are dispositionally lazy and uncooperative, or that the voters in your town who don't cast a ballot on Election Day are politically apathetic.

In each case, the research presented here should prompt you to look more deeply at possible subtle situational influences—what might be burdening the failing student, what features of the work environment may be discouraging employees from doing a better job, or what immediate barriers and beliefs are keeping so many of your fellow citizens from voting. It may even produce a more thoughtful response when you watch the nightly news and hear about horrendous acts committed in the context of intergroup conflicts, or when you read that a once lauded new CEO has failed to revive the fortunes of a faltering organization.* The wisest person in the room takes a close, detailed look at what can be done to change the situation—what barriers and disincentives need to be removed and what can be done to make desirable and constructive actions easier, and undesirable and destructive actions more difficult.

The fundamental attribution error leads to erroneous expectations about the consistency of behavior across different situations and unwarranted inferences about personal deficiencies (and unwarranted inferences about the virtues of those who have enjoyed great advantage in life).† It also leads to unwarranted pessimism about the value of social programs designed to remove barriers to success. We return to this issue in chapter 8 where we describe how relatively simple, inexpensive interventions can boost the academic performance of disadvantaged and stigmatized students. Throughout the remainder of this book, however, we urge you to keep the FAE in mind whenever we discuss how particular experimental manipulations or particular ways of posing problems turn out to have surprisingly powerful effects.

If you want to be the wisest in the room, discipline yourself not to rush to judgment about individuals until you know, and feel you truly appreciate, the situational forces and constraints that are making their influence felt. And as we discuss in the chapter that follows, there is a further lesson to be learned: the importance of attending not just to the objective features of situations, but to how the individuals facing those situations interpret them.

---

*Warren Buffett, perhaps the wisest investor in America, may be (suitably) less prone to the FAE. The "Oracle of Omaha" sagely noted that "when a manager with a reputation for brilliance tackles a business with a reputation for poor fundamental economics, it is the reputation of the business that remains intact."

† The exploration of situational vs. dispositional influences on behavior across situations and over time was initiated by Walter Mischel's ground-breaking text *Personality and Assessment*. Mischel and his colleagues have continued for almost half a century to refine our understanding of these issues.[21]

3

The Name of the Game

Today a hope of many years' standing is in large part fulfilled. The civilization of the past hundred years, with its startling industrial changes, has tended more and more to make life insecure. Young people have come to wonder what would be their lot when they came to old age. The man with a job has wondered how long the job would last.

This social security measure gives at least some protection to thirty millions of our citizens who will reap direct benefits through unemployment compensation, through old-age pensions and through increased services for the protection of children and the prevention of ill health.[1]

With those words, Franklin Delano Roosevelt signed into law the Social Security Act of 1935. It was not the law he wanted to sign. Although Roosevelt had long thought that U.S. citizens should have some level of cradle-to-grave protection against the misfortunes that life can deliver, the Social Security Act fell far short of that ideal.* So Roosevelt was beside himself when he learned that Sir William

---

* In the original Social Security Act, benefits were paid only to the primary worker— that is, overwhelmingly to men.

71

Beveridge, an English economist, was credited with creating just such a cradle-to-grave insurance program in the United Kingdom. "Why does Beveridge get his name on this?" Roosevelt complained. "It is my idea. It is not the Beveridge plan. It is the Roosevelt Plan."[2]

But Roosevelt knew that a program like Great Britain's was a political nonstarter here in the United States. Despite the devastation wrought by the Great Depression—gross domestic output cut in half, unemployment more than 25 percent, half of all elderly citizens unable to support themselves, ten thousand failed banks—most Americans were afraid of anything that smacked of socialism. And any program that taxed some people to help others, which any cradle-to-grave program would have to do, struck many people as socialistic.

To pass social security legislation, then, Roosevelt and his brain trust knew that his plan had to be structured and described in a way that obscured any such income transfer. It therefore was presented as a kind of savings account, accompanied by a kind of insurance policy: A portion of workers' earnings would be set aside each pay period, earning workers, after a number of years, a modest pension after retirement or various misfortunes. But then, as now, there were no real individual savings "accounts." Nor were workers collectively ensuring their own futures and those of their families by accumulating a pool of dollars. Social security was, and remains, a pay-as-you-go system. Money from current workers is used to meet the obligations owed to present-day retirees—that is, current generations of workers are taxed to provide income for earlier ones.

Roosevelt, who if not always the smartest in the room was certainly one of the wisest, understood the importance of framing the new system as one in which workers were prudently setting aside part of their own paychecks, and not as an intergenerational transfer of income. That framing not only made it easier to get the necessary legislation through Congress; it allowed retirees to feel that they were collecting something they had earned, not depending on younger workers to support them. This sort of framing can be important in matters of public policy and in many everyday decisions that we are all called on to make.

But the larger point we wish to make here complements the main message of chapter 2. Although people are greatly influenced by the specific features of the situation that confronts them, the wisest one in the room recognizes that it is not just the objective features of the situation that matter. No less important, and often more important, is the way people subjectively interpret that situation—the meaning it has for them in terms of their experiences, values, and goals, and in light of the social norms they see as relevant.

The Language of Politics and the Politics of Language

The great English essayist George Orwell wrote that "political language . . . is designed to make lies sound truthful and murder respectable, and to give an appearance of solidity to pure wind." You don't need to share Orwell's cynicism to acknowledge the validity of his observation. As the selling of the new Social Security system attests, those who control the language of a political discussion control the way the citizenry thinks and acts.

The Civil War was fought with guns, but the two sides differed in what they claimed the war was about—"states' rights" and the "right of secession" versus the "maintenance of the Union" in the face of the "southern rebellion" (and only later emancipation).

Ever since the *Roe v. Wade* decision of 1973 that affirmed a woman's right to abortion, "pro-life" and "pro-choice" advocates have engaged in a bitter political struggle, with one side implicitly labeling its opponents as "anti-life" and willing to countenance the "murder of unborn children" and the other implicitly labeling its foes as "antichoice" and intent on denying women the right to exercise "control over their own bodies." Both sides fully recognize that people's responses to this heated issue are likely to be determined by what they believe the issue is really about.

By the same token, as we contemplate immigration reform, it matters whether we call individuals who are in this country seeking work without legal authorization "illegal aliens" or "undocumented workers." It was no accident that soon after World War II, our country came to have a secretary of *defense* instead of a secretary of *war*. Nor is it an accident that today our leaders use terms like *enhanced interrogation* rather than *torture*, and *collateral damage* rather than *civilian casualties*. The names we give to plans, policies, and proposals determine what associations and images come to mind when we think about them. This in turn influences how positively or negatively we feel about them, what actions we favor, and the degree of urgency we attach to those actions.

Political activists across the ideological spectrum battle to control the images and associations we connect with particular threats. Excess meanings are exploited with great success. Public health proposals to deal with obesity are labeled by business interests as efforts to impose a nanny state, implying that such measures are the first step in a conspiracy to deny us many of the freedoms (and guilty pleasures) that come with adulthood. Taxes on wealthy estates are labeled "death taxes" to conjure up images of victims being further set upon during their time of grief.

Political progressives likewise conjure up images and associations that suit their purposes. They charge conservatives with creating gridlock in Washington, not just to indicate how difficult it is to pass legislation but to summon forth the irritation we all feel when stuck in traffic. In sounding an alarm about climate change, they tell us that if current trends continue, "the climate in Seattle will be like that of Tijuana" within the next few decades. It's a clever comparison. For most of the target audience at least, "Tijuana" carries a lot of excess baggage (danger, drugs, and general lawlessness) that makes the forecast seem ominous. But note that Tijuana's climate is virtually identical to that of La Jolla, California, just on the other side of the U.S.-Mexico border. Would the prospect seem so dire (especially to Seattle residents) if the threat involved having to put up with La Jolla's weather?

The Name of the Game and Why It Matters

Because people respond to their surrounding circumstances not as they are but as they are interpreted, the judicious use of terms and labels can determine the nature of the situation to which people believe they are responding. Language itself can therefore be a potent situationist influence. This was illustrated in a study Lee and his colleagues conducted, one that employed an old standby of behavioral science, the Prisoner's Dilemma Game. As you may know, the name derives from a scenario in which two suspects are being held on suspicion of a crime (say, burglary) that they did in fact commit. The police, however, have only enough evidence to convict them of a lesser crime (say, possession of stolen goods) and therefore need to get one suspect to testify against the other to obtain sufficient evidence to throw the book at one of them.

The suspects are interrogated separately, and each is invited to implicate the other in exchange for more lenient treatment. Each is told that if they both remain silent, they will be convicted of the lesser offense and receive two years in jail. If one suspect squeals and the other does not, the squealer will be set free, leaving his partner in crime to receive the maximum sentence for burglary of ten years. If both squeal, they are told, no special deal will be available to either one, although both will receive a less-than-maximum sentence of five years.

The defining feature of this dilemma is that regardless of what the other suspect does, each fares better if he squeals than if he remains silent (freedom instead of jail time if his partner remains silent, five years instead of ten if his partner squeals). Yet if both pursue this seemingly dominant strategy of informing on their partner, both end up worse off (five years in jail) than if both remain silent (two years in jail).

The laboratory version of the game is typically played for money, with two participants making separate decisions to "cooperate" or "defect." But the dilemma is the same. Again, regardless of what the other player does, each receives a better payoff for defecting than cooperating. In the example depicted in table 3.1, $8 instead of $5 if the other cooperates and nothing instead of a loss of $2 if the other defects. But again, each player fares less well if they both defect (both get nothing) than if both cooperate (both get $5).

Table 3.1: A Modified Prisoner's Dilemma Game

		PLAYER 1	
		Cooperate	*Defect*
	Cooperate	player 1 gets $5	player 1 gets $8
PLAYER 2		player 2 gets $5	player 2 loses $2
	Defect	player 1 loses $2	player 1 gets $0
		player 2 gets $8	player 2 gets $0

The stakes in Lee's study were somewhat smaller, and the game went on for five rounds, each with the same options and potential payoffs. But there were two special features of this study. First, half of the participants were students who had been specifically selected by the resident assistants (RAs) in their dorms as among the most likely to cooperate when playing the game (typical estimates by the RAs were 90 percent likely) and half were students the RAs nominated as being among the least likely to cooperate (typical estimates were 20 percent likely). These individuals were then recruited to participate, unaware that they had been nominated on the basis of their reputation for cooperativeness or selfishness. The second feature of the study was the name of the game presented to the students: Half of the nominated students were told they were playing the *Community Game* and half were told that they were playing the *Wall Street Game*.

The first finding of note is that the RAs' nominations proved to have no predictive power. None. The second is that the name of the game had a dramatic effect on the participants' decisions about whether to cooperate or defect, with the Community Game label roughly doubling the frequency of cooperation of both those deemed by their RAs as likely to cooperate and those deemed unlikely to cooperate. This was true for their first choice in the game as well as their choices over all five rounds (see figure 3.1).[3]

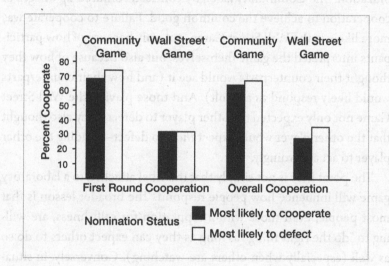

Figure 3.1. Cooperation rates among participants nominated as "likely cooperators" and "likely defectors" when the Prisoner's Dilemma game was labeled the Wall Street Game versus the Community Game. (From Liberman, Samuels, & Ross, 2002.)

Why would the label attached to the game prove to be a better predictor of who would cooperate than the players' reputations for cooperativeness? As we emphasized in chapter 2, this is partly due to the fact that people act less consistently across situations than is generally assumed. This is especially true when trying to generalize from how someone acts in a variety of familiar situations to one that is novel, like the Prisoner's Dilemma. But the failure of the participants' reputations to predict how they behaved was also the result of the label influencing what participants thought the game was "about," and hence what considerations were on their minds when they decided to cooperate or defect. The name of the game, in other words, determined what game they were playing and hence, how they played.

The Wall Street label led participants to think of the dog-eat-dog world of the financial trader, a world narrowly focused on profit maximization. The Community label, by contrast, conjured up images of cooperation to achieve the common good. Failure to cooperate was more likely in the Wall Street Game, not only because of how participants interpreted the game themselves, but also because of how they thought their counterparts would see it (and how their counterparts would likely respond as a result). And those playing the Wall Street Game not only expected the other player to defect; they also thought that the other player would expect *them* to defect—leading the other player to act accordingly.

The point here is not simply that the label attached to a laboratory game will influence how people respond. The broader lesson is that most people, even those with a reputation for selfishness, are willing to "do the right thing" as long as they can expect others to do so as well (especially when others are watching). Conversely, in situations where norms of self-interest reign supreme, even those who are generally community minded don't want to be seen as "suckers." No one wants to be a sucker, and few feel compelled to be a "saint." Most people just want to act appropriately and be a "good citizen," and it is their understanding of the surrounding context—including the label attached to it—that determines just what *appropriately* and *being a good citizen* mean.

How we interpret a situation guides how we act in two distinct ways. What we think the situation we're confronting is *about* determines how we think, feel, and act in response. Is an amendment to a bill in Congress an attempt to improve it or a political tactic to scuttle it? Is a friend's silence while we're talking about a budding romance a sign of approval or displeasure? How we interpret a situation also influences the meaning we assign to our own possible actions, thereby determining what we choose to do. Would I be a chump if I didn't try to maximize profit? Would it be unkind to say no?

How we interpret a situation, in other words, is at once an interpretation of the stimuli before us and of different possible responses. Everyone knows that at some level. But only the wisest in the room fully appreciates the extent to which responses are governed by those who control the way particular actions and situations are seen. The wisest in the room may not be aware of all the subtle techniques for doing so, but a wise person will certainly attend to the way options are labeled or framed.

Default Options Organ Donation: A Closer Look

To further appreciate the importance of the meaning people attach to the choices they face, let's revisit the remarkable findings on organ donation rates in Europe. Recall that opt-in countries like Germany (and the United States) have participation rates in the 10 to 20 percent range, whereas opt-out countries like France and Belgium have rates of more than 90 percent. At first glance, these massive differences invite a simple situationist interpretation: It's a bit easier to be a potential donor in an opt-out country than an opt-in country. Because people are sometimes lazy and prone to inertia, participation rates are bound to be higher in opt-out countries.

A straightforward situationist interpretation of this effect is certainly on the mark to a degree: Inertia and doing what's easiest are indeed a big part of the story. But in 2012, the two of us, along with

Tom's graduate student Shai Davidai, designed and carried out a series of studies to see whether there was more to it than that. In particular, we wanted to find out whether having an opt-in or an opt-out policy influences the very meaning people assign to being an organ donor.[4]

In an opt-in country, we reasoned, signing up to be a potential organ donor is likely to be seen as something that only particularly virtuous citizens do. In an opt-out country, in contrast, becoming a potential donor simply by not acting to exclude oneself from the program is something much less notable and altruistic—just ordinary good citizenship. It is something that only a person who was exceptionally selfish or misanthropic, or perhaps someone with some peculiar religious affiliation, would fail to do.

To test our conjecture, we told research participants about either the opt-in donation policy of the Netherlands or the opt-out policy of Belgium. We then asked them to rate how similar a variety of actions are to one another in the country in question (e.g., "paying your taxes," "letting others go ahead of you in line," "going on a hunger strike for a cause you believe in," and "volunteering for a dangerous military assignment"). Included in the list of actions was "donating your organs when you die."

By analyzing the overall pattern to these action-by-action comparisons (through a statistical technique called multidimensional scaling), it was possible to discern how close they are in meaning. The picture that emerged from this exercise was remarkable, and consistent with our conjecture about the meaning of being a potential donor (see figure 3.2). In the opt-in context of the Netherlands, the participants' similarity ratings indicated that they saw a willingness to donate as roughly akin to giving away half of one's wealth after one's death or volunteering for a dangerous military assignment. In the opt-out context of Belgium, in contrast, being a potential donor was seen in much less extreme terms—as something between letting others go ahead of you in line and volunteering some of your time to work with the poor.

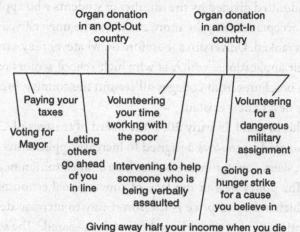

Organ donation
in an Opt-Out
country

Organ donation
in an Opt-In
country

Paying your
taxes

Voting for
Mayor

Letting
others
go ahead
of you
in line

Volunteering
your time
working with
the poor

Intervening to help
someone who is
being verbally
assaulted

Volunteering
for a
dangerous
military
assignment

Going on a
hunger strike
for a cause
you believe in

Giving away half your income when you die

Figure 3.2. Becoming a Potential Organ Donor in an Opt-In versus Opt-Out Country. Distances between each of the actions reflect their degree of perceived similarity.*

In short, our suspicion was confirmed. As the distances shown in figure 3.2 make clear, volunteering to be an organ donor in a country with an opt-in policy is seen as a much more substantial action than in a country with an opt-out policy. Having to opt in or opt out does more than simply make one option easier to exercise than the other. It also establishes the very meaning people assign to the act of being a potential organ donor.

Price as a Proxy for Value

A critical determinant of a university's ranking by *US News & World Report* or *The Princeton Review* is its acceptance rate: the number of

---

*The activities other than organ donation were rated very similarly by the two groups of respondents. Points on the figure for actions other than organ donation reflect the average ratings of the two groups.

students admitted divided by the number of students who apply. The lower the acceptance rate, the more exclusive the university, and the higher it is ranked. Universities therefore do whatever they can to increase their applications, which is why high school seniors are deluged with brochures from colleges all around the country, including many they never knew existed.

With this in mind, in early 2000 the board of trustees of Ursinus College adopted a proposal designed to increase applications that at first might seem counterintuitive: The board *raised* tuition nearly 20 percent. The policy flew in the face of conventional economic theory, by which a drop in price is the surest way to increase demand. Unconventional or not, it worked: Applications soared.[5] The strategy has been employed with equal success by a number of other colleges, including Bryn Mawr, Notre Dame, and Rice.

Although it is not what standard economic theory would recommend, it's easy to see why raising tuition would increase the number of applicants. Parents want to send their kids to high-quality, prestigious schools. But academic quality and prestige are hard to assess, and so they use price as an indicator of quality. If it costs a lot, they tell themselves, it must be good.

Ursinus's experience with raising its tuition to boost admissions highlights the same insight about human behavior offered by our earlier discussion of the impact of labels and defaults: People respond to their subjective interpretations of objective circumstances, not to the objective circumstances themselves. Potential applicants to Ursinus respond to what they understand a hefty tuition bill to mean (an exclusive, high-quality education), not to the dollars and cents themselves. Of course, price is not the only cue people use when they are uncertain of a product's value. Advertisers and marketers spend millions trying to find other proxies for value, and for luxury, power, and youth as well. They run focus groups to determine what kind of jungle animal it is best to name a car, or what type or color of con-

tainer suggests luxury to buyers of perfume, ice cream, and choco-
lates. (The answer, judging from the shelves in supermarkets and gift
shops, appears to be black.)

Meaning Making

The influence of subjective interpretation extends more deeply into
more areas of life than people generally appreciate. Indeed, an understanding of the full power and reach of subjective interpretation is
one of the things that separates the wisest person from everyone else
in the room. Is a parent's financial gift to an adult child an act of generosity, or an effort to exert control? Is a concession a sign of goodwill, or of weakness? How the adult child reacts to the gift and how a
concession from the other side is received depends on how they are
construed. If we want to understand the actions of other people, we
have to understand how they interpreted their circumstances and the
choices they faced—not the way *we* would interpret them or, rather,
the way we think we would interpret them if we were in their shoes.
Wise people recognize this and also take pains to ensure that their
own actions will be interpreted as intended.

So what determines how people assign meaning to different actions and circumstances? What determines whether an ambiguous
facial expression is seen as a smile or a grimace or a leer? And what
determines whether a stranger encountered outside on a dark night is
seen as a threat or simply another person out for a walk?

Some of the factors that influence how people are likely to interpret a given situation are pretty simple and familiar. But some are not
at all obvious, and a mastery of some of the general principles of how
interpretations are formed can make you wiser when it comes to exerting or resisting influence.

Context

Suppose you encounter a stranger on an otherwise empty sidewalk at night. Is it someone to fear? You're much more likely to come to that conclusion if you've just come from seeing a horror film than if you've just seen a romantic comedy. Psychologists describe this as a "priming" effect: What you saw at the cinema made notions of harm and mayhem more (or less) "accessible." That is, whatever happens to be on the top of your head because of prior events is readily applied to whatever stimuli you subsequently encounter. The same stimulus can therefore provoke very different reactions depending on whatever recent experiences you happen to have had.

More broadly, the surrounding context—what just happened and what is currently happening elsewhere in the environment—is one of the most powerful determinants of how objects, events, and propositions are interpreted. In a demonstration of this idea commonly used in introductory psychology courses, the same stimulus (see figure 3.3) is seen as a letter in the context of other letters but as a number in the context of other numbers.

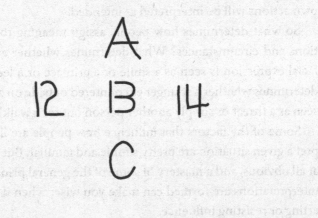

Figure 3.3 Is the symbol in the center a letter or number? It depends on whether you look from left to right or top to bottom.

As we'll see later in chapter 7 on conflict, the very same proposal can be seen as a helpful step toward resolution or a cynical ploy depending on who was thought to have offered it. It's impossible to always predict how others will respond to a particular word, deed, or proposal. But the wisest person in the room, or around the negotiating table, knows enough not to fall prey to naïve realism and simply assume that meanings are fixed, and shared by all.

Habit and Experience

Some ideas are sitting there on the top of our heads, ready to influence our interpretations, because we've recently dealt with them and others because we've frequently dealt with them. Consider how the sentence "he ran into the bank" might be interpreted differently by a bank executive versus a yacht owner. We all have particular categories or filters that determine what we notice and how we parse the world around us. The most accessible categories differ from person to person as a result of their interests, experiences, and concerns, and they may also depend on the specifics of the situation at hand.

Academics are prone to characterize people in terms of whether they are book smart or not; entertainers are likely to size up each other in terms of qualities like charisma or star power. The Steve Jobses of the world look at electronic devices in terms of whether they are elegantly designed, impoverished students consider whether they are worth the price, and aging academics ask whether they will be able to figure out how to use the damn things.

Motivation

If you want to know how a person is likely to interpret a given stimulus, it also helps to know her motivational state. This truth is captured in the cinematic cliché in which a shimmering image in the desert appears as an oasis to a parched, desperate traveler. In a clever investigation of this phenomenon, two of Tom's Cornell colleagues, Emily Balcetis and David Dunning, showed how people's desires can influence the way they resolve the ambiguity inherent in a number of perceptual illusions. In one study, for example, participants faced the final round of a laboratory task that would determine whether they experienced something positive (eating a bag of jelly beans) or something dreadful (having to eat a "bag of gelatinous and partially liquefied canned beans"). Their fate depended on whether the final stimulus that flashed on the computer screen in front of them was a farm animal or a sea animal. What was shown was the image depicted in figure 3.4.

As soon as the image appeared on the screen, the participants called out what they saw. The image appeared for only one second, long enough for them to see it clearly, but not long enough for them to spot the ambiguity. Supporting the idea that people often see what they want to see, participants were much more likely to say it was a farm animal if the appearance of a farm animal would spare them from having to eat the gelatinous beans, but to say it was a sea animal if a sea animal would spare them.[6]

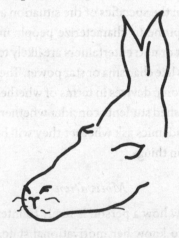

Figure 3.4 Horse or seal? It depends on how you look at it, or what you're motivated to see. (If you see the "V" at the top as ears, it's a horse; if you see it as a tail, it's a seal.)

But did the participants in this study really *see* what they wanted to see, or did they simply *report* seeing the stimulus that would give them a better outcome? Balcetis and Dunning ran a number of follow-up studies to be sure that the participants' motivation influenced their perceptions, not simply their verbal reports.*

The influence of motivation on people's judgments is of course widely recognized. It is not just the wisest ones in the room who exchange knowing glances when parents extol the brilliance, beauty, or artistic talents of their offspring. As we discussed in chapter 1, political partisans tend to think it was their candidate who did the better job in the debate. And hundreds of surveys have shown that men and women of all ages, regions of the country, and even social classes tend to rate themselves as above average on almost any positive dimension: more sensitive than average, more unbiased, better leaders, better drivers—you name it.[7] Perhaps the most remarkable finding is that even people who are in the hospital for injuries sustained in automobile accidents rate themselves on average as better than average drivers.[8]

---

*In one study that we'll describe in detail to give you a sense of how psychologists are able to make such determinations, Balcetis and Dunning quickly flashed actual words and mere letter strings ("flacter," "ombute") on a computer screen. Some of the actual words were related to "seal" (e.g., *blubber*) and others to "horse" (e.g., *cowboy*). The participants had to decide as quickly as possible whether the stimulus flashed on the screen was a word. The investigators reasoned that participants should be faster to identify a word like *blubber* if they had the idea of "seal" on their minds (as a result of just having seen it). The critical feature of their design was that some participants made these word vs. non-word assessments just *after* having been exposed to the ambiguous image in figure 3.4, whereas others made these assessments *before* seeing it. What the investigators found was that participants who did this task after seeing the ambiguous figure were faster to identify words like *cowboy* when it was a farm animal they wanted to see and faster to identify words like *blubber* when it was a sea animal they wanted to see. While all participants had the same motivation to see the type of animal that would serve their interests, only those who had already been exposed to the ambiguous figure were faster in identifying words related to it.

Part of this is simple human vanity. People show more of an above-average effect when their self-esteem has been challenged and they're in need of a boost.[9] But before you chalk up the above-average effect entirely to people's motivation to think highly of themselves, consider the possibility that most people really *are* above average, at least when their own criteria are taken into account. As the Nobel Prize–winning economist Thomas Schelling put it, "Careful drivers give weight to care, skillful drivers give weight to skill, and those who think that, whatever else they are not, at least they are polite, give weight to courtesy, and come out high on their own scale. This is the way that every child has the best dog on the block."[10]

Supporting this idea, researchers have found that the above-average effect is much stronger on traits that permit multiple interpretations ("talented," "sensible") than on traits that are more narrowly defined ("tall," "punctual").[11] It's easy for people to have different "objects of judgment" in mind when considering whether they are athletic, artistic, or altruistic, and the object they select tends to be one that favors their own talents. So it should not be a surprise that people so often judge themselves as above average.

People are therefore not exactly deceiving themselves when they show the better-than-average effect. We tend to organize our lives around our strengths. We pursue areas in which we have enjoyed success and expect continued involvement to pay dividends. Young men who are stronger than their peers choose football as their sport and therefore live in an athletic world that emphasizes being big and strong. Those who are more slightly built, in contrast, might choose tennis or badminton. Their world is one in which being athletic is to be blessed with superior hand-eye coordination.

By the same token, and much more important, those who see good citizenship as a matter of paying taxes and keeping their property in good shape, those who see it as a matter of working for causes they believe in, and those who believe it is a matter of getting out and protesting when the government is not living up to what they believe are its obligations all live their lives and spend their time and energies accordingly. They can then all claim, at least by their own criteria, to be "better-than-average" citizens.

Temporal Proximity

Suppose someone asks you whether you'll help mobilize voters for your favored candidate in next week's election. Your answer would likely depend on your calendar of commitments and the specifics of the duties involved (Drive voters to the polls? Make phone calls or knock on doors, which could be awkward? Ask people for money, which could be even more awkward?). Suppose instead that someone asks whether you'd be willing to help with similar electioneering efforts in two years. In that case, your answer would likely depend on more abstract considerations such as your sense of civic duty and what you see as fulfilling your personal values.

When looking far off in the future we see the forest; when looking close at hand, we see the trees. This difference in perspective influences the very meaning we assign to events. Going to college is about learning and personal growth; *being* in college is about studying, turning in assignments, and dealing with immature dormmates.[12] These differences in perspective can then lead to conflict between what we commit to do far in advance ("Going to exotic places is the only way to really get away from it all") and what we feel like doing when the moment arrives ("How am I going to communicate when I don't speak the language? Where's my passport? Who will look after my dog Buster while I'm away?"). If we want our choices to reflect our abstract values, it's therefore a good idea to choose, or imagine choosing, from a more distant perspective—for example, by imagining how we're likely to feel looking back at a decision a year or so after the fact.*

---

* Our late colleague Amos Tversky advised that when deciding whether to accept an invitation to give a talk next year, you should imagine that the invitation is for a talk next week: After all, when you actually begin to try to fit your preparation for the talk into your busy schedule, it *will* be for next week.

A similar sort of distance can be achieved by thinking about what decision you'd recommend for someone else. Events we experience ourselves are psychologically closer than events others have experienced, and so we think of them in more detailed, concrete terms. That's why people often find it easier to figure out what choice to recommend to others than to make themselves: For better or worse, thinking about the matter from the more distant perspective of someone else makes it easier to put complicating details aside and focus on what seems most important. An important component of wisdom is perspective. The wisest in the room therefore toggles back and forth between different perspectives to get the most comprehensive view of a particular decision.

Frame and Fortune

In a popular and obviously apocryphal story, the great Yankee catcher Yogi Berra places an order at a New York pizzeria. When asked whether he'd like the pizza cut into four slices or eight, Yogi supposedly responds, "Better make it four; I'm not hungry enough to eat eight."

The humor in this story comes from the assumption that no one—or hardly anyone—would be so dim as to think that the same pizza would be any less filling cut into four large slices than eight smaller ones.* Yet psychologists over the past thirty years have demonstrated time and again that the tiniest change in how a question is worded or how an option is described can radically alter how it is understood—and therefore how people respond.

Consider a study that Tom conducted in conjunction with a large

---

* If Yogi were aware of the studies on overeating that we discussed in chapter 2, he might realize that having the pizza cut into eight slices could be a pretty good strategy for avoiding weight gain. Because people unconsciously monitor the number of slices they have eaten, Yogi would in fact be more likely to eat four large slices than eight small ones.

insurance company. Half of the respondents, drawn from a national sample of relatively affluent households, were asked whether they could comfortably *save* 20 percent of their income, and the other half were asked whether they could comfortably *live on* 80 percent of their income. Of course, to save 20 percent of your income is to live on 80 percent of it. Nevertheless, whereas only half of the respondents thought they could save 20 percent of their earnings, four out of five thought they could comfortably live on 80 percent.

This difference in reactions cannot be chalked up to simple financial illiteracy. People find beef that is 80 percent lean more appealing than beef that is 20 percent fat.[13] They are more impressed by condoms whose manufacturers boast of a 95 percent success rate rather than a 5 percent failure rate.[14] They are more supportive of taxes on the rich when the existing level of income inequality is described in terms of how much more the rich earn than the median wage earner than when it is described in terms of how much less the median wage earner earns than the rich.[15]

Some of these effects of the language used are the result of very particular associations people have to specific words. The frames are sui generis. As we noted earlier, people respond differently to policies related to *illegal aliens* versus *undocumented workers* because one term evokes more negative associations than the other. A very different set of negative associations leads people to react more negatively to *torture* than *enhanced interrogation,* and still another set of negative associations leads people to express more concern over the prospect of a *mosque* being built near the site of the former World Trade Center than an Islamic *cultural center* being built there. The brand Chemlawn elicits powerful negative associations now that it did not have when the lawn care company was founded, which is why it is now called Trugreen.

But some principles of effective framing have broad application. The fact that saving 20 percent of your income seems harder than living on 80 percent of it, and the thought of eating beef that is 20 percent fat seems more unappealing than eating beef that's 80 percent lean illustrates one of these principles. We explore these principles in the remainder of this chapter. Knowing about them should help you be a more effective advocate for policies you favor. It should also help you resist clever attempts to influence you and those you care about or consult on important matters.

Losses and Gains

So what is the link between our reluctance to save 20 percent of our income, our distaste for meat that's 20 percent fat, or our aversion to products with a 5 percent failure rate? All three, psychologists claim, are the result of *negativity dominance*. Holding objective magnitude constant, bad things hurt more than good things feel good. Getting an unexpected $500 check in the mail feels good, but not as much as getting an unexpected $500 bill feels bad. This is why a piece of meat that is 20 percent fat is less desirable than a piece that's 80 percent lean. The former highlights the weightier negative information; the latter ushers it to the background. Negativity dominance is especially relevant to everyday persuasion because many outcomes can be equally well described in the language of good or bad, or losses and gains. Hundreds of studies have demonstrated that logically equivalent phrasings are by no means psychologically equivalent.

Daniel Kahneman and Amos Tversky have done the most to shed light on the ways in which numerical framing can influence people's judgments and decisions, and so our discussion of this insight starts with one of their most famous studies.[16] Participants were presented with the following dilemma:

> Imagine that the country is preparing for the outbreak of an unusual disease, which is expected to kill 600 people. Two programs to combat the disease have been proposed:

- If Program A is adopted, 200 people will be saved.
- If Program B is adopted, there is a ⅓ chance that 600 people will be saved, and a ⅔ chance that no one will be saved.

What choice would you make? If you would elect to save the 200 lives with certainty, you're in the majority. Seventy-two percent of the respondents in the original study (it has been replicated many times) were *risk averse*: The chance of saving 600 instead of 200 lives doesn't seem worth the risk of not saving any at all. Better to go for the sure thing and lock in those 200.

However, Kahneman and Tversky also presented a different group of participants with a different framing of the same choice. This time the options were as follows:

- If Program C is adopted, 400 people will die.
- If Program D is adopted, there is a ⅓ chance that nobody will die, and a ⅔ chance that 600 will die.

What choice would you make under these circumstances? If you'd opt for the "certain" option this time, dooming 400 people to certain death, you'd be in the minority. Most people who saw this version seemed to be *risk seeking*, although a better description would be that they were *loss averse*. They so hate the idea of accepting a certain loss that they are willing to take a big risk to avoid it. In fact, 78 percent of the participants said they would rather take a chance on saving everyone, at the risk of saving no one, than letting 400 people die for sure.

The kicker, of course, is that saving 200 out of 600 is the same as letting 400 die. And a one-third chance of saving 600 *is* a one-third chance of nobody dying. The preference for choosing the sure thing or rolling the dice was heavily determined not by some stable attitude toward risk but by how the choice was framed.

Inspired by these results, Lee and David Fetherstonhaugh asked travelers at the San Jose airport if they would be willing to work an extra three years—to retire at age sixty-eight instead of age sixty-five—to gain an increase of $2,500 in their annual pension benefit, from the $10,000 available at age sixty-five to $12,500. Others were asked whether they would be willing to work those extra three years in order to avoid a $2,500 reduction in their pension, from the $12,500 available at age sixty-eight to $10,000 for retiring at age sixty-five.

Responses to these two ways of framing the same choice were dramatically different, especially among those earning less per year than the median respondent ($60,000). When the $2,500 per year was presented as a gain for working until age sixty-eight, roughly two-thirds of the low wage earners said no; it wasn't worth staying on the job for the extra three years. But when that same $2,500 was presented as a penalty they could avoid by working longer, more than two-thirds of them (71 percent) said it was worth the extra three years of work.[17]

Economists skeptical of psychological research on decision-making biases frequently question whether these sorts of findings apply to the choices made by experienced decision makers dealing with important concerns in their professional lives. One study tackled that question by confronting practicing physicians with a hypothetical decision involving two treatments for lung cancer: (1) radiation, which presented no immediate risk of death but offered less favorable longevity statistics, and (2) surgery, which presented a nontrivial risk of immediate death but more favorable long-term statistics.[18] What the investigators varied was how these statistics were described. Some of the physicians were given the information framed in terms of mortality rates, and others were given the same information framed as survival rates. Consider how you would respond first to the options in the left column of the page and then to the options in the right column:

Mortality Framing	Survival Framing
Surgery	*Surgery*
10 percent die during treatment	90 percent survive treatment
32 percent will die within 1 year	68 percent survive at least 1 year
66 percent will die within 5 years	34 percent survive at least 5 years
Radiation Therapy	*Radiation Therapy*
0 percent will die during treatment	100 percent survive treatment
23 percent will die within one year	77 percent survive at least 1 year
78 percent will die within five years	22 percent survive at least 5 years

When confronted with the choice framed in terms of mortality (the left column), the physicians were evenly split between surgery and radiation: Exactly 50 percent opted for each. For them, the benefit of decreasing immediate mortality by choosing radiation seemed as attractive as the benefit of increasing longer-term survival through surgery. For those shown these data as presented in the right column, however, the overwhelming majority (84 percent) opted to tolerate the increased risk of death during surgery in order to increase the chances of longer-term survival. In the investigators' words, "We attribute this result to the fact that the risk of perioperative death looms larger when it is presented in terms of mortality than when it is presented in terms of survival."

By the Numbers

On Tom's desk at this moment are solicitations offering daily delivery of a prominent newspaper for a mere $1 a day, upgraded internet service for only $30 a month, and a way to "save nature in Europe" for a trifling 3 cents a day. How can any reasonable person refuse? Why hasn't he jumped at these opportunities? For one thing, his enthusiasm wanes when the costs are calculated on a per year rather than a per day basis—$365 a year for the newspaper and $360 a year for faster internet service. (And please don't ask why he hasn't yet saved the flora and fauna of Europe for a mere 11 euros a year.)

These organizations recognize that the prospect of spending a relatively small amount is more palatable than spending a large amount. But as numerous studies have shown, most people focus on the raw numbers presented to them rather than doing the math that would help them make informed choices. For the same reason, people are more likely to buy expensive brand-name products when they are priced in a strong currency like the British pound that results in a relatively small price tag (318 pounds for an Apple iPad with retinal display) than when priced in a weak currency like the Mexican peso that results in a relatively large price tag (6,395 pesos for the same iPad).[19]

An especially common version of this phenomenon is what psychologists call *denominator neglect*. If you want people to be impressed by an amount, choose a large scale ("$365 a year"); if you want them not to be impressed, choose a small scale ("only a dollar a day"). The effects of strategically choosing the right scale (i.e., the right denominator) can be dramatic. In one study, respondents judged a disease that kills 1,200 out of every 10,000 afflicted individuals to be more dangerous than one that's twice as lethal, killing 24 out of every 100.[20]

This is not to say that people never pay attention to the denominator. In the early 1980s, the A&W fast-food restaurant chain introduced a burger with a third of a pound of beef to compete with McDonald's popular quarter pounder. Although most customers preferred A&W's new burger in taste tests, it was a big disappointment in the marketplace. When focus groups were run to get to the bottom of this paradox, A&W discovered that many customers thought a burger with one-third of a pound of beef was less generous than one with one-quarter of a pound. Customers were attending to the denominator, just not very intelligently: The smaller "3" led many to conclude that one-third is smaller than one-quarter![21]

People are more likely to attend to a denominator—appropriately or not—when it is something they can attach real meaning to, not merely an abstract numerical value. Consider a well-known thought experiment in which participants are asked whether they would drive across town to save, say, $15 on a $49 iPod shuffle they've decided they need. Most say yes. But when asked whether they would drive across town to save $15 on a needed $649 iPhone, most say no.

From a purely rational perspective, it is unreasonable to value $15 over the time and nuisance involved in driving across town in the first case but not the second. A savings of $15 on a $49 iPod purchase (31 percent) is undeniably more of a bargain than saving $15 on a $649 iPhone (2 percent). But what the participants overlook is that the relevant denominator—the cost of the iPod or the iPhone—should not influence their calculation about whether it is worth driving across town to save $15. The strategic choice of denominators can also influence people's decisions about energy savings—a specific dollar savings seems large when expressed as a fraction of their *heating bill*, smaller when expressed as a fraction of their *utility bill*, and smaller still (and perhaps not worth the trouble) when expressed as a fraction of their *household expenses*.

Mind the Gap

Suppose that after undergoing genetic testing, your doctor tells you that you have a 25 percent chance of developing a severe neurological disorder. How much would you pay to lower your risk to 24 percent? Probably not much. Suppose instead that your doctor tells you that you have a 1 percent chance of developing the disorder. How much would you pay to lower your risk to zero? If you're like most people, you'd pay a LOT more to get your risk down to zero. Doing so involves a change in kind rather than degree—from "a chance" to "no chance."

The same principle applies at the other end of the probability scale. How much would you pay to increase your chances, from 75 percent to 76 percent, of winning the privilege of kissing your favorite movie star? What about from 99 percent to 100 percent? Again, most people would not pay much (or anything) for a 1 percent increase if it just gives them a 76 percent chance, but they would be willing to pay quite a bit for a 1 percent increase that makes the outcome certain.

The psychological difference between options at different points on the certainty scale has additional consequences. For one thing, the closer one gets to certainty, the more impact a message has. Reducing the chance of something bad from 4 percent to 2 percent will strike most people as more important than reducing it from 24 percent to 22 percent.

This likely played a role in the cancer treatment choices made by physicians that we described earlier. A tendency to prefer a treatment described as having a 90 percent survival rate over one described as having a 10 percent fatality rate may have involved more than an asymmetry in how people respond to the prospect of losses and gains. Psychologically, 90 percent seems closer to 100 percent than 10 percent does to 0 (in the same way that the difference between 90-pound and 100-pound barbells feels much smaller than the difference between a 10-pound weight and nothing). As a result, a 10 percent chance of death in the fatality frame seems substantial (so far from zero!) at the same time that the chances of not surviving in the survival frame seem remote (90 percent is so close to 100 percent!). The broader lesson here is that our sensitivity to events near or at the end points of the probability scale can be exploited to make potential actions or outcomes seem more or less dangerous, more or less appealing, or more or less worthy of our attention.

Select or Reject?

Many times a choice comes down to two options: Cornell or Stanford, a Subaru or Volvo, the female candidate from finance or the male candidate from HR. And when such a choice is made, two things, by necessity, happen at once: One option is selected and the other is rejected. So it shouldn't matter whether a person is asked to choose one or to reject one, should it? They're just different ways of asking the same thing.

But we hope by now we have convinced you that different ways of saying the same thing don't always produce the same response. So it probably won't surprise you to learn that it *does* matter whether decision makers approach the choice between two options as a matter of selecting one or as rejecting one. When focused on selection, people tend to think of things that warrant selection. When focused on rejection, in contrast, people tend to think of things that warrant rejection—on reasons for ruling out one or the other option.

What this means is that a safe, middle-of-the-road option will fare better relative to one with notable pluses and minuses when rejecting than when choosing. The Princeton psychologist Eldar Shafir demonstrated this tendency when he asked participants to settle a hypothetical custody dispute.[22] When asked to which parent they wanted to award custody of the child, a majority sided with the mixed-bag parent (very close relationship with the child, but lots of work-related travel) over the parent with moderate rapport with the child and moderate job-related demands on time and availability. But when asked which parent should be *denied* custody, a majority made the opposite recommendation. In other words, the very same parent was paradoxically deemed both more worthy and less worthy of having custody of the child.

The lesson should be clear. If the candidate you'd like to get the nod from your boss, your working group, or your family is the flashier, riskier one, pose it as a choice of which to select. If your candidate is the less flashy, less risky option, frame it as a choice of which to reject.

Near the beginning of this chapter, we quoted George Orwell on the ability of language to shape political thought. The research we then discussed can seem, well, Orwellian: The findings we reviewed can give the impression that people's judgments and decisions are at the mercy of how a skilled manipulator chooses to frame an issue through the language used.* That is certainly one way to look at the research on framing. The Orwellian threat is real. But as we noted in the previous chapter on situationism, people are not passive puppets on a string. They actively seek out the meaning of the stimuli and events that happen around them. And the wisest one in the room considers alternative ways of framing issues and choices, especially when they are controversial or the stakes are high. As we'll see in the next chapter, while the frames they adopt (or are led to adopt) influence how they choose to act, their actions, in turn, powerfully influence their framings and interpretations.

---

* In working on conflict resolution in Northern Ireland, Lee took note of the 2001 change in the name of the police authority. What had been the Royal Ulster Constabulary (which to Catholics connoted a police force designed to protect the interest of Protestants who identified themselves as British) became the Northern Ireland Police Service (which connoted an agency responsible for the even-handed protection and security of the entire community, Catholic and Protestant alike). This change was designed not simply to make citizens more accepting of an unsatisfactory status quo. It was designed to reinforce the message of change in policing objectives and in the larger objectives of political leaders intent on ending violence and forging a better intercommunal relationship.

4

The Primacy of Behavior

When Roger Federer and Rafael Nadal met in the finals of the 2006 French Open, Federer, who is often referred to as tennis's GOAT (Greatest of All Time), was at the top of his game. He had won the previous Wimbledon, U.S. Open, and Australian Open tournaments. With a victory at the French, he would become only the second man in professional tennis history to win all four major tournaments in a row—tennis's Grand Slam. Interest in the match was heightened by the fact that the nineteen-year-old Nadal had defeated Federer in the semifinals of the French Open the year before. This was Federer's opportunity for revenge.

Federer seemed well on his way to getting that revenge when he raced out to a 5–0 lead in the first set. Nadal then held serve and won his first game of the match. But rather than exhibiting the physical demeanor of someone who had merely delayed an inevitable loss of the set, Nadal enthusiastically sprinted to the baseline to receive Federer's serve in the next game. In fact, he looked for all the world like a player who was *ahead* 5–1, not behind. Nadal went on to lose that game, and the set. But he then won the next three sets (6–1, 6–4, and 7–6) to win the match. Did Nadal's show of confidence reflect an awareness of some weakness in Federer's game, or a planned change of tactics that might turn the tide? Or did his physical display of energy and confidence somehow *allow* him to elevate his game?

What tennis fans witnessed that day confirmed a bit of wisdom that tennis coaches have stressed for years. When things are going badly, players are told, bounce on the balls of your feet, straighten your shoulders and back, and assume the posture you would naturally assume if you were playing well. It's the tennis version of "fake it 'til you make it." You can't play the bold brand of tennis that's needed to win against top opponents with a posture of defeat.

The wisdom of that advice goes far beyond tennis and sports. Everyone knows that the way we feel influences the way we behave. When we're feeling down, we move more slowly. When we're upbeat, or angry, we move more quickly. But psychologists have shown that the opposite is also true: that our posture and the way we conduct ourselves while carrying out different actions can influence the way we feel and, like Nadal, the results we achieve.[1]

Folk wisdom conveys this same message. Whistle while you work (to make it more enjoyable); sing a happy tune when you are feeling afraid or blue (to elevate your mood). Earlier generations were even told to whistle while walking past a graveyard to counteract the deeper fears of encountering a ghost.

Psychologists have explored the influence of how people act on how they feel in a wide range of circumstances. But two very wise commentators on human affairs, one an early twentieth-century American philosopher and psychologist and the other a Greek poet who lived twenty centuries earlier, seemed to appreciate this direction of influence long before the evidence from experimental research made its way into academic journals.

James's Radical Theory of Emotion
and Ovid's Recipe

More than one hundred years ago, the pioneering psychologist William James offered a startlingly counterintuitive hypothesis about emotion. Common sense tells us that the emotions we experience dictate the way we respond, but James suggested that something like the reverse is actually the case: that our experience of emotion is the experience of our bodies responding to events. The experience of fear, for example, is the experience of our heart pounding, or that of our face contorting itself, or even that of our leg muscles contracting as we run away from a threat. In a famous passage, he maintained that "we feel sorry because we cry, angry because we strike, afraid because we tremble, and not that we cry, strike, or tremble, because we are sorry, angry, or fearful, as the case may be."[2]

A later theory offered by social psychologists built on James's insights by adding the notion of emotional labeling.[3] The theory maintained that although James was onto something important, the physiological cues associated with emotion are relatively diffuse, leaving our experience open to the influence of situational cues and labels.* So we attach the label *fear* to the arousal we are experiencing when there is something in the environment we regard as frightening. And we apply the label *joy* (or perhaps *relief*) to the arousal we experience when we see or hear something we are especially glad to encounter.

James's theory and later modifications have turned out to have

_____

* The psychologist most responsible for this theory, Stanley Schachter, was Lee's PhD advisor and mentor, and a major influence on the way both of us have thought about psychology and conducted our research. He was particularly adept at making connections between theory and real-world events and experiences, and then crafting clever experiments to explore those connections.

some problems. (For one thing, facial expressions and other bodily responses to positive and negative events are more differentiated than these theories assumed.) But the idea that our emotions might be heightened or dampened or completely transformed by altering our physical actions has proven to be sound. In one famous study, for example, researchers had students rate how amused they were by a series of cartoons—in some cases while holding a pen with their teeth, thereby adopting a "smiling" expression, and in other cases while holding the pen with their lips, thereby preventing a smile. Consistent with the idea that the cues provided by the way we are acting influence the way we feel, students who looked at the cartoons with the smile found them significantly funnier than the students who looked at them with an expression akin to a frown.[4]

If the same bodily sensations can be labeled in different ways, it's possible to get confused about exactly what it is we're feeling. While our environment might trigger one emotion, we might end up feeling another. This idea was anticipated by the Roman poet Publius Ovidius Naso, who lived at the time of Christ and became known in the English-speaking world as Ovid. In *The Art of Love*, he told his contemporaries that to stoke the ardor of wives or mistresses (or anyone else one fancies), attendance at gladiatorial contests is just the ticket—just the ticket, that is, to produce strong feelings of arousal that lend themselves to being labeled, or rather *mis*labeled, as feelings of lust.

More modern versions of Ovid's recipe for kindling romantic interest include scary movies or roller-coaster rides at the amusement park, or even the local gym, where the combination of elevated heart rates, sweat, and lightly clad bodies offers excellent possibilities for similar mislabeling.[5] This is also one of the reasons that "makeup sex" following an intense quarrel often proves to be so passionate and gratifying.

Ovid's recipe was tested in an intriguing study that took place on the swaying Capilano Suspension Bridge in British Columbia, a structure that produces in most people a kind of uneasiness that might normally be labeled fear or anxiety. There, young men encountered an attractive female interviewer who asked them to fill out a questionnaire. Included in the questionnaire was a request to write a brief story to go with a photograph showing a young woman covering her face with one hand and reaching out with the other. The interviewer also mentioned that if they had any additional questions about the experiment, they could contact her, and she provided her phone number. Another group of young men had the same encounter on a lower, more stable, and less "arousing" bridge.

Which participants showed more sexual content in the stories they wrote, and which were more likely to call with a few "follow-up questions"? As the investigators had predicted, it was those who had their brief encounter on the arousing suspension bridge. The researchers followed up this study and found that evidence of heightened romantic interest was apparent only when the encounter occurred *during* the bridge crossing, when the swaying bridge and gusts of wind were giving rise to an elevated heart rate, rapid breathing, and other symptoms of arousal. When the encounter occurred *after* the men had crossed the bridge, and enough time had passed for their physiological arousal to subside, the "recipe" no longer worked.[6]

Body over Mind

As Ovid recognized, people sometimes fail to keep straight the messages coming from the mind and body. Research has confirmed that arousal produced by one emotion (fear) can get mixed up and feed a second, unrelated emotion (lust). Indeed, researchers have shown just how much cross talk there is between body and mind. In one study, for example, individuals who were induced to nod their heads (a movement normally associated with agreement) while ostensibly testing a set of headphones were more favorably disposed to the messages they received over the headphones than were participants who were incidentally induced to shake their heads (a movement normally associated with disagreement).[7]

Similar effects follow from other gestures we associate with positive versus negative reactions. In one study, research participants evaluated information they encountered while pulling their hands inward (a movement associated with acceptance, as when we accept a wad of cash), while others evaluated the same information while pushing their hands outward (a movement associated with rejection or avoidance, as when we push away something that has a disagreeable taste or smell). As predicted, those pulling in evaluated the information more favorably than those pushing out.[8]

What about the very different associations people have to giving the "thumbs-up" gesture versus "giving the finger"? Does mimicking these gestures influence people's concurrent assessments? To find out, a group of researchers hid their hypothesis from their participants by leading them to believe that the study was an investigation of "multitasking." The participants were asked to read about a character named Donald, and while doing so, to simultaneously move their hands through a motion detector—some by extending their middle finger upward, others by extending their thumb. As predicted, those with their middle fingers extended judged Donald to be rather hostile; those with their thumbs pointed upward judged him to be likable and smart.[9]

Another demonstration of this sort of cross talk between body and mind, one with considerable implications for the planet, was provided by a pair of Tom's former students, Jane Risen and Clayton Critcher, who asked people about the threat posed by global warming.[10] What they varied was the temperature of the room in which the questions were posed. Those polled in a particularly warm room indicated that they thought that global warming was a much more serious problem than those polled in a cold room. In fact, self-described political conservatives in a warm room expressed as much concern about global warming as self-described liberals in a cold room.*

The research on bodily influences on mental states provides some tips that can help you master some of your own thoughts and feelings. If you're feeling down or lacking confidence, take a tip from Rafael Nadal: Assume the posture you'd naturally assume if you were on top of your game.

The effectiveness of this particular self-help strategy was explored by Dana Carney and Amy Cuddy, who had research participants assume postures associated with people who have high or low status or power. High-status people tend to take up a lot of space—they put their hands behind their head with their elbows out; they put their hands on their hips; they put their feet up on a desk or an extra chair; and so on. Low-status individuals take up less space—they fold in on themselves, with their hands crossed over their torso, their hands touching (and partly covering) their faces, and so on. When participants were asked to strike these poses, those who assumed the posture of a powerful person experienced a surge in testosterone and a drop in the stress hormone cortisol. Those who assumed a low-power pose experienced just the opposite: a drop in testosterone and a spike in cortisol.[12]

The researchers also had participants assume one posture or the other right before taking part in a mock job interview (one made rather stressful by the interviewer's maintaining an inscrutable demeanor and offering no supportive verbal or nonverbal feedback of any kind). The interviews were tape-recorded and scored afterward

---

*Public opinion surveys in the United States and Australia have shown similar effects. Hotter-than-usual days prompt higher levels of concern about the climate changes that will challenge us all in the not-too-distant future.[11] One could argue that the local temperature carries some information about broader weather patterns and so respondents are not being irrational by upping their belief in global warming when the temperature is hot. The same cannot be said about the studies that manipulate the obviously artificial temperature of the room in which respondents are filling out their surveys.

by judges who knew nothing about the purpose of the study or what pose each interviewee had earlier assumed. The participants who earlier had mimicked a high-power pose were rated as more impressive in their interviews and more deserving of landing a job than those who had mimicked a lower-power posture. So attending to your actions, instead of concentrating on how you "really feel," can help you, like Nadal, win the day. Whistling while you work, or doing whatever else you do when feeling upbeat, can get you through a boring or laborious task, and it can help chase away the blues. And taking a cold shower really can be a good idea when you are about to act impetuously.

I Act; Therefore I Believe

A common cliché is that what sets us apart from all other animals is our intelligence. We certainly do have cognitive capacities unmatched by any other creatures, and we are unique in our capacity to guide our actions with reflective thought. But as one of Lee's undergraduate professors put it (he does not remember which one), "Whenever you think of people as animals, you get a little smarter. And whenever you think of animals as being like people, as creatures that reason and react as we do, you get a little dumber." One of the most fundamental similarities between *Homo sapiens* and all other organisms is that we have evolved first and foremost to act effectively in the environment that confronts us. Behavior, in that sense, is primary. The added ability to engage in reflective thought was a later evolutionary development. Given that evolutionary history, it is hardly surprising that while our thoughts often determine our actions, the reverse is also true: Our actions often determine our thoughts. Indeed, one of the most consistent and remarkable findings in the behavioral science literature over the past century is that people's behavior is often more predictive of their attitudes than their attitudes are of their behavior.[13]

A number of theories have been offered to explain the influence of actions on beliefs. Two of them have been especially influential, and both lead to the same conclusion: Once people have acted in a way that seems consistent with a particular belief, they are inclined to endorse that belief. One theory was offered by the most famous social psychologist of his era and perhaps the cleverest experimentalist our field has ever produced. The other was put forward by a young upstart who challenged that celebrated senior psychologist and initially invoked the wrath of the field's establishment. We shall depart from the conventional treatment of these two theories by discussing them in the reverse order in which they were developed. We do so because it is the upstart's later account that relates most directly to the research we have discussed thus far, and it is the celebrated theorist and experimentalist whose work holds the key to the important takeaway message we offer later in this chapter.

Self-Perception Theory: When Doing Is Believing

When a child bumps her head and starts to cry, one of her parents is likely to tell her that it "hurts" or that she's "in pain." The child thus learns what words apply to those feelings. But the child is also getting a critical lesson about her internal experience and what it means. She learns that she's "nervous" or "excited" before the ballet recital and "afraid" of the dentist and "embarrassed" by the reception her behavior is getting from disapproving adults. Part of coming to understand and label what we're feeling, in other words, comes from attending to what we're doing and to the situation in which we are doing it.

This idea, a staple of the philosophy of mind, was a starting point for Daryl Bem, the young upstart in our story. His self-perception theory holds that when internal cues available through introspection are weak, ambiguous, or absent, we infer the nature and strength of

our beliefs and priorities from our actions and the surrounding circumstances—just as we do when making such inferences about other
people.[14]

How much do you like Italian versus Mexican food? Your answer,
Bem claimed, comes from noting how often you frequent Italian versus Mexican restaurants (while taking into consideration differences
in convenience and price that might have influenced your choices).
In other words, you consider exactly the same information you would
consider if you were figuring out the food preferences of a friend or
neighbor.

How do you feel about rock concerts versus folk music, or football versus baseball? Well, how much have you been willing to pay for
tickets for one type of concert or the other, and what do you remember watching on TV when you were alone in a hotel room with no
one's preferences but your own to consider? How religious are you?
How often, you would ask yourself, do you attend religious services
that are not connected to a birth, marriage, death, or some other social ritual? And do you find yourself offering silent prayers or looking skyward and giving thanks when something you hoped for takes
place or something you dreaded did not?

In the 1950s, at the height of the Cold War, more than a few
Americans invested in concrete bomb shelters in their basements and
backyards. Although these purchases presumably reflected the level
of the buyers' fear of a nuclear exchange with the Russians, a Bemian
analysis suggests that the buyers would likely feel more fearful as a
consequence of their purchase—even if the purchase had as much
to do with a smooth sales pitch or the desire to conform to whatever
the neighbors are doing. By the same token, today's parents who buy
every child-safety device on the market and monitor every movement
of their children's outdoor play thereby elevate their estimates of the
dangers posed by the very calamities they're trying to avoid (and by
their actions, they also elevate the level of fear their youngsters feel).

This process of inferring internal states from external behavior can apply even to what would seem to be directly discernible states like hunger or romantic interest. "I just ate a second sandwich," you tell yourself, "so I must have been hungrier than I thought." "I find that I keep walking down the street where she lives, on the chance we will meet," you muse, "so I guess I must really be smitten." Again, the idea is that knowledge of your own internal state is largely arrived at by the same inferential leap from observed behavior to private feelings and priorities that you would make about anyone else who acted the same way under the same circumstances.

This strikes most people as wildly counterintuitive. We insist that we "just know" how hungry we were or, by the same token, we insist that we just know who we're attracted to and what we believe. A theory that maintains that we *infer* these things seems just plain wrong. Bem, as we noted, added the proviso that we resort to such inferences only to the extent that more direct, internal information is "weak, ambiguous, and uninterpretable." But his most important insight—and his theory's message to the wisest in the room—is that what we get from introspection is indeed weak, ambiguous, and uninterpretable far more often than most people imagine.

Many of the signals coming from our stomachs are indeed hard to read, and so we infer how hungry we are. Romantic interest can be difficult to gauge, as the misattribution study on the Capilano Bridge illustrates. Even the traces of our seemingly important beliefs are weaker than most people would expect. For example, 90 percent of those who changed political party affiliation between the 1972 and 1976 elections incorrectly recalled their earlier affiliation.[15] Furthermore, when students' attitudes toward busing to achieve racial integration were challenged and changed by someone armed with very persuasive arguments (on either side of the issue, it should be noted), they insisted that their new beliefs were ones they had held all along.[16] In short, it seems that we know the contents of our own minds less well than we think, and so we're often in the same position as an outside observer, who must infer what we think or feel.

Dissonance Reduction:
Motivated Changes of Mind

Bem's ideas were greeted coolly by the academic establishment in part because they were put forward as an alternative to a theory proposed earlier by Leon Festinger, the leading social psychological theorist of his era. Festinger's theory had a very different starting point: It proposed that people are motivated to reconcile discrepancies in their actions, beliefs, values, and priorities.[17] To some extent, Festinger's theory of *cognitive dissonance* (a term now common far outside of academic psychology) was a variant of much older notions of rationalization and self-justification. But Festinger and his colleagues did more than repackage older ideas. They sharpened our appreciation of how this process of dissonance reduction operates with a series of nonobvious findings that constituted one of the most interesting chapters in the history of social psychology. In so doing, they fleshed out one of the most important principles for anyone who wants to influence the attitudes of others.

Festinger's theory followed from his earlier work on group dynamics and what he termed "pressures to uniformity." He had previously noted that when differences of opinion arise in a group, they produce a kind of tension that the group members work to resolve, especially if the issue producing the disagreement is important. That tension, he had argued, is diminished only when agreement is achieved and harmony restored—usually by the majority pressuring the minority to go along. Festinger's newer claim was that what plays out interpersonally in the dynamics of groups also takes place in the internal dynamics of our individual minds. That is, we feel a kind of psychological discomfort whenever certain attitudes we hold clash with others, and especially when our behavior seems inconsistent with our values, priorities, and beliefs. That discomfort, in turn, motivates us to reduce the dissonance in whatever ways we can.

By focusing on these cognitive processes that operate entirely in the head of the individual, Festinger helped usher in a period in which social psychology became a lot less social. But in fact, dissonance reduction can be a very social enterprise. We help one another feel better about potentially upsetting inconsistencies in our thoughts and deeds. Friends assure us that we deserve to splurge on a vacation when we're feeling dissonant about our impetuous purchase of airline tickets soon after resolving to reduce our credit card bill. They tell us that it's okay to have a fattening dessert in spite of a stated intention to reduce our calorie intake. They insist that no real harm was done when we neglected to fulfill an obligation. And as we will see in chapter 7 when discussing intergroup conflict, and in chapter 9 when discussing the problem of climate change, these collective efforts at dissonance reduction can have consequences that are far less benign.

Examples of dissonance reduction have been offered by wise observers of human foibles ever since Aesop's fable of the fox that eased his frustration by deciding that the grapes beyond his reach were sour. People who miss the banquet take comfort in the fact that they avoided overeating. Those who have a blind date cancelled (or receive no follow-up to the end-of-the-date promise "I'll call you") decide that the match would never have worked. People who endure hardship for a cause, whether a noble or ignoble one, value it more—and the greater the hardship, the greater the value attached to the cause.

People also find ways to rationalize their failures. An economic misadventure becomes a "great learning experience." A more-strenuous-than-expected hike becomes a demonstration of one's fortitude and great preparation for future adventures. People are also adept at rationalizing their failures to get started on challenging or tedious tasks ("I really need to straighten out my files before getting down to work," or "I need to send Jennifer congratulations on her engagement before trying to sort out the mess in my garage," or "I'll wait until I have a period of time when I won't face any interruptions before tackling my tax forms"). And the list of things people come up with to rationalize their failures to exercise more, eat healthier, do more to curb energy consumption, or give money to those in need goes on and on.

Festinger and his students had a sharp eye for common instances of dissonance reduction, including their own. Despite the then-emerging research on the perils of smoking, Festinger persisted in the habit and offered all sorts of justifications for doing so—while acknowledging them for what they were: justifications.* And his students exchanged knowing glances when he gushed about the car (a Nash) he had purchased, because his own theory made it clear that his great affection for the vehicle was not something he maintained *in spite of* its unlovely lines, gas-guzzling appetite, and too-frequent repair bills. Instead it was something he felt *because of* those unfortunate features. But it was the laboratory studies the Festingerians conducted that shaped and energized the field of social psychology.

Reducing Dissonance about the Choices We've Made

The first wave of studies Festinger and his students carried out explored a familiar type of dissonance reduction—the sort that occurs after we've decided between two options, perhaps two candidates running for public office, two tempting items on a restaurant menu, or two vacation destinations. He showed that after making these decisions, a "spreading of alternatives" takes place. That is, once we've made our choice, we become increasingly confident that it was the right one. The more we ponder the matter, the more certain we become that the newcomer we voted for despite her lack of experience will do a better job of reforming outdated programs than the old stalwart we supported last time. After placing our restaurant order, we re-

---

*Nevertheless, in the late stages of his fatal illness, Festinger took pains to insist that while he was succumbing to cancer, it wasn't *lung* cancer.

duce our dissonance about the sizzling delights of the steak we didn't order by deciding it was overpriced. We further remind ourselves that the salmon we did order was recommended by our server as being especially fresh that night. We might reduce our dissonance even further by telling ourselves that we can spend the calories we saved by treating ourselves to that tempting chocolate mousse.

One early study confirmed a subtler dissonance theory prediction by showing that the spreading apart of alternatives is most pronounced when the alternatives are close together in appeal (when there is therefore a lot of dissonance about the alternative relinquished).[18] Another study highlighted the way justification processes kick in with particular vigor right after a decision is made by asking bettors at a race track about their horse's chances of winning either as they approached the betting window, before they had placed their bets, or after they left the window, when they were fully committed and had money on the line.[19] As dissonance theory would predict, the bettors expressed greater confidence that their horse would win after they had placed their bets than before. Other studies have shown that the same thing happens in elections: Voters are more optimistic about their candidate's chances of winning when they are interviewed on their way out of the polling station than on their way in.[20]

One lesson here is that there are pronounced psychological benefits to commitment. Put differently, although it can seem appealing to "keep my options open," and there can be tangible benefits of doing so, failing to commit also comes with psychological costs. It can seem appealing to put off the choice of a career as long as possible, but many people discover all the pluses of a given line of work only after choosing it. The prospect of marriage can conjure up fearful metaphors like the ball and chain, but the full power of dissonance reduction will be exercised only once a commitment is made.

The tension between the desire to keep options open and the benefits of closing them off was nicely illustrated in a study conducted by Harvard's Dan Gilbert and Jane Ebert. The study involved a less momentous decision and a more modest commitment than the ones we just described. The investigators asked aspiring photographers to spend a few days taking a dozen photographs and then to develop two of them into prints during a subsequent darkroom session. The photographers were then asked to choose and take home with them their favorite of the two prints, with the other to be kept on file in the researchers' office. Some were told they could change their mind later and exchange the prints if they wished to do so; others were told the choice was final. When asked how the option to change their selection would influence how much they ended up liking it, most of the participants thought it would make no difference at all. But in fact, those who could not alter their choices liked the photographs they selected significantly more than those allowed to keep their options open. Only those who were fully committed to their choice reaped the hedonic benefits of dissonance reduction.[21]

Turning Reinforcement Principles on Their Head

The more people are paid to do something, the more they will like doing it. That seems reasonable, doesn't it? Given a choice, nearly everyone would opt for higher rather than lower compensation. However, a classic dissonance experiment showed something that may at first seem surprising—that the *smaller* the payment received for doing something disagreeable (and hence the more dissonance experienced), the greater the tendency to conclude that it really wasn't so disagreeable after all.[22]

In this study, students who showed up for what they hoped would be an interesting psychology experiment were assigned an utterly mindless and boring task—turning pegs inserted into slots on a board, one-quarter turn at a time, until each peg was back to its original orientation. Upon completion of the task, the experimenter explained that he was studying the effect of expectations on people's performance and that he needed their help with the next participant. Specifically, he needed them to tell the next person that the task they had just performed was very enjoyable. What varied in this study was the amount of money the student was offered for that bending of the truth. For some it was $1 (the standard payment in 1959 for participation in an experiment); for others the payment was $20 (at that time more than the price of a lunch for two at one of New York's finest restaurants).*

Because the experimenter made this request in a difficult-to-resist manner, all participants agreed to do what they had been asked. The focus of the study was what the participants would say when later asked how much they had liked (or, more accurately, how *little* they had *disliked*) the boring peg-turning task. The counterintuitive prediction of the dissonance theorists was confirmed: Those who were paid $20 and felt amply compensated for their lie (and hence felt little if any dissonance) rated the task as extremely boring. Those paid only $1 for their lie (and hence needed to reduce their dissonance about what they had told their peer) rated the task as relatively enjoyable.†

This process can be seen in numerous areas of everyday life. People who freely choose an occupation that offers low pay for difficult work (think of schoolteachers) or uncertain rewards in a field where talent is no guarantee of success (think of artists, musicians, novelists) feel

---

* In 1962, New York's Le Pavillon, considered at that time the finest restaurant in the United States, priced its daily luncheon special at $7.50 per person.

† When Festinger first talked about his work, he delighted in describing his procedures without explaining his hypothesis and inviting the audience to predict whether the large or small reward would produce more positive ratings of the task. Most people, heavily influenced by the reinforcement theories of that era, predicted that the larger reward would have the more positive effect.

compelled to justify or rationalize their choice. Although they may continue to grumble about the low pay or the life of uncertainty, they also tell us how much they love their work and how fulfilling it is, and why other careers would have been unsatisfactory.

Many people have noted a parallel in the experience of parenting. Raising a child inevitably involves difficult moments and continuing challenges—sleep deprivation, pronounced menu restriction, endless chauffeuring, and later, as John Updike put it, "the odorous, clamorous throng of dermatological disasters" who come to woo one's daughters. But parents very often say that raising a child is the most gratifying experience of their lives.

Might the very price parents pay to raise a child be one of the reasons they say it's so rewarding? A dissonance theorist would certainly think so. Support for the idea comes from the fact that in previous eras, when children were thought of as valuable contributors to a family's economic well-being, relations between parents and children were less affectionate than they are today. As one of Tom's former students, Richard Eibach of the University of Waterloo, put it, "Children's emotional value began to be culturally idealized just as their economic value to families declined."[23] That trend, of course, is just what dissonance theory would predict.

To explore the role of dissonance reduction in parents' views of the child-rearing experience, Eibach and Steve Mock gave some parents only information about the average financial cost of raising a child to the age of eighteen ($193,680 in the Northeast United States). Other parents were given that information along with information about the financial and practical support children provide as they tend to their aging parents. All of the parents then rated their agreement with a number of statements about the value and pleasures of parenthood, such as "There is nothing more rewarding in this life than raising a child" and "Nonparents are more likely to be depressed than parents." Consistent with the idea that parents idealize the raising of a child in part to justify all they put into it, those who were reminded only of the costs agreed with these statements significantly more than those who were also reminded of the economic benefits that children can provide their parents in their later years.*

What we see in all of these dissonance studies is essentially an inversion of everyday logic. We know that those who love doing something, even if it is difficult, will do it for little or no pay (think again of artists and musicians or amateur athletes). Turning this around, the $1-versus-$20 study showed that people who chose to do something distasteful for modest pay report that it wasn't all that distasteful. We also know that someone who truly values something will endure suffering to get it. The parenting study shows that people who suffer for something will feel psychologically compelled to value it.

This is the psychological principle behind the challenging initiation rituals we find in fraternities, elite military units, urban gangs, and all sorts of other groups that require the type of cohesion, loyalty, and commitment that allows them to function together in trying circumstances. The nonobvious twist that the Festingerians added is that the very circumstances that make us feel the most dissonance about our actions (i.e., low compensation, high effort, or high costs endured, especially when we had a lot of freedom in deciding to take those actions) are the ones that make us most inclined to decide that we enjoyed them or greatly value what we accomplished.

Once the principles of dissonance theory are understood, their influence can be seen all over. Consumers seem to like products that require a bit of self-assembly (think IKEA) more than comparable products that require no such investment of energy (and no need to justify that investment).[24] They also seem to value products more if they pay a high price for them.[25] Part of the reason most people endorse the proposition that "you get what you pay for" is that those

---

* Eibach and Mock also asked participants how *uneasy, uncomfortable,* and *bothered* they felt. Further supporting the idea that it was dissonance that led to the idealization of parenthood, those who reported the most discomfort before providing their thoughts about parenthood were the ones most likely to extol the virtues of parenthood.

who pay a lot feel a need to justify their purchase. In an especially telling study, participants were given an energy drink at either the regular or discounted price and then asked to solve a number of difficult word puzzles. Those who got the discounted drink were less motivated to prove to themselves that the drink was effective. Or so it would seem, because they solved significantly fewer puzzles than the participants who had paid the full price for the energy boost.[26]

Using a technology that was developed long after the early dissonance studies—an fMRI machine that records the amount of activity in different areas of the brain—researchers have been able to document that high prices change not just what we say about products but how we feel about them deep down. Research participants in a recent study were given small amounts of wine. Some were told that the wine cost $90 a bottle and others told a bottle cost $10. You will not be surprised to learn that those who thought they were drinking more expensive wine rated it more highly. What the researchers were able to show, beyond those ratings, is that the fMRI recordings indicated more activity in the brain regions associated with the experience of pleasure when participants thought they were drinking more expensive wine.[27]

Getting the Ball Rolling . . . with Just Enough of a Push to Overcome Resistance

The central message of chapter 2 was that while you can try to change someone's behavior by targeting the person's heart and mind, sometimes it's best to target behavior directly. The additional lesson here is that if you target behavior in a psych-wise manner, the heart and mind will follow. Your child may not like doing household chores (Who does?). But in the course of doing them faithfully, he or she will come to place a value not only on a clean household, but also on doing what needs to be done in life and on keeping up with tasks that can otherwise pile up and overwhelm. The key to reaching difficult, long-term goals and developing the necessary values and motivation is to get the ball rolling. Long ago the Babylonian Talmud anticipated the "primacy of behavior" with the following commentary: "One should always occupy himself with Torah and good deeds, [even if] it be not for their own sake, for out of good work misapplied in purpose there comes [the desire to do it] for its own sake."[28] The author of that directive, we venture to guess, was the wisest rabbi in the room!

Both dissonance theory and self-perception theory add something important and nonobvious to the general prescription that action leads to belief. If you want initial actions (doing chores, practicing the piano, studying Torah) to lead to corresponding changes in attitudes and values (to produce "internalization," psychologists would say), the inducements used to spark those actions should not be heavy-handed. When it comes to offering incentives, applying pressure, or providing justifications, *less is more*. Be cautious, in other words, about offering big rewards or dire threats to get your kids to do their chores or their homework or to act in socially responsible ways. They'll comply, but they'll see it as something they were coerced to do, not something worth doing for its own sake.*

By the same token, whereas *subtle* pressures and *mild* inducements can lead people to feel that their behavior reflects their beliefs and preferences (as it did for those paid only $1 to say a boring task was enjoyable), *obvious* pressures and *strong* inducements can have the reverse effect: They can lead people to feel that they only acted as they did because of those pressures and constraints. Consider what happened in an experiment in which students were rewarded with points

---

*Note, however, that there is danger in not exerting *enough* pressure: Failing to do so can lead to the opposite negative consequence. Those who do not yield to the pressure will seek a way to reduce whatever dissonance they feel from *not* reaping the benefits of compliance—perhaps by deciding that what they neglected to do was especially boring, difficult, or distasteful or by deciding that what they did and were punished for doing was especially gratifying.

they could later exchange for prizes every time they played a novel math game. In one sense, the point system worked: The children played more math games when the reward system was in place. But in a more important sense it failed: After the rewards were removed, they played the math games less often than before the reward program had been instituted. Something that originally had seemed to be interesting and fun came to be something done only to get points, not to learn or to have fun.[29]

This finding—indeed all of the research discussed in this chapter—reinforces the idea explored in chapter 3 that it is not the stimulus itself that drives behavior, but how the stimulus is understood. The impact of incentives and constraints on motivation and behavior depends on how they are construed.

In a provocative exploration of this idea, nursery school children were asked to draw a picture with what was then a novel drawing tool: felt-tip markers. Some were offered a prize for drawing a picture with the markers; others received the prize unexpectedly, after they had already drawn their picture; still others were offered no incentive at all. When the markers were later introduced into a free play period, the children who had drawn a picture in order to get a reward played with them significantly less often than children who had not been "bribed" to draw their picture. In essence, the promise of a reward turned play into work. But when the prize was unexpected—when it was experienced not as a bribe but as a bonus—it did not decrease the children's interest in playing with the markers.[30]

Note the parallel to professional athletes who became successful in their sport in part because they loved playing, and the more they played, the more their skills increased. But after being in the big leagues for a number of years, they worry about how their contracts compare to those of other players, and they hold out and threaten to retire rather than take a pay cut that would lower their salary from a kingly sum to a princely sum. Wise athletes, and anyone else fortunate enough to be well paid for doing what they love, can make themselves happier by reminding themselves why they chose their callings and seeing their high salaries as bonuses, not as inducements or even bribes to continue their efforts.

Focus on the Self

When someone acts in a way that is unfair, immoral, or unethical, they are often told, "Take a good look at yourself." The advice derives its power from the fact that there is a particular type of inconsistency that people find especially troubling—inconsistency between their actions and their sense of themselves as competent, principled, and moral. As a result, making people literally *self*-conscious—that is, focusing their attention on what their actions convey about the kind of person they are—can facilitate desirable behavior.

One electoral study highlighted this link between self-regard and behavior by documenting the effect of a simple change in language. Prior to Election Day, some potential voters were asked, as is customary in preelection surveys, whether they intended *to vote*, while others were asked whether they intended to *be a voter*. The effect of labeling the targeted action with a noun rather than a verb was a ten-percentage-point difference in one study and an eleven-point difference in another— more than enough to swing the outcome of many elections (if, for example, a campaign knew that those ordinarily less likely to vote favored their candidate).[31] Of course, if a candidate's campaign staff took pains to identify potential supporters and to pose this psych-wise question only to those individuals, the benefit would be even greater.

Investigators continue to find clever ways to promote desirable behavior by focusing people's attention on the relationship between their sense of self and their moral standards. One study examined contributions to an honesty box in the coffee room of an English university. Anyone could serve themselves tea or coffee, with or without milk, but they were expected to pay a suggested amount for whatever they took. (The layout of the room made it unlikely that anyone failing to pay would be observed.) The investigators alternated the image on a banner printed above the suggested prices for the tea, coffee, and milk—flowers on some weeks and eyes directed at anyone looking at the banner on other weeks. Remarkably, nearly three times as much money was put into the honesty box during weeks when the eyes were displayed than during weeks when flowers were displayed.[32]

In a follow-up study, some of the same investigators examined the effect of the presence of posters featuring images of eyes or flowers on littering. Again, the eyes did the trick. The amount of littering when the eye posters were present was half the amount observed when the flower posters were on display. Moreover, the eye posters seemed to have a larger effect when there were fewer people in the café than when it was busy—that is, when there were few other "eyes" already on the potential litterers.[33]

The desire, indeed the need, to see oneself in a positive light can lead people to behave in ways that are consistent with self-esteem and with the values that society expects everyone to uphold. But it can also lead people to justify actions that violate such values, and it is to this darker side of human psychology that we now turn.

Rationalization: An All-Too-Human Frailty

We all rationalize from time to time. We justify the purchase of things we don't need ("This new gadget will make me more efficient") or the consumption of food we *really* don't need ("I'll have an extra piece of pie because tonight is a special occasion"). As we noted earlier, and have experienced in writing this book, the failure to get started on work produces its own supply of rationalizations ("I'd better check my email again. There might be something important there, and I really should wait for Greg to send me his latest article before tackling that last section of chapter 8"). The wisest one in the room recognizes rationalization when she sees it, including instances when she is the one rationalizing. Perhaps the surest way to spot your own rationalizations is to ask how you would respond if someone else offered the same justification.

Rationalizing an occasional high-calorie treat or a break from a tiresome task is relatively harmless. Less benign are rationalizations that relate to our duties as citizens ("I would have voted, but the line was too long, and besides, my candidate didn't really have a chance"). We have a special obligation to take a clear-eyed look at our justifications for actions that are self-serving or that shortchange others. The countless rationalizations we offer as individuals and as a nation to justify our failure to address the challenges posed by global warming (discussed in chapter 9) is a case in point. ("I would be willing to do my part, but my efforts would just be a drop in the bucket . . . and the real villains are power companies that refuse to stop burning fossil fuels . . . and the Chinese who won't cooperate. In any case, the scientific evidence is not definitive—and it would hurt job creation just as the economy is making a comeback").

Note that the best rationalizations are those that have an element of truth. Whether you vote or not will almost certainly have no influence on the outcome of an election. Nor will the amount of carbon you personally put into the atmosphere make a difference in the fate of the planet. And perhaps it really *should* be up to governments rather than the charities that are soliciting your contributions to feed the hungry and homeless in America or save children around the world from crushing poverty and abuse. But the fact that these statements are true doesn't mean they aren't also rationalizations that you and others use to justify questionable behavior.

This uncomfortable truth is crucial to an understanding of the link between rationalization and evil—an understanding that starts with the awareness that sane people rarely, if ever, act in a truly evil manner unless they can successfully rationalize their actions. Hollywood films notwithstanding, villains who proudly embrace evil are virtually nonexistent in real life. The problem is that people are extraordinarily adept at rationalizing. This applies not only to personal misdeeds, but also to the greater sins of omission and commission associated with genocide, slavery, apartheid, war atrocities, and the denial of basic human rights and human dignity. A further problem is that in contrast to the kind of dissonance reduction shown by the research participants in the studies by Festinger and his colleagues, the process of rationalizing evil deeds committed by whole societies is a collective effort rather than a solely individual enterprise.

Perpetrators are encouraged to rationalize their deeds by leaders and their propaganda machines, who insist that " 'they' deserve what is being done to them," or that what is being done serves some noble end or necessary goal (two common justifications for wartime atrocities). After the fact, perpetrators join together in maintaining that they were only "obeying orders." Bystanders to evil, meanwhile, similarly rationalize by saying, "It wasn't me, it was them"; "I was powerless to do anything about it"; or "No one could dare oppose those in power." These sorts of rationalizations often work hand in hand with denial. The defenders of slavery simultaneously insisted on its economic necessity and refused to acknowledge the depths of its cruelty.

The lessons of the Nazi Holocaust have been a subject of active debate since the end of World War II, as have the policies of strategic bombing that leveled Axis cities and caused hundreds of thousands of casualties, to say nothing of the atomic bombs that were dropped on Hiroshima and Nagasaki. It is clear that the Holocaust depended on monstrous deeds by thousands, but also on small acts of complicity by hundreds of thousands—people who sold the barbed wire or bought goods produced by slave labor or accepted deposits of ill-gotten gains in Swiss banks, or even those who just cheered when others cheered, or simply remained silent in spite of their misgivings. The situationist thrust of social psychology raises difficult moral issues when it comes to discussing such dark chapters in human history.

Hannah Arendt's controversial "banality of evil" thesis may have been overdone when it was offered as an analysis of the crimes of

Adolf Eichmann and other high-ranking Nazi war criminals.[34, 35] But there is no denying the evidence that most of the low-level perpetrators of the Holocaust led unexceptional lives before and after. And absent the particular historical situation in which they found themselves, it is unlikely they would have committed any acts of particular evil.[36] The excuses they offered about obeying orders, or doing their duty as officers in the military, or being duped by a leader whose maniacal evil was matched only by his oratorical powers, are both explanations and rationalizations. They have been offered, with mixed results, by countless others called to the bar of justice for war crimes and by millions more whose sins were ones of omission rather than commission. But the strength of our condemnation is probably not sufficiently tempered by an appreciation of the forces and constraints that operated on them in a manner akin to the step-by-step process we mentioned in considering the Milgram experiments.

The wisest person in the room thinks carefully about the situational factors that play a role in provoking evil deeds, trying hard not to excuse or deny personal responsibility but to understand the importance of addressing the forces and constraints that influenced the perpetrators.

Quiet and Not-So-Quiet Heroes

Andre Stein was eight years old when the Nazis occupied his birthplace of Budapest, slaughtering his mother and nearly everyone in his extended family. Tortured and left for dead, Stein somehow survived and later wrote a chilling book about the horrors that he and so many others endured. After he built a life in his new homeland of Canada and became a sociologist and psychotherapist, he remained heavily burdened by the memories of those horrors. At the suggestion of a theologian who felt Stein might gain some relief from that burden by making contact with some of the Christians who had helped hide and rescue Jewish children, Stein found a number of such individuals in his adopted homeland. He recounted their wartime efforts in a book bearing the title *Quiet Heroes*.[37]

Stein's collection of narratives reminds us that any reasonably comprehensive analysis of individual and collective rationalization of wrongdoing must look as well to the opposite end of the moral spectrum—at the actions of individuals who resisted evil at great personal risk and sacrifice. Here too, issues of rationalization are front and center. Stein's goal was to uncover any common denominators of the men and women who risked their lives to rescue people who were merely neighbors or even strangers. But he found himself frustrated in his efforts. No such common denominator emerged.

Some "quiet heroes" were religious, some were not; some were driven in part by ideology and some were not. Nor were there any particular similarities in personality or personal history. Instead, Stein discovered, in yet another echo of Milgram's illuminating research, that the path to heroic action began with small steps and minor commitments. Agreeing to hide a child for a night or just offering some food to a desperate family led to further steps and commitments, such as keeping the child hidden for a longer period of time when it became clear that leaving the hiding place would mean certain death. This led to further escalations in risk taking, such as a dangerous train trip to get medicine when a child was sick.

But what seemed even more notable about these quiet heroes, and what truly set them apart, was their unwillingness, or perhaps even their inability, to engage in the same sorts of rationalizations as virtually all their neighbors. Their neighbors found ways to blame the victims, claiming that they should have left while they had the chance. The quiet heroes acknowledged that for most victims, escape had not been possible and that the real issue was what was now to be done.

Their neighbors claimed to be powerless to do anything or to have felt obliged to put the safety of their own families above the safety of strangers. The quiet heroes said they had just done what they saw could be done and that the risks they undertook, at least initially, were small in light of the fates facing those they sheltered if no one came to their aid. Their neighbors focused on day-to-day concerns and didn't allow themselves to see the issue in broader moral terms. The quiet heroes could not maintain that narrow perspective. They asked themselves, "What would it say about me if I remained indifferent to the fate of these children? What kind of person would I be? And how will I look back on myself when the war is over and normal life returns?"

In the course of conducting these interviews, Stein noted how many rescuers ultimately left their homeland. It is unclear to what extent they felt obliged to leave communities that had tolerated atrocities without offering any resistance, and to what extent their continuing presence was not welcomed by those who had failed to act. But it is clear that the majority who rationalize inaction in the face of evil and the minority whose brave actions present a continuing reminder and reproach to the rationalizers do not make comfortable bedfellows.

The White Rose

An inspiring story of resistance under Nazi rule is that of the White Rose. Led by a sister and brother, Sophie and Hans Scholl, and their philosophy professor, Kurt Huber, this small band of German youths succeeded in distributing a series of mimeographed anti-Nazi leaflets from June 1942 to February 1943. They also inscribed graffiti on the walls of buildings. Their identity was soon discovered and they were summarily sent to the guillotine, displaying great courage to the end.

Today the symbol of the group, the white rose, is displayed in several German cities and towns in remembrance. In a sense, their actions were futile, doomed from the outset given the might and cruelty of the regime they confronted. To some, the monuments to their sacrifice convey the message that there were at least some Germans brave enough to openly voice what many of their countrymen felt but dared not express. To others, the message is a more burdensome one: that even in the face of the overwhelming pressures to accept rather than oppose evil, there is a choice—and to do nothing, to remain silent, to rationalize rather than act, is to be complicit.

The monuments to the youth of the White Rose also raise a disturbing question. Why is this particular example of resistance to Nazism given such prominence while other larger, more sustained, and more successful instances of resistance are so little acknowledged and celebrated? There were priests who successfully sheltered children and spoke out forcefully against euthanasia of those with physical or mental disabilities. There were successful efforts by Aryan women with Jewish husbands to secure their release from the camps. Most notable, perhaps, there were the prewar efforts of Communist groups to take to the streets and challenge Hitler's rise to power, efforts that thousands paid for with their lives.

Is the selective celebration of the White Rose itself an invitation and an aid to rationalization? Does it encourage people to feel that the only choice was that of acceptance and survival, or useless resistance and a grisly death—and that only martyrs and saints can be expected to choose the latter?

The wisest in the room recognize that the rationalization of evil, and of inactivity in the face of evil, is as great a threat to humankind as the cruel motives of the perpetrators. We hope that none of our readers will ever face the stark choices of the citizens of Nazi Germany. But we also hope they will pause to consider what opportunities exist today to individually and collectively address ills and evils in our own country and around the rest of the world in ways that are both brave and effective.

5

Keyholes, Lenses, and Filters

Any psychologist who uses historical events to illustrate a scientific principle runs the risk of cherry-picking supportive examples. Still, the picking is much easier in some cases than others. And when it comes to examples of tunnel vision, the picking is especially easy when considering the U.S. 2003 invasion of Iraq.

Right before the invasion, Secretary of Defense Donald Rumsfeld predicted that the war "could last six days, six weeks. I doubt six months"—a slight miscalculation, as the war was not declared over until December 2011. Vice President Dick Cheney added, "I really do believe we will be greeted as liberators." Even Cheney, notorious for his reluctance to yield to contradictory information, would have a hard time with that one, as more than four thousand U.S. soldiers lost their lives in the conflict. In another ill-fated prediction about the invasion and its aftermath, Andrew Natsios, head of the U.S. Agency for International Development, estimated that "the American part of this will be $1.7 billion. We have no plans for any further-on funding for this." Most current estimates of the cost to U.S taxpayers for reconstruction are around $60 billion (out of a total cost of the war to the United States of $1.9 trillion, as estimated by the Congressional Budget Office).[1]

Faulty judgments also plagued the United States as it went about the business of reconstruction. Decision after decision flowed from an overarching belief that "the free market" would bring about the best results. Thomas Foley, the director of private sector development for the Coalition Provisional Authority, announced on his arrival in Iraq that he planned to privatize all of the country's state-owned enterprises within thirty days. Told that the sale of assets by an occupying force would violate international law, he insisted, "I don't give a shit about international law. I made a commitment to the President that I'd privatize Iraq's businesses." So U.S. troops and the Coalition Provisional Authority often turned a blind eye when government property was commandeered for private use.

Peter McPherson, who served as director of economic policy for the Office of Reconstruction and Humanitarian Assistance in Iraq and initially supported such an approach, stated, "I thought the private enterprise that occurred sort of naturally when somebody took over their state vehicle, or began to drive a truck that the state used to own, was just fine." The chaos that ensued when existing institutions were torn down made a mockery of these grandiose beliefs about the power of market forces. As one member of the reconstruction team put it, "We were so busy building a capitalist economy that we neglected the big picture. We squandered an enormous opportunity and we didn't realize it until everything blew up in our faces."[2]

It is easy to be blinded by ideology. In this case, a strong faith in the power of private markets blinded government officials to the fact that markets are anything but free when there is no government around to enforce basic rules of competition, let alone when warlords, tribal leaders, and just plain thugs can enforce their will on society through the barrel of a gun. The problem is not limited to a capitalist worldview. Ideological blindness is an equal-opportunity malady, afflicting judgment all across the political spectrum. An anticapitalist ideology, for example, blinds many on the Left to the value of cost-benefit analysis, and it led the environmental movement to be slow to embrace market-based approaches to environmental problems, such as cap-and-trade systems.

Ideologies and preconceptions are lenses and filters. They make it easy to see and grasp some things but harder to see and understand others. If you're convinced that a supportive home environment is essential for healthy development, you'll have no trouble spotting examples of successful people with parents who are quick to praise and slow to criticize. But you are likely to overlook the narcissists who come from such homes or the happy high achievers whose parents are stingy with praise and quick to find fault.

Ideological blindness is only one source of tunnel vision. It is the nature of preconceptions that they make it easy to see some things (the light at the end of the tunnel) and hard to see others (everything else). We see people, actions, and events from a narrow perspective—through a narrow keyhole. At whatever scale or level of analysis you might choose, our access to the information out there in the world has limits. These limits start with the simple fact that our eyes are located at the front of our head, and so we take in only roughly 180 degrees of the 360 degrees that the world has to offer, and we focus on only about one-thirtieth of that range.* Call that restriction number 1.

A further limitation is our ability to keep only five to nine separate pieces of information in mind at any one time.[3] If you try to think of more things at once, something's got to give. If you focus on a tenth item, the second, fifth, or something else will fall away, lost to memory and your conscious attention. Our limited attentional capacity constitutes restriction 2.

Moreover, what we see is the product of the lenses, ideological

---

* The precise span of human vision differs from person to person, expands when the eyes can move, and varies with the criterion employed. With the eyes kept still, people can take in roughly 120 degrees of visual angle. With the head still but the eyes free to move, people can take in roughly 180 to 200 degrees of arc. Much of that, however, consists of peripheral vision, which is relatively impoverished. The degree of visual angle that provides resolution sufficient to read text is a mere 6 degrees.

or otherwise, that we bring to the task at hand or the ones provided by others. The lenses we look through constitute restriction 3. As we noted in chapter 3, when a question is framed a particular way, we tend to think within that frame. When shown the death rates associated with two different medical options, for example, people compare those rates, without considering what the options would look like in terms of corresponding survival rates. Recall that even experienced physicians deciding between surgery and radiation therapy for cancer patients succumbed to this framing effect.

Finally, the world doesn't always play fair: It highlights some information but casts other information in the shadows, yet another restriction in what we see and consider. The net result is that the information we can access most readily is often but a small fraction of the information we need, and often a biased sample at that. The wisest in the room understands that the information most readily available is often not the best guide to effective action and therefore takes some simple concrete steps to get a broader, more complete, and more accurate view.

Two Minds, One Brain

You're on vacation in Switzerland, and you're told that the afternoon's temperature will be 19 degrees centigrade. Should you bring a jacket or sweater? If you grew up in a country that uses the centigrade scale, you know the answer immediately because you know what that temperature feels like. But if you grew up using the Fahrenheit scale, you'll have to do some math ("multiply 19 by ⅘ and add 32") to arrive at 66.2 degrees on the scale with which you're familiar.

This example highlights the fact that people think in two very different ways. Much of our thinking happens quickly and automatically and is based largely on associations. Growing up in a country that uses the centigrade scale, a person learns to associate different temperature labels with different atmospheric conditions. He or she therefore "just knows" whether to take along extra clothing when the temperature will be 19 degrees centigrade. This process, which unfolds with no conscious guidance, is often called "intuitive" or "reflexive" thought.

The thinking that people do when translating unfamiliar centigrade labels onto the more familiar Fahrenheit scale is quite different. That sort of thinking is more plodding and deliberate, and often consists of following explicit rules ("multiply 19 by..."). It is also the type of thinking that people describe as "rational" or "reflective" thought.

Sometimes the rational mind calls the shots. As you prepare for a flight, you see a newspaper headline about a twister that is forecast to wreak havoc in the Midwest and your first thought is "I hope we aren't flying over Kansas." But after a bit of nostalgic and very conscious reflection, you realize that your fear is not due to any statistics you've read, or any recollections about where giant or recent tornados have occurred. Rather, it was due to your vivid "memory" of the tornado that whisked Dorothy and her little dog, Toto, to the land of Oz.

Other times the intuitive mind is sovereign. If you're a baseball fan, you know that commenting on a no-hitter in progress can't possibly influence whether the opposing team gets a hit. But you can't help feeling that it would do just that, and so, by baseball tradition, you avoid any reference to the zeroes on the scoreboard (no runs, no hits)—at least when it is your team's pitcher who's mowing down the opposition. Or if you're a parent who keeps your fingers crossed when your daughter is about to speak her lines in the school play, you're acquiescing to the more magical associations that the intuitive mind calls up.

Wisdom doesn't require that we never act on nonrational impulses and impressions. But it does require some understanding of how our two different "minds" interact. Especially important is the need to recognize that our intuitive impressions are based simply on whatever information comes our way. Our intuitive mind does not take into account that the information available to it may be incomplete or misleading. That is the province of deliberate thought. To overcome this limitation, we have to develop habits of mind (and data-gathering procedures) that broaden our view and give us access to more of the information we need. It is the job of the rational mind to consider whether there is some important information that isn't available, isn't salient, or hasn't been considered—the dog that *didn't* bark in the night for Sherlock Holmes fans (thereby revealing the intruder to be someone familiar). Part of being wise is accepting this burden, seeking out what's hidden, and not contenting ourselves with looking at the world through a keyhole or a single distorting lens.

Note how this connects to the idea of naïve realism discussed in chapter 1. It is our intuitive assessments that especially feel like they are direct assessments of "the way things are." Understanding that others might see and experience things differently is a job for the slower, more rational mind.

The intuitive mind is more impulsive than the rational mind, and more likely to act—to render a judgment and lean toward a course of action—without surveying information beyond its immediate attention. This helps explain some of the most common errors of everyday judgment: specifically, that many mistakes are made not because the right answer is too hard but because the wrong answer is too easy.[4]

It is these "too easy" and "too tempting" conclusions that judgment and decision-making researchers have brought to our attention and helped us understand. Consider one of the most noteworthy studies in that research tradition, brought to us, once again, by those masters of the convincing example, Amos Tversky and Daniel Kahneman. Respondents read about the following individual:

> Linda is thirty-one years old, single, outspoken, and very bright. She majored in philosophy. As a student, she was deeply concerned with issues of discrimination and criminal justice, and also participated in antinuclear demonstrations.[5]

They were then asked to indicate how likely it was that Linda would have pursued various activities or occupations later in life. In particular, they were asked to rank the likelihood of the following activities and occupations: a teacher in an elementary school, a psychiatric social worker, a member of the League of Women Voters, an activist in the feminist movement, a bank teller, an insurance salesperson, a bank teller who is active in the feminist movement.

The notable result is that most participants thought it was more likely that Linda would be a bank teller who is "active in the feminist movement" than simply "a bank teller." Intuitively, that seems right. Linda does not seem to fit our image of a bank teller, but we can readily imagine her as a *feminist* bank teller. When you add her interest in the feminist movement (which seems likely given what we know about her apparent political leanings), the match is quite a bit better.*

But then you realize, once you think about it for a moment, that that *can't* be right. Anyone who is "a bank teller and is active in the feminist movement" is necessarily a bank teller, and so the former can't possibly be more likely than the latter! It's basic logic. The conjunction of two events (bank teller and active in the feminist movement) cannot be more likely than either of its constituent elements alone (bank teller; active in feminist movement).

But even after we consider the problem logically, the wrong answer continues to feel right. The correct solution, then, is not too hard; the wrong (and intuitive) solution is too easy. As the noted paleontologist Stephen Jay Gould put it, "I am particularly fond of this example because I know that the third statement [feminist bank teller] is least probable, yet a little homunculus in my head continues to jump up and down, shouting at me—'but she can't just be a bank teller; read the description.'"[6]

---

*Were the participants in this study somehow confused? When *bank teller* and *bank teller active in the feminist movement* were both options, did some think the first option meant a bank teller who was *not* in the feminist movement? To rule out this alternative explanation, Tversky and Kahneman showed that even when some participants rated the likelihood of Linda ending up a bank teller and others rated the likelihood of her ending up a bank teller in the feminist movement, the latter was rated as more likely than the former.

What, then, are some of the insidious ways in which we rush to unwarranted judgments and bad decisions—or are led there by skillful persuaders? How can we protect ourselves from the most common pitfalls? What steps does a wise person take to make sure that all relevant information is available? And how does a wise person know when to slow down and override immediate gut impressions? An important component of wisdom, surely, is knowing when to trust intuition and when to be leery.

Seek and Ye Shall Find

Suppose your boss decides to host a dinner party and invites a number of potential clients. You are told about a client who will be seated next to you, "I think she's politically conservative, but you should find that out." How would you do so? If you're like most people, you'd ask questions designed to tap conservative sentiment: "Does your blood boil every time you have to go to the Department of Motor Vehicles?" "Do you think public education would be improved if schoolteachers didn't have tenure and they were hired and fired based on their performance, just like everyone else who works for a living?"

What you would *not* do, most likely, is ask questions likely to tap *liberal* sentiment: "Isn't it a travesty that some of the richest people in the country are taxed at a lower rate than their secretaries?" "Don't you think the government should be doing more to shore up our crumbling infrastructure?" Your questions, in other words, would follow what psychologists call a "positive test strategy,"[7] a particular version of what's more commonly known as the *confirmation bias*. Concerned about whether a dictatorship is developing weapons of mass destruction? It's the most natural thing in the world to look for evidence that it is, and less natural to look for evidence that it is not. Will a new product be welcome in the marketplace? Again, it's natural to look for signs that it will be and less natural to look for signs that it will not.

The search for confirmatory information is so natural because it seems to follow directly from an unassailable proposition: If something is true, there should be evidence for it. So we look for that evidence. That's fine as far as it goes. The trouble, of course, is that to determine whether something is true, it's necessary to survey both the evidence for and against it. Our most natural inclinations, then, are likely to leave us with an imbalanced assessment. Supportive information will almost always be at the front and center of our attention; contradictory information will often get lost in the shuffle. Contradictory information might surface, of course. Reality has a way of making itself known. But it often does so too late, after a critical decision has been made.

Consider the results of a provocative study in which one group of participants was asked to ascertain whether tennis players who work out strenuously the day before a big match tend to do well and win their matches.[8] The participants could do so by consulting whatever information they wanted from a list provided by the experimenter—a list that included the number of times players worked out strenuously the day before and won their subsequent matches, the number of times they did not work out strenuously and nonetheless won their matches, the number of times players worked out strenuously and lost their matches, and the number of times they did not work out strenuously and lost their matches. Different participants asked to see different subsets of these different types of information, but by far the most frequently requested type was the information that would be consistent with the notion they were testing: the number of times players worked out hard and won.

A second group was asked the logically equivalent question: whether tennis players who work out strenuously the day before a big match are more likely to *lose* their matches. These participants were also told they could consult any of the same four categories of information. What were they most interested in examining? It was the number of times players worked out hard and lost. Again, that is, the participants were most interested in the information that would support the idea they were evaluating.

Note how remarkable this is. These participants had no stake in the outcome. They probably didn't care one way or the other whether working out before a match makes a player more or less likely to win. Nevertheless, they were substantially more interested in looking at information consistent with the idea they were testing.

We're all familiar with the tendency for people to look for support for what they want to believe. Few people were surprised, for example, when it was revealed that members of the Bush administration who wanted to topple Saddam Hussein's regime tended to grasp at any information, however weak, that Iraq was developing weapons of mass destruction. But what many critics of the Bush administration found distressing is the degree to which congressional leaders, ordinary citizens, and members of the press were swayed by the weak evidence supporting the administration's claims, without giving appropriate attention to evidence challenging those claims.

The confirmation bias runs deep. It affects people's judgments and decisions even when they're thinking most dispassionately. That is why Emory University psychologist Scott Lilienfeld refers to the confirmation bias as (harking back to an earlier war against Saddam Hussein) "the mother of all biases."[9]

To see how pervasive the bias is, consider a study that was done in the 1980s, before the unification of Germany.* One group of participants, from Israel, was asked which pair of countries was more similar to one another, East Germany and West Germany or Ceylon (now Sri Lanka) and Nepal. The overwhelming majority thought that East and West Germany were more similar to one another. Fine; it's hard

---

* This study was not designed to explore the confirmation bias, but to test a formal model of similarity (and explain why having a dog is a bit like having a child, but having a child is nothing like having a dog). But the predicted (and observed) effect here depends on the tendency for people to look for information consistent with the proposition (i.e., similarity, dissimilarity) being tested.

to argue with that assessment. After all, they were both inhabited by Germans who shared a common heritage and language and prior to World War II had been part of a single nation. But when another group was asked which pair of countries was more *dis*similar to one another, a similarly strong majority said East and West Germany—presumably because one exemplified the communist East and the other the capitalist West. Thus, East and West Germany are thought to be both more similar and more dissimilar than Ceylon and Nepal, something that makes no logical sense.[10]

But it does make *psychological* sense. When asked to assess the relative similarity of East and West Germany versus Ceylon and Nepal, the participants looked for evidence of similarity—that is, things the two countries shared. With more knowledge about Europe than Asia, they could think of more things that East and West Germany shared and so they judged them to be more similar. But when asked to assess which two countries are more dissimilar to one another, the second group of participants looked for evidence of dissimilarity—of things that are distinct about one country or the other. Again, because these participants knew more about Europe than Asia, they could think of more ways in which East and West Germany differ from one another.

The confirmation bias can thus give rise to striking contradictions. Similar inconsistencies can emerge, as we saw in chapter 3, when there are two applicants for a position and only one can be hired. You might think of the task as a question of which applicant to select, in which case you'll mainly consider which applicant has more of the attributes that are important to the job. You'll look for evidence to *rule in* the right candidate. But you might instead think of it as a question of which applicant to reject, in which case you'll be more inclined to look for things that *rule out* the weaker applicant. Because it's possible for one candidate to have both more positive and more negative attributes, it's possible to both pick that candidate if you're picking and reject that candidate if you're rejecting.[11] You might pick Bill Clinton over another candidate to represent your company (or political party) because of his many obvious personal and political assets, but also reject him as a representative of your company (or party) in favor of another candidate because of Clinton's equally obvious baggage.

Sometimes the confirmation bias influences the information you seek from outside sources—the questions you ask an interviewee, the terms you type into a search engine, or the information you consult in a database. But other times the information you consult is already in your head, just waiting to be called up. What gets retrieved, however, is also subject to the confirmation bias. When considering whether "people who have a glass of wine every night tend to live longer," whether "Californians tend to be laid-back," or whether "bad news tends to come in threes," you're likely to think first and foremost about examples of aged drinkers, easygoing Californians, and plane crashes, hurricanes, or murders that happened in quick succession. We'll outline some ways of overcoming this particular bias later in this chapter. But first let's consider some of the other lenses and filters that can narrow and distort your perspective and compromise the quality of your judgments.

Seeing What You Want to See

Suppose you were told that whatever ethnic or national group you belong to—Canadian, Croatian, Costa Rican, what have you—is not as intelligent, or moral, or as true to their word as most other groups. Would you reflexively look for evidence to support that claim? Of course not. As we alluded to earlier, people's desires and rooting interests influence how the confirmation bias plays out. The more you want a proposition to be true, the more inclined you are to look for evidence that supports it.

But if you're Canadian, Croatian, or Costa Rican and you don't want your intelligence or integrity called into question, you're likely to look for evidence against the slur directed at your group—to recall Canadians, Croatians, or Costa Ricans who won the Nobel Prize in Chemistry or were celebrated for their service to humanity. (And if you are a member of one of these groups, you are especially likely to have that sort of information at the top of your head.) In this case, you'd be looking for information that would disconfirm the proposition. Indeed, the term *confirmation bias* has been used in many ways, sometimes as the unmotivated "positive test strategy" we have described, and at other times to refer to the commonly held idea that if you want something to be true, you tend to seek out and seize on evidence to support it—and that if you *don't* want something to be true, you seek out information that would call it into question.

This bias distorts people's evaluations of things that really matter to them, like their health. Participants in one study were given a test to ascertain whether they had a (fictitious) enzyme deficiency that would lead to pancreatic disorders later in life, even among those who were not currently experiencing any symptoms whatsoever. The test consisted of having participants deposit a small amount of saliva in a cup and then putting a piece of litmus paper into the cup. Some were told they would know they had the enzyme deficiency if the paper changed color; others were told they would know they had it if the paper *did not* change color. The paper was such that it did not change color for any of the participants.

How did they react? Just the way you'd expect people motivated to get good news (and avoid bad news) to react. Those who did not want the litmus paper to change color did not keep it in the cup very long (a minute and fifteen seconds). But those who did want it to change color looked really hard for evidence of that change. They kept the paper in the cup a half-minute longer on average (a minute and forty-five seconds). And they took additional steps to discover the desired color change, engaging (as the investigators put it) "in a variety of different testing behaviors, such as placing the test strip directly on their tongue, multiple redipping of the original test strip (up to 12 times), as well as shaking, wiping, blowing on, and in general quite carefully scrutinizing the recalcitrant . . . test strip."[12] What participants wanted to see influenced where and how they looked.

What We Bring to the Table

The great English philosopher Francis Bacon described a further source of confirmation bias almost four centuries ago.

> The human understanding when it has once adopted an opinion draws all things else to support and agree with it. And though there be a greater number and weight of instances to be found on the other side, yet these it either neglects and despises, or else by some distinction sets aside and rejects, in order that by this great and pernicious predetermination the authority of its former conclusion may remain inviolate.[13]

Bacon was referring to the human tendency to evaluate information in a way that leads people to persevere in their initial beliefs, whether hasty first impressions or the dogmas of their political or religious group. This bias is all too familiar to anyone who has been frustrated by the reluctance of those on the other side of some contentious issue to "look at the evidence" or "learn the lessons of history." It is also familiar to those of us who have been accused, in turn, of not looking at the evidence or not heeding the lessons of history by someone on the other side who, we believe, is cherry-picking historical examples or offering up unconvincing arguments. Both experiences reflect the tendency for people to accept at face value evidence that supports their beliefs while subjecting contradictory evidence to critical scrutiny.

Bacon would have shaken his head knowingly at the event we described earlier regarding the decision to invade Iraq—the administration's acceptance of flimsy evidence that Iraq was actively developing nuclear, chemical, and biological weapons, and its dismissal of the misgivings of seasoned diplomats and Middle East experts who questioned the administration's assessments and offered evidence incompatible with its claims.

Of course, it is reasonable to some extent to interpret evidence in light of existing beliefs. If you receive an email offer from Nigeria promising you a huge sum of money if only you agree to act as a middleman for some dubious transaction and send a few thousand dollars as a token of your good faith, you would be wise to hit the delete button. It is also reasonable to be skeptical about evidence that seems implausible and is at odds with well-established knowledge and theories. The philosopher David Hume famously maintained that extraordinary claims require the support of extraordinarily convincing data, and it is his dictum that we wisely follow when we read of alien abductions, Bigfoot sightings, or reports of psychic prophecies.

But there is a cost to excessive willingness to assimilate data to existing beliefs or theories. It makes it hard to shed plausible but erroneous beliefs, or to win acceptance of initially implausible new theories (such as the idea that diseases are caused by microscopic organisms rather than miasmas or a sorcerer's evil spells). When carried to an extreme, the rejection of evidence that doesn't fit current beliefs can make it impossible to learn from personal experience or the results of empirical research. In fact, viewing data through the prism of existing beliefs can even lead to a strengthening of those beliefs even when logic dictates that they should become less rigidly held.

Lee and his colleagues explored this possibility in the context of the persistent debate about capital punishment and its effectiveness as a deterrent to murder.[14] The participants in their experiment, all of whom were either strong proponents or opponents of the death penalty, were given capsule descriptions of two studies that spoke to the issue of deterrent efficacy. One compared homicide rates in adjacent states. The other compared murder rates in particular states before and after they had adopted or dropped capital punishment. What the participants didn't know was that the investigators were not reporting actual data—instead they manipulated which outcome went with which methodology, so that every participant read about one study supporting their views and one study supporting the views of the other side of the debate.

Two notable findings emerged. As you might expect, each side thought that whatever type of study offered data supporting their position, whether it was a state-by-state comparison or a within-state historical comparison, was more methodologically sound and more informative. The nature of the study didn't matter; what mattered was the conclusion it supported. A logician would have no problem with that: All things being equal, it's reasonable to assume that empirical methods that yield evidence confirming existing beliefs are more sound and more informative than methods producing data at odds with existing beliefs.*

But a logician would have a big problem with the second result. Participants on both sides of the debate reported that they were now more sure of their position than they had been before reading about either study. The logical transgression here can be described succinctly: It's okay to interpret data in light of a prior theory, but it's not okay to then use that same "processed" data to validate that theory. Failing to heed that dictum increases the heat that accompanies debate about empirical questions and it prevents society from making wise and reasoned decisions based on dispassionate evaluation of evidence.

---

* It would be perfectly reasonable, for example, to conclude that a new technique for dating human fossils is reliable and valid if it yields results very similar to those obtained with existing methods, but to have doubts about its validity if it yields results much different from existing methods. You would show a similarly justifiable bias in evaluating the claim that Jack has spoken ill of you—that is, to take the claim at face value if you have reason to believe that Jack is an enemy, but to harbor doubts and give Jack the benefit of the doubt if he is a good friend.

Widening the Keyhole

What does a wise person do to overcome this pervasive bias in human judgment? The solution is easy to state but difficult to follow, or at least difficult to follow consistently. What you need to do is to slow down and consciously look for information that challenges whatever proposition you are evaluating, especially if the proposition conforms to your current views or preferences. Does vegetarianism promote good health? Your first instinct, especially if you're a vegetarian, will be to think of healthy vegetarians you know. But don't stop there. Try to think of vegetarians who suffer from various ailments. In fact, to draw a statistically valid conclusion, you need to consider whether the proportion of healthy to unhealthy vegetarians is really any higher than the proportion of healthy to unhealthy nonvegetarians.

The same is true when evaluating, say, the relationship between extroversion and effective leadership. Outgoing, personable leaders, effective ones especially, will almost automatically spring to mind. But as we noted in our earlier discussion of the confirmation bias, you can't stop there. If you were a political scientist who wanted your thesis about the role of extroversion in effective leadership to be taken seriously by your colleagues, you would have to determine whether the proportion of extroverts versus introverts among effective leaders is any higher than it is among ineffective ones, or even among the population at large.

If that sounds excessive for many everyday purposes, at least get in the habit of getting beyond the mind's impulse to consider mainly supportive cases. Instead, adopt the "consider the opposite" strategy that decision scientists recommend. Studies have shown that when people are encouraged to ask themselves, "Why might my initial impression be wrong?" or "Why might the opposite be true?" they tend to show less of a confirmation bias and, as a result, make far more accurate assessments.[15]

For many centuries the Catholic Church used just such a procedure when deciding whether a potential saint should be canonized. Starting in 1587, it appointed a *promotor fidei*, or promoter of the faith, whose job it was to build a case against canonization—to speak out against the candidate's character, question the magnitude of the candidate's contributions to the faith and to humanity, and exercise skepticism with regard to any miracles the candidate was said to have performed. It continues to be a wise practice to assign someone the role of devil's advocate, but it is not as widely used as it needs to be. For example, after Quaker Oats suffered from its expensive ($1.8 billion) and ill-fated acquisition of the beverage company Snapple, the company's CEO, William Smithburg, admitted, "We should have had a couple of people arguing the 'no' side of the evaluation."[16]

As it happens, John Paul II eliminated the practice of appointing a devil's advocate for canonization decisions and, predictably, the rate at which church members have been deemed worthy of sainthood has skyrocketed. From 1000 CE to 1978, fewer than 450 saints were canonized; in the relatively short time since John Paul II's papacy, more than 480 have been.[17] Interestingly (and controversially), John Paul II was himself recently canonized, in the fastest path to sainthood in modern church history, without having to pass the scrutiny of a *promotor fidei*.

If appointing a devil's advocate is not possible, there are other ways a wise person can "widen the keyhole" and avoid distorting lenses and filters. When it comes to making consequential decisions, for example, you can compare how you think about the pros and cons right now with how you imagine you'll think about them ten years from now. Or you might consider what you'd recommend for a friend or what you think someone you respect would recommend. As we saw in chapter 3, you can shed light on the best product, proposal, or person to *select* by turning the question around and also asking which is the right one to *reject*.

Some decision analysts recommend conducting a "premortem," that is, assume that a decision has gone horribly wrong and ask yourself what information you'd want to gather to find out why.[18] Get that information now. All of the tools for avoiding confirmation bias belong in your tool kit if you want to be the wisest one in the room when it comes to evaluating claims, proposals, and courses of action.

Hidden in the Shadows

According to an old joke, an economist is someone who always wanted to be an accountant . . . but didn't have the personality for it. Whether you think it's funny or not (which is likely to depend on whether you're an economist or an accountant), you have no trouble getting the joke. Your intuitive mind quickly and effortlessly accessed a stereotype about accountants, retrieved some propositional knowledge about the kinds of things most people aspire to, and detected an incongruity that it recognized as the thrust of the joke. The intuitive mind does a great job of dealing with information presented to its attention and accessing information stored in memory. It readily uses information that's readily available. But it doesn't do a good job of deciding whether the information available is misleading or unrepresentative.

That job belongs largely to the rational mind, and it is a difficult one even when all the potentially relevant information is readily available. Even then, as we've seen, the intuitive mind may seize on some information at the expense of other, equally relevant information. But the world doesn't always play fair. It hides some things and highlights others. It is entirely the rational mind's job to correct for any such imbalances. The intuitive mind can't determine when information that has immediately commanded its attention has done so unfairly, or for reasons having nothing to do with its value in making accurate assessments and sound decisions. The distinguished decision-making scholar Robyn Dawes presents a telling example in his book *Rational Choice in an Uncertain World*. He noted that *Discover* magazine once ran a story advising readers that they should "know where the exits are" when they board a plane and rehearse how they would exit in case of an emergency landing. Why? Someone had done a study of individuals who had survived airplane crashes and crash landings and found that 90 percent of them had their escape routes mapped out beforehand.[19]

That statistic, 90 percent, sounds impressive. But a moment's reflection prompts some second thoughts—including the realization that the investigator obviously hadn't interviewed anyone who died in those crashes. It is therefore entirely possible that 90 percent of those victims had similarly mapped out their escape routes (as they are advised to do by their flight attendants). In fact, it's possible (although unlikely) that an even larger percentage of the victims had taken that precaution, meaning that doing so is actually hazardous to one's health.

The point here (again) is that when deciding whether a given practice has an influence on health and well-being, it is necessary to compare the proportion of good and bad consequences that follow from the presence versus the absence of the practice in question. The further point is that unless one's rational mind sends a "hold-on" signal that cancels the intuitively compelling conclusion, one can end up making egregious mistakes.

One such mistake we all make involves our assessments of what others think of us—specific others, that is. We are pretty accurate in anticipating whether our friends, family, coworkers, and fellow club members as a whole think that we're hot-headed, clever, trustworthy, or talkative. But we're not very accurate when it comes to knowing what *this* coworker or *that* club member thinks of us. Indeed, when office mates, college roommates, or discussion group members are asked to rate one another on these traits and then each person is asked to predict how he or she will be rated by each of those other individuals, the predictions are only modestly aligned to reality. That is, the correlation between Joe's ratings of Jennifer and how Jennifer thinks she'll be rated by Joe is close to zero. As one investigator who does this type of work put it, "People seem to have just a tiny glimmer of insight into how they are uniquely viewed by particular other people."[20]

Although our lack of insight into what specific other people think of us may seem surprising at first glance, it becomes much less surprising when we remind ourselves that critical information (in both senses of that word) is typically hidden from us, at least by strangers, acquaintances, or relatively distant friends. That is, we generally fail to give each other accurate feedback about our true feelings. If you think Carlos is too talkative, or Lou is too boastful, or Sally too eager to show off her Ivy League education, you're far more likely to complain about it to a third party than to bring it to the attention of Carlos, Lou, or Sally. It's hardly surprising, then, that people tend to think they'll be evaluated more favorably by others than they actually are.

One important exception: People are accurate in anticipating the *status* they are granted by other members of their group. When it comes to status, we do get accurate feedback. If we act as if we have more status than we actually do, the group will cut us down to size. And if we report a more modest assessment of our status than we deserve, the group will let us know about that too.[21]

A number of superstitions depend on asymmetries in available information. If a loved one dies shortly after you have dreamed of his or her death, the earlier dream will surely stand out.[22] But those dreams tend to be forgotten whenever, as is almost always the case, the premonition is not followed by a confirmatory event. The same is true of many other beliefs: "I always need something right after I've thrown it away," "It always rains right after I water the lawn," and "I'm more likely to be called on by my professors if I haven't done the assigned reading."[23]

The superstitious beliefs of sports fans, even sports fans with PhDs, that what they're doing in their living rooms might have an effect on a contest taking place hundreds or thousands of miles away offer many examples of the same idea. Fans believe, or at least act as if they believe, that commenting on a streak of good performance (wins against a particular opponent, free throws made by a favorite player, or successful completions by a quarterback) will somehow make the streak come to a halt. Others, out of some combination of tradition and conviction that it will make a difference, turn their baseball caps backward to spark a rally or wear the same "lucky shirt" or sit in the same "lucky chair" to increase (or avoid jinxing) their team's prospects. Instances in which these actions pay off stand out. Failures are little noted nor long remembered.

It is difficult to make broad statements about what makes some information salient and renders other information relatively inaccessible. But it is easy, as we have done, to offer many telling examples. The reasons that real estate agents can maintain that "buyers are liars" (because clients who end up exceeding their "absolute ceiling" are more memorable than those who don't), that some parents insist that "my kids always seem to bother me when I'm on the phone" (because otherwise their requests aren't really a bother), and that negotiators can be convinced that "you have to be tough or they'll walk all over you" (because they can't see the results of an approach—not being tough—they don't follow) are all different from one another. But some of the causes clump together in categories. Social psychologists have identified some systematic ways in which everyday life highlights some information and hides other information in the shadows. A wise person is aware of these asymmetries and knows when extra steps are needed to make visible information that would otherwise be hidden.

Casting Our Own Shadows

Your child thinks she has real talent in math so she studies extra hard in her math class, attempts to solve the bonus problems in her homework assignments, and dives into the book of math puzzles you bought her after hearing her say that math seems to be "her thing." Not surprisingly, it turns out to be her strongest subject.

A financial guru opines on television that stocks are overpriced by historical standards and that a dip in the market is likely in the near future. His followers sell their equities and invest in bonds and precious metals. Sure enough, the stock market softens.

You doubt that anyone as lovely as Jennifer could care for you, so you never suggest going out for coffee, you avoid looking at her, and you're reserved in her presence. She remains distant.

All of these are examples of an important behavioral science concept that has made its way into popular consciousness: the self-fulfilling prophecy. We think something is true and act in ways that make it true. More pertinent to our discussion of seeing the world through keyholes and filters, Tom introduced the concept of *seemingly fulfilled prophecies* to describe the (related) series of events whereby our beliefs lead us to act in ways that make the belief *seem* true—that prevent us from encountering evidence that it is not.[24]

If you think Anya is hostile, you're likely to give her a wide berth, thereby making it unlikely that you'll get to see that she is actually warm and friendly. If you think one of your employees lacks the talent to succeed at the next level, you won't give her the chance to prove you wrong. If you believe your company should hire only graduates from prestigious business schools, you'll look around and see all sorts of dedicated, hard-working, and talented Ivy Leaguers in your organization. What you won't get to see are all the dedicated, hard-working individuals you turned down because they graduated from less prestigious schools—and are now exercising their considerable talents elsewhere.

In all these situations, the conclusions drawn—she's hostile; he doesn't have what it takes; our personnel department is really on top of things—seem entirely reasonable and well supported by the available evidence. What the wisest person in the room might be able to make you see is the role you yourself have played in the creating of that evidence.

Another common social dynamic that keeps critical information hidden from view is what behavioral scientists call *pluralistic igno-rance.*[25] The phenomenon occurs whenever people hide their true thoughts and feelings because they have an exaggerated sense of how much others would disapprove. The resulting schism between private thoughts and public behavior only reinforces the false norm, which makes it even harder for individuals to express how they really feel. The group as a whole therefore remains ignorant of its actual beliefs.

Pluralistic ignorance plays an important role in all sorts of trou-blesome phenomena. Consider the excessive alcohol consumption that takes place on college campuses. Students think that their peers are more enthusiastic imbibers than they are themselves, which leads them to act as if they like to drink more than they actually do in order to fit in. The shared pretense reinforces the erroneous belief about the popularity of drinking and the likely reaction to students who don't join in on the fun.[26] This leads to more alcohol consumption, which reinforces the original belief, and so on.

To break this vicious cycle, researchers in one study had groups of students type in their answers to survey questions about alcohol and alcohol consumption on campus. As they did so, their aggregate responses were projected for everyone to see. Follow-up surveys ad-ministered two months later revealed that those who received this real-time information about their peers' attitudes reported consum-ing 20 percent less alcohol than students in a control group who did not receive information about the true norms.[27] Getting a glimpse at everyone's unguarded responses eliminates the impulse to put up a false front aimed at a false norm.

Pluralistic ignorance also plays a role in career burnout. People tend to think that they will be highly regarded (and not one of the ones to be let go if the budget is cut) if they are seen as someone who can handle the job without stress, strain, or self-doubt. So they hide their doubts and difficulties, leading anyone experiencing simi-lar doubts and difficulties to assume that there's something uniquely wrong with them—that they can't handle the job as well as their peers. This only serves to increase the stress of the job, leading some to conclude that they just aren't cut out for it.

As one person who was interviewed in a study of burnout among health care professionals put it, "I did get rattled and upset at times— like the first time a patient died. And I would be feeling panicky and angry and sad, but I would be fighting any expressions of those feelings because I knew they were not professional. Everyone else seemed to be handling things okay, which made me feel even worse—like a real failure and a weakling who wasn't cut out for this kind of work."[28]

An important component of wisdom, then, is knowing when and how *you*—and your behavior—have influenced the very information you are using to form judgments and make decisions. Who are you not hearing from? Have you made it hard for others to tell you the truth? Is the energy you've devoted to a pet project the reason it looks better than the projects you've neglected?

The Sounds of Silence

We've all been in this situation: The person in charge of the meeting suggests, to get things started, "Let's go around the room and see what everyone thinks." The results are often disappointing. Rather than leading to a free flow of ideas, the range of possibilities under discussion quickly narrows. Two processes limit the diversity of opinion, one deliberate and the other unintentional.

First, self-censorship often sets in. People are reluctant to step on each other's toes. As a consequence, positions that are at odds with an emerging consensus tend not to be expressed. Group members thereby offer tacit support for positions with which they disagree. In extreme cases, people end up explicitly advocating positions they would never endorse privately ("I agree with what my esteemed colleague from accounting just said . . ."). This sort of self-censorship is especially common when the stakes are high and the group members want the reassurance that comes with apparent consensus. In those cases, a type of "groupthink" emerges whereby the critical scrutiny that should be devoted to an issue gets truncated by the pressure to achieve consensus.

Irvin Janis, a social psychologist who helped pioneer the study of group decision making and who coined the term *groupthink*, argued that these sorts of social pressures were responsible for some of the most misguided decisions in American political and military history. His list included the failure to heed warnings about a possible attack on Pearl Harbor by the Japanese, the Bay of Pigs invasion aimed at overthrowing Fidel Castro's regime in the early 1960s, and the decision to escalate the war in Vietnam later in that decade.[29]

The Senate Intelligence Committee that examined the Bush administration's decision to invade Iraq in 2003 cited groupthink as a reason for the administration's miscalculations when it came to claims that Iraq was developing weapons of mass destruction. The committee maintained that the deliberations that led to the invasion "demonstrated several aspects of groupthink: examining few alternatives, selective gathering of information, pressure to conform within the group or withhold criticism." This narrow focus is so common that the military has its own name for it, *incestuous amplification*, which *Jane's Defense Weekly* defines as a tendency whereby "one only listens to those who are already in lock-step agreement, reinforcing set beliefs and creating a situation ripe for miscalculation."[30]

In these sorts of high-stakes deliberations, and when evaluating less weighty matters as well, a much less conscious process further contributes to a premature convergence of opinion: Group members unknowingly end up talking about information they share rather than information that is unique to each of them.[31] Suppose Bob knows a lot about the history of a new product's development as well as the size of the market for it, but knows very little about the product's technical specifications. Suppose that Chelsea knows a lot about both the product's history and its technical specifications, but nothing about the market for the product. Chances are that Bob and Chelsea will spend the bulk of their time talking about what they both already know—the product's history—and miss the opportunity for each to learn from the other. Information that everyone knows is easier to talk about because there is more common ground for discussion and doing so often leads to a more congenial meeting as well.

What can be done to combat these twin sources of convergent thinking? There's a simple lesson here. To combat self-censorship, don't start a meeting with "Let's go around the room and have everyone say what they think." That tends to dampen the generation of ideas. It is much better to have everyone write down their ideas and any pertinent information that needs to be discussed and then have someone read everyone's thoughts out loud. The facts, options, and considerations that then get discussed tend to be more far ranging, leading to more informed deliberation. Dividing into small brainstorming groups and then sharing the fruits of each group's efforts is another way to prevent the premature narrowing of the discussion.

Overcoming the common knowledge effect is more difficult. Simply having the group deliberate longer in the hope that hidden information will eventually come out tends not to help much. Nor does increasing the number of people in the group in the hope that it will promote greater diversity in what gets discussed. Including people known to have diverse areas of expertise can help, but doing so tends to be most effective when someone has been assigned the task of ferreting out hidden information and making sure that those with specialized knowledge and diverse viewpoints are heard.[32] The wisest one in the room may suggest just such a strategy. That wisest person can be you.

Looking Back and Moving Forward

When people try to define wisdom, they often emphasize practical knowledge and social acuity over intellect or "book smarts." As we mentioned in the introduction, Merriam-Webster offers "good sense" as its final definition of wisdom, a definition that highlights the ability to apply what one knows when dealing with the opportunities and challenges of everyday life. It is in the spirit of that perspective on wisdom that we offer the final four chapters of our book.

We wouldn't have written this book (or ever pursued careers in social psychology) if we didn't think the wisdom our field has to offer could help in dealing with a wide range of pressing problems and practical concerns. In very general terms, we have suggested that in tackling any applied behavioral problem, it is essential to understand the details—especially the hidden and subtle details—of the web of situational forces acting on the individuals whose behavior one wants to change (chapter 2). But it is also essential to understand how those forces are interpreted by the individuals who face them (chapter 3) and to be aware of the various filters and lenses that guide, and potentially distort, their interpretations (chapter 5).

We began our discussion, however, with the most common source of human misunderstanding that wise men and women have called attention to over the centuries: the tendency for people to regard their own perceptions and reactions as if they are a direct, objective, and veridical reflection of how things "really are" rather than the product of subjective interpretation (chapter 1). We also introduced a critical insight about the link between beliefs and behavior: The actions that people take not only reflect what they feel and believe; they can powerfully *influence* their feelings and beliefs downstream (chapter 4). Indeed, an understanding of the human need to make sense of our actions, and in many cases to justify or rationalize those actions, can be a valuable tool in addressing applied problems.

In our first five chapters, we have focused mainly on what goes on in the mind of the individual. Before proceeding further, it is worth considering the ways in which the factors described in these five chapters come together in a given society or culture. Without our being aware of it, our culture provides the lenses and filters through which we perceive the events that take place around us and the challenges and opportunities that present themselves. But culture is not something that is just "in the head." It includes the material features of our environment—the kinds of houses we live in, the design of our shops, schools, and meeting places; and it also includes the laws and customs that dictate much of our behavior. Directly and indirectly it determines the options that are open to us and what actions are deemed virtuous or scandalous or even unthinkable.

When we think of cultures, we tend to think of *other* cultures—especially those that differ from our own in marked ways, cultures in which people engage in strange practices, eat strange foods, indulge in strange superstitions, and have strange notions about what constitutes a life well lived. Nowhere is naïve realism more apparent than when we reflect on the views and behavior of people in other cultures—when we take our own ways of living for granted and think of the ways of people in other cultures as something to be explained by the particular demands of their ecology or their particular history. We find it hard to appreciate that it is our culture that much of the world regards as strange. In fact, anthropologist Joe Heinrich and his colleagues have coined the acronym WEIRD (for Western, educated, industrialized, rich, and democratic) to alert us to the features of our culture that distinguish us from much of the rest of the world.

With the principles discussed in our first five chapters, and this cautionary note about our particular cultural lenses in mind, we turn in part 2 to four important issues that individuals and societies everywhere face. In chapter 6 we sketch the outlines of a psych-wise perspective on human happiness and the lessons that contemporary research has to offer on the characteristics of happy versus unhappy people and societies, and on what we can all do to live happier lives.

In chapter 7 we focus on a persistent threat to human happiness and well-being, the conflicts that arise because different people want and need different things, and feel that their wants and needs are more legitimate than those of the people with whom they disagree. In this chapter we take an especially close look at the psychological barriers that prevent groups locked in conflict from reaching agreements that could leave both parties better off.

In our final two chapters we focus on what we term a "tough problem" (chapter 8) and an "even tougher problem" (chapter 9). The tough problem is that of improving the classroom performance of at-risk student populations. In particular, we discuss some promising psych-wise intervention strategies that, although modest in scope, can set in motion virtuous cycles whereby students and educators reinforce each other's efforts in ways that produce significant gains in achievement. The even-tougher problem is that of dealing with climate change. For the most part, we consider the psychological dimensions of the problem that make it difficult to marshal the resolve and resources that will be required if our heirs are to continue to enjoy the relatively benign conditions under which humans have thrived over the past several millennia. But we also offer some potentially useful strategies for practitioners and responsible citizens who want to alert their peers to the dimensions of the problem and begin to address it.

Part 2

WISDOM APPLIED

6

The Happiest One in the Room

On the evening of October 14, 1993, Mark Zupan and a group of teammates on Florida Atlantic University's soccer team went out drinking at Dirty Moe's, a bar that catered to the college crowd with low-priced drinks and a lax approach to keeping minors at bay. After downing a number of free drinks from fans who had been at the game, Zupan said he was feeling "shit-housed" and left the bar around midnight looking for a place to sleep it off. He chose the back of his friend's pickup truck.

His friend, Chris Igoe, was not feeling so well himself at that point. He passed out in the bar and was rustled awake by a bouncer at 2:00 a.m. and told the bar was closing and he had to leave. He got into his truck, convincing himself that he could safely drive the two miles to his dorm. He couldn't. He took an exit off I-95 at too great a speed and lost control of his truck, slamming it into a fence. The collision catapulted Zupan out of the truck and into a drainage canal.

Zupan lay in the brackish water, unable to move or feel anything in his legs. Igoe, not knowing that Zupan had been lying asleep in the back of his truck, was unaware of his friend's misfortune. So when an off-duty police officer handcuffed Igoe and took him away and a tow-truck driver took away Igoe's vehicle, Zupan was left lying in the ditch, his arm clinging around a branch to keep his head above water. When he was finally discovered the following day, he was rushed to the hospital, where a devastating diagnosis was delivered: His spine was severely damaged and he would spend the rest of his life as a paraplegic.

You might imagine that anyone suffering such a fate would sink into a deep depression, never to achieve the same level of happiness again. But Zupan, who went on to become a champion wheelchair rugby player, doesn't see it that way. Instead, he maintains that:

> In truth, my accident has been the best thing that could have ever happened to me. I'm not trying to be glib when I say this, or rationalize my mistakes, or offer you a steaming bowl of bullshit-flavored Chicken Soup for the Soul. What I am saying is that it has been the single most defining event of my life. And without it, I wouldn't have seen the things I've seen, done the things I've done and met so many incredible people. I wouldn't have become a world-class athlete. I wouldn't have come to understand my friends and family the way I do, and feel the kind of love they have for me and I have for them.[1]

Zupan's capacity to make the most of life since his traumatic accident is a remarkable triumph of the human spirit. Many people say they "would rather die" than live as a paraplegic. But while Zupan's accomplishments are exceptional and inspiring, his recovery and positive outlook are not as unusual as you might assume. Most people who lose the use of their limbs go on to live satisfying lives with just about as much joy (and about as much sadness and frustration) as everyone else. In fact, in one study, 86 percent of a sample of men and women paralyzed because of spinal cord injuries said that the quality of their life was "average" or "above average." One in four said that their life was close to "ideal."[2]

Stories like Mark Zupan's offer powerful testimonials to the human capacity for *adaptation*. We all suffer misfortunes and losses from time to time. But even when terrible events hit us hard and knock us down, most of us gradually get back up again. In the face of adversity, adaptation is our greatest asset, and something we all tap into when things are bleak. And knowledge of this capacity can help us serve as a source of support and perspective when others face adversity. But a wise person knows that simply saying "Don't worry; you will get over it" or "Look on the bright side" is not likely to prove helpful. Nowhere is naïve realism, which we discussed in detail in chapter 1, more evident than when someone tells you that your feelings are not appropriate to the situation, or when you tell someone that your outlook for their future is more realistic than their own.

Of course, the same psychology that gets us beyond disappointment and trauma limits our ability to sustain strong positive feelings. A friend claims that she will never again be troubled by minor annoyances if the tumor her physician is biopsying turns out to be benign. A working mother insists that she would be much happier if only her boss would give her the 10 percent pay raise she is asking for—and that she would be in a perpetual state of euphoria if she hit it big in the lottery. A brother insists that he would be the happiest man in the world if the person of his dreams says yes to a marriage proposal. The reality is that although such outcomes do bring joy, it is a joy that fades predictably, and often quickly, with the passage of time.

It is no great revelation that people get used to changes in their circumstances and that the pain or joy they bring diminishes over time. As we noted in our preface, the words of the early Sufi poets, echoed in the Hebrew Bible, encapsulate that insight: "This too shall pass." The empirical surprise for even the wisest among us is just how powerful adaptation tends to be. Indeed, although four out of five people who have lost the use of their limbs rate the quality of their lives as average or above, fewer than one out of the five doctors and nurses who attend to patients with spinal cord injuries believe *their* lives would be similarly satisfying if they were to suffer such an injury.[3]

Zupan's Happiness

What is it these medical professionals fail to appreciate when they imagine what it would be like to find themselves in the predicament of their patients? To understand Mark Zupan's experience and that of others who have coped with adversity so well, we need to consider what he means when he says, "My accident has been the best thing that could have ever happened to me." Which "me" is he talking about? If he is talking about the author of the book *Gimp*, the man who has overcome great misfortune and fashioned a rewarding life for himself, his claim does not seem farfetched. But it certainly doesn't apply to the man who spent those hours of agony lying in the ditch on the day of his accident, or the man who endured the months of surgeries, catheterizations, and painful physical rehabilitation. Nor, in all likelihood, does it apply to the man who faces a physical challenge just to get out of bed each morning rather than simply hop out the way most people do.

The Mark Zupan who reflects on the totality and meaning of his life is very different from the Mark Zupan who experiences it moment to moment, and it's possible for those two different selves to have very different sentiments about the accident. Zupan can believe with the utmost sincerity that it was the "best thing that ever happened to him" yet acknowledge that he would not choose to reexperience the accident if he could "live life over again," much less recommend it for a son, niece, or stranger.

This distinction is captured in part by the difference between moment-to-moment pleasure (or the sum or average of such moments) and what philosophers have called *eudaimonia*—the broader sense of well-being that comes with the feeling that one's life is worthwhile, meaningful, and well lived. Studies in which volunteers agree to be beeped by a smartphone and report what they're doing at that moment and how happy they are highlight this distinction. Volunteers in these studies consistently rate watching television as pleasurable.[4] But after spending a day watching TV, few of us feel much satisfaction. The moment-to-moment consumer of television is happy, but the retrospective evaluator who has spent hours watching reruns and reality TV shows is not. Both perspectives are valid: The person watching television is no doubt experiencing some pleasure, but the ennui and self-criticism that often set in after hours in front of a television screen are real as well.

The same contrast is familiar to any parent. Much of the moment-to-moment and day-to-day experience of raising a child—staying calm during weeks of colic, staying awake after predawn chauffeuring to swim practice, and staying civil during periods of adolescent rebellion—is anything but enjoyable. Yet many parents say that raising a child and persevering through such difficulties is the most rewarding thing they have ever done in their lives.[5]

There is something else to bear in mind when we consider Zupan's assertions about his good fortune: the narrow focus of attention and the filters or lenses that govern our perceptions and judgments that we discussed in chapter 5. When asked to consider a fate like Zupan's, we focus on the prospect of becoming a paraplegic and the consequent loss of mobility, which is obviously terrifying. The transition from someone who takes running, walking, standing, and getting out of bed for granted is indeed traumatic. We get that right. Paraplegics are often depressed for months after their accidents. And even long afterward, the daily limitations and travails are a source of frustration. But what we don't appreciate when we consider what it is like to be a paraplegic is that those coping with their disability don't spend all their time *being* paraplegics.

They are also fathers who enjoy their child's triumphs, foodies who salivate over duck breast in an orange pomegranate sesame sauce, or readers who dive into the latest novels of their favorite authors with at least as much pleasure as those who don't share their disability. In fact, we suspect that their pleasure in these activities is heightened. The sight of their child laughing, the touch of a loved one, or the irritation felt when watching election coverage on that "other network" become the focus of attention and dominate the emotional landscape. At those moments at least, paraplegics' lives are not much different than they would be had they never lost the use of their limbs.

This narrow focus of attention also influences how people think about taking steps that might change their lives. In one study, people living in the Midwest were asked whether they'd be happier if they lived in California. This naturally leads to a focus on the most obvious difference between the two locales: the weather. Given the common preference for blue skies and comfortably warm temperatures over gray skies and snow, most respondents said they would be happier in California. But surveys make it clear that the average person in the Midwest is just as happy as the average Californian.[6] What the participants in this study failed to consider is that most of the time, the weather, or even more consequential changes in our job or physical health, is not on our minds as we go about the business of day-to-day living.

The wisest in the room appreciates the implications of this focusing effect when making personal decisions and offering advice to friends. The wisest in the room also appreciates that overall assessments of the quality of life are not a matter of simply adding up moment-to-moment experiences of pain and pleasure. Instead, such assessments are dictated by the broader meaning we give to our everyday experiences. Was the day spent cleaning up the beach a boring but dutiful exercise, or was it a satisfying opportunity to act in accord with important values in the company of like-minded companions? Consider the story of two NASA janitors asked to describe their jobs. One said it was to clean up and maintain the physical plant. The other said it was to help put an astronaut on the moon. It is not difficult to guess which one found his job more satisfying.

The Well-Calibrated Pursuit of Happiness

Even for those determinants of happiness that are familiar to all of us, some (like adaptation) turn out to be even more powerful than you might assume. Others (like money) turn out to have less impact than we assume when we contemplate the future and make choices we think will make us happier. People are happier, and certainly less stressed, when their financial situation improves, but the cliché that money can't buy happiness is also largely true.[7] Winning the lottery does make people happier—just not as much as they had hoped, or as much as the rest of us assume we would be if we received the same windfall.[8]

It will also surprise few people to learn that when it comes to wealth and material goods, it matters a lot how we stack up in comparison to those around us, a fact nicely captured by H. L. Mencken's definition of wealth as "any income that is at least 100 dollars more a year than the income of one's wife's sister's husband."[9]

It would also surprise very few people to learn that happiness researchers have found that satisfying social relationships and simply being with others contribute to happiness.[10] So does service to others.[11] But here too, recognizing the strength of these relationships, and the particular ways in which they make their influence felt, is a key to becoming wiser.

Who Are the Happiest in the Room?

Some people you know just seem happier than others, and research confirms that there is a pretty high correlation between how happy people say they are and how happy their friends and coworkers say they are. What's their secret? In part, of course, the answer is to be found in the circumstances of their lives. People with good jobs and satisfying relationships are, on average, happier than those without such blessings. As Sigmund Freud put it in a letter to Carl Jung, "Work and love, love and work—that's all there is."

But Freud clearly left some things out—like play, for example, or laughter, or stopping to enjoy the beauty of nature. More broadly, both everyday experience and empirical research indicate that objective factors like the quality of a person's work or social life don't tell the whole story. Some people seem happier or unhappier than others regardless of their circumstances. There are numerous clichés about seeing glasses as half-empty or half-full, or counting one's blessings, or making lemonade when life hands you lemons. But there also are some intriguing research hints that happy people respond to life's challenges in ways that protect them from the dissatisfaction less happy people experience in those very same situations.

Consider the finding, discussed earlier, that people who choose between two attractive options tend to denigrate the option they rejected (as a way of reducing cognitive dissonance). But happy people do this less than others. At least that was the finding in a pair of studies Lee and his former student Sonja Lyubomersky conducted. In one, college students chose between delicious desserts; in the other, high school seniors rated colleges that had accepted them for the coming year. In both cases, the happier the students said they were, the less likely they were to downgrade the rejected alternatives. The happiest participants in these studies got to savor the black forest cake without deciding that the linzer torte (which they might choose to enjoy tomorrow) looked a bit stale and unappealing. And they could also look forward to attending Swarthmore or Columbia or their state university without denigrating the schools they declined to attend (and without alienating classmates who chose those schools).*[12]

---

*It is not that happy people fail to protect themselves against more substantial threats to their self-esteem or well-being. The happy seniors in this study did not refrain from denigrating the schools that had rejected *them* (while feeling no need to denigrate the ones they rejected). In fact, they did so even more than the less happy students.

People often engage in social comparison in a way that can diminish the pleasure they take in their good fortune (think Mencken here). In another study, participants who were asked to teach a math lesson to children got feedback indicating that they had done a "good job." In some cases they received only that feedback; in other cases it was accompanied by information that a peer had done an *even better* job. How much did this comparison diminish the participants' pleasure in their performance? A great deal in the case of those who rated themselves as relatively unhappy—and not at all in the case of those who rated themselves as happy.[13]

Happy people also differ from their peers in how they think about their past. When Israeli military veterans were asked to reflect on the highs and lows of their service, the happier veterans were more inclined than their peers to treat their memories of good days as a continuing source of happiness, and less inclined to draw contrasts between the present and those "good old days." The happier veterans were also less likely to treat memories of their worst military experiences as a continuing psychic burden and source of unhappiness.[14]

Findings like these raise a critical question about the direction of influence. Do some people, out of psychological wisdom and personal experience, see the world and react to events in ways that make them happy? Or are some people—through genetic makeup, fortunate parenting, or exposure to the right role models—simply happier and therefore prone to see and react to the world in ways that further advance their happiness?

Both processes likely operate in a kind of virtuous cycle (or, in the case of unhappy people, a vicious cycle). The important message from this kind of research, however, is that there are things a wise person can do to be happier. Chapter 4's discussion of the primacy of behavior offers some tips: Act like a happy person, and you will find it easier to be one. Don't waste your energy denigrating paths not taken or choices not made. Avoid social comparisons that put you at the short end of the stick. Savor the great times you had and the blessings you enjoyed in the past rather than dwelling on what may be lacking in your life today. But also seek out experiences that will contribute to your happiness right now. Unfortunately, this sort of advice is much easier to offer than to follow. If that weren't the case, there would be fewer long faces in the world.

Countless books offer specific advice about how to enhance your happiness and sense of well-being. Many of them are by well-respected researchers whose own research provides the basis for their advice.[15] You can find them in the psychology section of your local bookstore. We won't summarize that vast literature here. Nor will we urge you to have a rich social life, choose a warm and compelling mate, or find a gratifying career—things that are strongly linked to happiness but aren't fully within a person's control. (You can't just decide to have a rewarding social life, an adoring and exciting partner, or a fulfilling career.) Instead, we offer a few practical ideas that we believe are particularly useful in the pursuit of happiness. They are based on principles that the two of us have gleaned from our own empirical work and have found to be supported by our own personal experiences and observations of our friends and colleagues. Most important, they involve things that are under your personal control.

Mind the Peak and End

Imagine you and your family are planning a trip to Kauai, Hawaii's "garden isle." Like most people, your budget is limited and you have to make some trade-offs. One option is to economize a bit—by renting a condo a quarter mile from the beach and avoiding restaurant meals—so you can stay for two weeks. The alternative would be to stay for a shorter period (perhaps only a week) and use the savings to splurge a bit—rent a house right next to the beach, treat yourself to a slack-key guitar performance by a local legend, and take a helicopter flight over the island on your last day. What would you choose?

Psychological research provides a clear answer to these sorts of quantity-quality trade-offs: Choose the shorter, more memorable vacation. When you're back at home or at work, two pleasant but less memorable weeks won't feel any different from one. But savoring your memories of walking right onto the beach in the morning and then again at sunset, playing the album of the musicians you heard live as you sipped that rum concoction, and remembering what it looked like to see the Na Pali coast from the air are experiences you will draw on for a lifetime.

The message here applies well beyond vacation planning. Pioneering research by Daniel Kahneman and colleagues has documented a "peak-end" rule. What we recall about any experience—what lives on and determines our long-term sense of enjoyment or pain—is generally governed by what it was like at its most extreme moment and what it was like at the end. As Kahneman noted, this idea was nicely captured by a line in Milan Kundera's *Immortality*: "Memory does not make films, it makes photographs." What stands out are the exceptional moments captured in those photographs. You will remember, as an abstract proposition, that a two-week vacation in Hawaii lasted two weeks. But your overall sense of the vacation and the feelings that linger will not depend much on duration.

In one study that illustrates this fact of hedonic life, Kahneman had one group of participants watch a series of short video clips of pleasant images—puppies, penguins diving into the water, waves crashing on the beach. Another group saw clips of decidedly unpleasant images—a gruesome mutilation, the aftermath of the Hiroshima bombing, industrial-scale slaughter of animals. In both cases the length of these presentations varied for different participants, all of whom were asked to adjust a dial from moment to moment to indicate how pleasant, or unpleasant, each segment was to them. Afterward, the participants were asked how enjoyable or unpleasant the overall experience had been.

What Kahneman and colleagues found was that the length of the presentation had little effect on participants' overall assessments of how good or bad their experience had been. Seeing a lot of terrible stuff didn't make the experience much worse than seeing much less. What best predicted the participants' overall ratings was how good or bad their experience was at its best or worst moment and how good or bad it was at the end. How gruesome a mutilation is plays a big role in the impression it leaves; how long we have to witness the mutilation plays very little role. How cute a puppy looks has a big effect on our overall assessment; how long we get to look at puppies hardly registers.[16]

A surprising real-world implication of the peak-end rule was demonstrated in a study of people undergoing diagnostic colonoscopies without sedation, a procedure that is particularly painful when the scope is inserted farthest into the colon. Normally, that point comes at the end of the procedure, after which the doctor quickly removes the scope. Patients typically remember the whole experience as very painful—so painful that many never follow the recommendation to repeat the procedure five years later. Applying the lesson of the peak-end rule to this problem, Kahneman and colleagues had doctors try something different. Instead of removing the scope immediately after the most painful period in the procedure, they had the doctors pull the scope out *most* of the way, letting it linger inside the end of the colon for a short (and a medically unnecessary) additional period.

This extra period of time, it should be emphasized, is not pleasant. Indeed, it is rather unpleasant—just not as unpleasant as the period beforehand when the scope had been inserted most deeply. Even though the patients who were subjected to this additional period of discomfort obviously experienced more pain, they rated the overall experience as less traumatic than patients undergoing the procedure in the standard fashion. Indeed, 70 percent of these patients signed up for the recommended follow-up procedure, a notable increase over the 50 percent rate among participants in the study treated in the usual "in-and-out" manner.[17]

The lesson for hedonic management should be clear. When planning a vacation, for example, it's a good idea to sacrifice some of the length of the trip if it allows you to experience a more sublime high point. If you can make that sublime moment happen at the very end, all the better. If not, make sure the trip at least ends with something pleasant—a last evening watching the sunset or a nice brunch—rather than a couple of frantic hours running around buying gifts and souvenirs followed by a hasty packing session before rushing to the airport. By the same token, when you are doing a string of unpleasant chores, resist the temptation to leave the toughest and most tedious to last. Even better, try to end your labors with a chore that is at least somewhat pleasant.

You'll Always Have Paris

Suppose you are one of the many Californians who like to drink wine but have a limited budget. Would it be better to spend your limited resources on a wine rack that would allow you to store your wine in the proper atmospheric conditions in your basement, or on an afternoon wine tasting trip to some nearby vineyards? Choices between durable goods like the wine rack and fleeting experiences like the wine tasting (or any other choice between a single pleasurable experience and the acquisition of a more durable asset) may seem easy to make if we think in conventional investment terms. Given that the asset will be around for a long time while the experience will come and go in a flash, isn't the asset the more prudent investment? Prudent, perhaps. Wise? Perhaps not.

Research and personal reflection alike suggest that there's something overlooked in that seemingly prudent calculation. We're all familiar with how much fun it is to get a new couch, car, or cappuccino maker. The fabric on the couch smells fresh and clean, the car's engine purrs along without the slightest arrhythmia, and the froth put out by the cappuccino machine is luxuriantly rich. But before long we fail to notice the smell of the new fabric, stop attending to the sound of the engine, and experience the stuff on top of the drink as just foam. For most of us, and for most possessions, things soon fade into the background of our mental landscape, providing little continuing benefit.

Experiential purchases are less likely to disappear from that mental landscape. When people are asked to rate their most significant material or experiential purchase from a given time period—the past month, the past year, or the past five years—they report that their experiential purchases are more satisfying, provide more happiness, and represent money "better spent."[18] Material and experiential purchases tend to provide just as much happiness initially, but the thrill of material goods tends to fade, while the enjoyment derived from experiential purchases endures.[19]

Experiential purchases live on and provide more enduring enjoyment in the stories we tell, the memories we cherish, and the enhanced sense of identity and personal development we gain. As Humphrey Bogart memorably said to Ingrid Bergman at the end of *Casablanca*, "We'll always have Paris." Indeed, experiences don't just endure; they often become better with time as we embellish the best elements and downplay the worst. A camping trip during which it rained endlessly, a bear stole most of the food, and the couple in a nearby tent screamed at each other until the wee hours of the morning becomes, with time and in the telling and reminiscing, not the "camping trip from hell" but the *"hilarious* camping trip from hell."*

---

*The distinction between material and experiential goods is not cut and dried. Bicycles and cars are clearly material goods, but they are also vehicles for experience. Also, some possessions—mementos in particular, like the family matriarch's wedding ring or a child's first baseball mitt—are likely to become ever more valuable as the years pass. But they do so because they serve as tokens of experience—as prompts to mentally relive the treasured experiences to which they are tied. In fact, when research participants are asked to think of a purchase such as a television or box set of music CDs in either material or experiential terms, those led to think of it in experiential terms report being happier with it.[20]

Differences in adaptation and the warmth of memories are not the only reasons that experiential purchases tend to provide more enduring satisfaction than material goods. They are also less likely to spark comparisons of the sort that diminish enjoyment—comparisons with what other people have or we had previously. Imagine, for example, that you just bought a new laptop computer. No sooner have you taken it out of its box and examined all its features than you learn that an acquaintance also just purchased a laptop for roughly the same price, only his is undeniably better than yours—faster processor, more RAM, higher-resolution screen. How bothered would you be? A lot! It's not fun when others, especially those you don't particularly like, outdo you. In fact, merely reading an ad for a more attractive computer at a comparable or lower price, something that is bound to happen before too long, is likely to make you feel some regret.

But now imagine that you spent the money not on a laptop but on a beach vacation where the weather was fine, the locals were friendly, your companion was great company, and you got the downtime you needed. Here too, suppose you discover that someone else, even someone you don't like, also vacationed at that beach but the weather was even better, the hotel a step up in quality, the food more sumptuous, and the prices paid for everything lower. Or simply suppose that you saw an ad for an even fancier beach vacation at an even better price. How bad would you feel about *that*? Would the unfavorable comparison diminish your satisfaction as much as it would for the inferior laptop? Though you might wish you could trade laptops with your rival, would you entertain any such wish to trade vacations?

Research by Tom and his former student Travis Carter suggests that pleasure is much less subject to adverse comparisons when it comes to experiences like vacations or concerts than possessions like laptops or large-screen TVs.[21] People who waste time, money, and emotion trying to keep up with the Joneses when it comes to their car, their condo, or their clothes are much less likely to do so when it comes to where they vacation, where they dine out, or how often they go to the theater. Experiences, in other words, tend to be evaluated more on their own terms. We are less likely to be troubled when we're outdone by the experiential purchases of others. We don't wish we could trade our vacations or concert experiences with those of our peers, just as we don't wish we could trade our memories, photos, or stories—even when the ones we'd receive would be seen by a dispassionate evaluator as "better."

Things and experiences also differ in the hedonic consequences that follow from comparing the present and the past. Once you've owned a superior vehicle, appliance, or high-tech device, it is hard to go back to an inferior model. But after you've dined out at a high-end restaurant, the offerings at your local burger joint or pizza parlor are still delicious (evolution, which disposes us to enjoy salt, fat, and sweetness—the staples of junk food—takes care of that). When it comes to material goods, then, things that were luxuries for our grandparents (automatic dishwashers, television sets, air-conditioning) came to be seen as necessities and taken for granted by our parents. And things that were luxuries to our parents (a second car, a flat-screen TV, cell phones) are now seen as ordinary entitlements for middle-class Americans.

Psychologists refer to this as the "hedonic treadmill"—having to run ever faster and accumulate more and more just to stay in place hedonically.[22] The idea of a hedonic treadmill explains why there has been essentially no intergenerational increase in happiness despite a massive increase in the wealth and standard of living of the average citizen in developed countries.[23]

Experiences also tend to provide more enduring satisfaction because they foster social connection. Most experiences are shared: We go out to dinner with friends, take vacations with family, and enjoy concerts, hikes, and sporting events with fellow enthusiasts. Even when we dine or vacation alone, we are quick to share our experiences with others when back at home or back at work. People tell more stories about their experiences than about their material goods, and they (and their listeners) enjoy it more when they do.[24] In one study that speaks to this difference, pairs of college students were asked to have a get-acquainted conversation and were restricted to talking about either material or experiential purchases they had made. Afterward, those who had talked about their experiences reported liking the conversation and their conversation partners more than those who had talked about their possessions.

Experiences build other types of personal capital as well. People treasure some of their material possessions, and some even become parts of their identity. But it is our experiences and what we make of them that make us who we are. Our possessions might be important parts of our lives, but they rarely become important parts of *ourselves*.[25] That is why such a prominent theme in literature and film is the emptiness experienced by individuals who, looking back on their lives, realize they've engaged too much in material pursuits and too little in developing meaningful relationships and pursuing meaningful experiences.

A wise person knows this, of course. That is why characters in literature or film who devote so much energy to material pursuits are virtually never seen as wise and generally either meet a sad end or (like Scrooge) come to see the error of their ways.

Although to this point in our book we have mainly discussed what a wise individual would do, it is important to note that the same can be said of wise societies. Some communities and societies prioritize experiential pursuits and provide the parks, trails, beaches, bike lanes, and public spaces that make it easier for people to have satisfying experiences. (The system of national parks that Theodore Roosevelt wisely took the lead in establishing—and which the novelist and conservationist Wallace Stegner famously dubbed "the best idea we ever had"— is a case in point). Those who prioritize low taxes and private wealth creation at the expense of building up these sorts of public experiential resources are likely diminishing society's collective well-being.

Get Up and Go

In the fall of 1975, Bruce Springsteen leaped into pop culture orbit. With the release of *Born to Run*, his simultaneous appearance on the covers of *Time* and *Newsweek*, and a run of historic performances at New York's Bottom Line and LA's Roxy Theater, Springsteen and his E Street Band became a worldwide phenomenon. The rock critic Jon Landau (later to become Springsteen's manager) famously wrote at this time, "I saw rock and roll's future, and its name is Bruce Springsteen."

Shortly after their series of concerts at the Roxy, the E Street Band traveled to the University of California campus at Santa Barbara to perform in the cozy confines of Robertson Gym. Tom, then an undergraduate on a tight budget, was urged by his hipper classmates to buy a ticket and experience a piece of this historic run. Alas, the appeal fell on deaf ears, resulting in a frequently revisited sense of regret that persists to this day.

Examples like this are typical of people's most commonly reported regrets. Most of us tend to focus on things that we failed to do rather than things we did but turned out badly. When research participants are asked to list their biggest regrets, they report more regrets of inaction than action by a two-to-one margin. When asked more specifically whether their biggest regret in life involved something they had done or something they failed to do, three times as many respondents named the latter.[26] We can't quite endorse the sentiments of the aging roué who said, "I spent the bulk of my youth on wine, women, and song—the rest I just wasted." But there is much wisdom in Henry James's observation: "I don't regret a single 'excess' of my responsive youth—I only regret, in my chilled age, certain occasions and possibilities I didn't embrace."[27]

Studies make it clear that when it comes to such commonly experienced dilemmas as "Should I or shouldn't I?" "Do I jump in or stay out?" or "Is now the right moment?" it is cautious inaction rather than impulsive action that we most likely come to regret. Some of this caution is warranted, of course. It is neither wise nor a blueprint for happiness to act on every impulse. Nike's injunction to "Just do it" is too broad and too simple. Some actions breach trust and harm others. They can lead to a lifetime of regret (not to mention lost friendships, broken marriages, or incarceration). Throwing caution to the wind in how one drives, sails, or climbs, and in the way one ingests calories, alcohol, or carcinogens, can result in a short lifetime.

Nevertheless, the broad lesson here is that we humans are active, goal-striving creatures who seem most happy when we're doing something active. Teddy Roosevelt captured this element of wisdom in his constant exhortation to himself, and to his sons, to "get action." Or, as the renowned happiness researcher David Lykken put it, "It is interesting that . . . most of the things that can be counted on to give us a welcome . . . lift above our individual happiness set-points are active rather than passive, and usually also constructive—activities that have a useful product."[28]

The "flow" state, in which a person experiences a deep sense of well-being from being completely immersed, or lost, in an activity has rightfully received a great deal of attention in the scientific literature on happiness.[29] One can't, however, get into a flow state without taking action. The action need not be something physical like gardening or hiking: Consider the vast difference between the two sedentary activities of reading (or for that matter writing) and watching television. But getting outside one's comfort zone and actively engaging in the world, if not physically then at least intellectually or artistically, is an important key to finding happiness.

The evidence that action promotes well-being goes beyond people's most common regrets. For example, recall that when people are beeped by their smartphones and asked to report what they are doing at that moment and how happy they are, watching television comes out fairly well. It ranks below socializing with friends or making love, but well ahead of preparing meals or taking care of the kids. But when researchers ask about more enduring types of satisfaction, they find a strong negative correlation between the amount of TV watched and reported well-being.[30] Watching television—or playing video games or checking Facebook—is much like eating doughnuts or pizza: A little can be great, but more than a little is a recipe for lethargy and self-recrimination.

Further support for the link between taking action and enhanced well-being comes from studies of self-esteem during adolescence. It surprises no one to learn that self-esteem tends to dip during the teen years, and the decline is particularly pronounced for girls. But girls who participate in organized sports suffer much less of a drop.[31] Being active seems to provide a buffer against a very common threat to well-being. Both of these findings are correlational, so the usual uncertainties and cautions apply. It is certainly possible, for example, that self-esteem prompts participation and lack of self-esteem discourages it, or that having supportive parents both builds self-esteem and makes participation in extracurricular activities more likely. However, our reading of the research reinforces the idea that if you are feeling a little blue, it is wise to *do* something. Go for a walk, call a friend, start that classic novel you've long intended to read, plan a dinner or vacation, or, better still, look for a way to make someone else a bit happier.

The idea that happiness and well-being are advanced by being active is also consistent with the notion that happiness serves an evolutionary function. As Tom's Cornell colleague Shimon Edelman says in his aptly titled *The Happiness of Pursuit*, "There are good reasons why the accumulation of experience feels good and promotes happiness. The urge to explore, accrue information about the world, and use it to dodge the 'slings and arrows of outrageous fortune' . . . makes evolutionary sense. Feeling good about mastering novelty through learning appears to be the currency with which the brain is bribed into leaving the couch and venturing outside."[32]

This, then, is the psychology behind the often-quoted phrase that "life is a journey, not a destination." Evolution has made it hedonically rewarding to act on and learn about the world. It is striving and making progress that promotes happiness; having something (a prized material good, an award, a title) is a poor substitute. This is also the psychology behind the hedonic treadmill. Achieving is gratifying, but the achievement itself quickly becomes old hat, relegated to the background and no longer able to provide much of a boost as we set our sights on new goals and new arenas in which to strive. As Shakespeare pointed out, "Things won are done; joy's soul lies in the doing."[33]

You can try to fight this element of our nature by vowing to savor your accomplishments, stop and smell whatever roses you've encountered, and scale back, want less, and live more simply. But it is a fight, and one that's not easy to win. A wise person, at least in our particular society, accepts the fact that whether we are working or playing, or enjoying the pleasures of good company and beautiful surroundings, we're happiest (and acting most in accord with our evolved nature) when we're striving and being actively engaged with the world.

The Two Faces of Happiness

Suppose that sometime tomorrow you could feel a pure, undiluted version of whatever emotion you choose. What would it be? Unless you had vengeance on your mind, it probably wouldn't be anger. And unless you wanted to continue to pine over an unrequited love, it probably wouldn't be sadness either. It's positive emotions we generally want to feel. But which ones? Would you rather feel thrilled or calm? Excited or peaceful? Your answer to this question, it turns out, is likely to depend on your ethnic heritage and your age.

In a remarkable series of studies, Lee's Stanford colleague Jeanne Tsai has shown that there are pronounced cross-cultural differences in preferences for what she calls high-arousal and low-arousal positive emotions.[34] People in the highly individualistic societies of Western Europe, Australia, New Zealand, Canada, and the United States take their happiness shaken and stirred, favoring thrills and excitement over calm and tranquility. They seem to believe in Emerson's claims that "nothing great was ever achieved without enthusiasm" and that "the world belongs to the energetic." People in the more interdependent societies, including China, Taiwan, Korea, and Japan, tend to have the opposite preferences. They take to heart the words of Lao-Tzu—"If people can be clear and calm, heaven and earth will come to them"—and the Buddha—"Even as a lake, deep, extremely clear and tranquil, so do the wise become tranquil having heard the Teaching."

Children in these two different cultures get exposed very early to what Tsai calls their societies' "ideal affect." An analysis of bestselling children's books in the United States and Taiwan, for example, found that the characters in the U.S. books had broader smiles and were engaged in more arousing activities. Predictably, then, when children in the United States and Taiwan were shown two happy faces, one with a big, broad smile and one with a more modest smile, the American kids were more likely than their Taiwanese counterparts to say the one with the broad smile was happier and the one they'd rather be. The Taiwanese kids, in fact, often found the broad, toothy smiles scary. A similar analysis showed that the celebrities and fashion models gracing the covers of magazines in the West tend to have big, broad smiles, whereas those in the Far East tend to have more demure smiles.

These differences in ideal emotions influence the activities people in different cultures pursue throughout their lives. When asked to describe their ideal vacation, European Americans tend to describe outings that include more physical activities and fewer relaxing activities than Asian Americans. The music favored by East Asians tends to be quieter and more soothing than that favored by people in the United States and Western Europe. These are average differences, of course. There is no shortage of East Asians who enjoy bungee jumping, skydiving, and snowboarding, and a great many European Americans and Europeans like nothing more than reading, relaxing, and listening to the Moonlight Sonata. What this research has uncovered is that the widely shared stereotypes of the subdued Asian and the extroverted, action-oriented American have a grain of truth to them.

It is interesting to note how closely these stereotypes mirror the ones most of us in the Western world have about the young and the old. The young are thought to seek enjoyment in vigorous activity and the old to look more toward quieter, calmer pursuits. When Peter Townshend of The Who wrote, "I hope I die before I get old," he was likely referring to the transition from a life of intensity and gusto to one of more sedate pleasures. These pairs of stereotypes come together in the Western world's celebration of youth and the East's reverence for age.

By the way, Townshend was more worried about growing old than is justified by research findings on well-being—a fact that the seventy-year-old Townshend now probably appreciates. Although people tend to believe that happiness declines with age, in fact the opposite is true. Older people have more of a knack than the young for thinking about outcomes and events in ways that promote happiness.[35] The happiness that older people enjoy is indeed more centered around serenity than excitement, but it is genuine happiness just the same.[36] The wisest in the room understands that it is a better bet to embrace rather than resist the transition from high-arousal to low-arousal positive emotions that comes naturally with age.

There is a second lesson here as well—one that connects to the idea of naïve realism discussed back in chapter 1. Westerners might assume that happiness can come only from excitement and enthusiasm—that that's what happiness *is* (think Emerson and Townshend). But that is just one way of being happy, and the preferred positive emotions of East Asians and older people in the West are no less real or legitimate. The views and priorities of a culture or age group are just that, views and priorities, not a veridical assessment of the way things truly are.

Dividing the Pie Wisely

There are a lot of inspiring findings in the scientific literature on happiness. But perhaps the most heartening is that people appear to derive more satisfaction from spending money on others than on themselves. The University of British Columbia's Elizabeth Dunn and Harvard's Michael Norton have driven this point home in a number of studies.[37] In one, participants were given either $5 or $20 and asked to spend it on themselves or on someone else or a charity by 5:00 p.m. that day. When contacted after that deadline, those who had been asked to spend the money on others reported being happier. In another study, respondents in Canada and Uganda were simply asked to think of a time they spent money on themselves or on someone else. When later asked to fill out a subjective happiness scale, those in both countries who had been randomly assigned to recall a time they gave to others reported being happier.

This is not an alien idea, of course. People have long been taught that it is better to give than to receive. The Jewish sage Hillel noted, "If I am not for myself then who shall be for me? But if I am only for myself, then what am I?" And legendary UCLA basketball coach John Wooden used to tell his players that "it is impossible to have a perfect day without doing something for someone else."[38] Still, it is reassuring to see that this is an empirically reliable effect, not just something people want to be the case.

Do the hedonic benefits of altruism apply beyond the voluntary acts of individuals to the policies of nations and the distribution of wealth? Do countries that achieve greater economic equality also tend to achieve greater collective happiness? We examine that question a bit later in this chapter. But let's first consider a narrower question: What sort of wealth distribution do people (or, more specifically, Americans) think is best for society as a whole? Given the polarization that dominates the current political landscape in the United States, it might seem that people at different points along the political spectrum would have very different views on this question. Liberals might champion something like the "nanny states" of Denmark or Sweden, so that the least advantaged members of society would have a measure of security and dignity and their health, educational, and nutritional needs taken care of. Conservatives might insist that such a state breeds dependency and fails to adequately reward effort, initiative, and the exercise of personal responsibility.

But there is actually much less polarization on this issue than you might expect. When Michael Norton and Dan Ariely asked a representative sample of Americans how much of the overall wealth in the United States "should" belong to the top 20 percent, the bottom 20 percent, and each quintile between, they found very little disagreement. Men and women, liberals and conservatives, the wealthy and those of modest means all largely agreed on what the ideal wealth distribution should be.[39] Political conservatives and liberals might disagree on how to get there, and on what the right combination of tax and government spending policies might be, but they tend to agree on what the right level of inequality would look like. And what they agree on, you'll probably be surprised to learn, is a distribution pretty close to that of Sweden!*

Very few conservatives, of course, would respond affirmatively if they were asked explicitly whether our country would be better off overall if the wealth in the United States were distributed the way it is in Sweden. But when they are asked, without reference to any specific country, what percentage of the overall wealth should belong to different fifths of the population, the conservative respondents suggested an ideal wealth distribution that matches what actually exists today in Sweden.

Not only do most Americans agree on what constitutes the best distribution of wealth, but if the goal is maximizing collective happi-

---

*Note that Norton and Ariely's respondents were asked about the distribution of *wealth*, not *income*. As Thomas Piketty documented in his recent bestseller, *Capital in the Twenty-First Century*, it is ever-growing disparities in wealth rather than income that most challenge people's notions of a fair society.

ness, they're right. Research indicates that great disparities of wealth can stunt overall well-being in a society. To be sure, the privileged enjoy what they can do with their wealth and they get satisfaction from being much better off than their neighbors. But few people enjoy seeing others in want and despair. Such comparisons can prompt guilt in those enjoying economic prosperity. And the poorest can feel distressed when they confront the gap between their own circumstances and those of others leading more comfortable lives, to say nothing of the rich and famous.

The economist Robert Frank and political scientist Adam Levine examined various objective indicators of well-being in the one hundred most densely populated counties across the United States that vary in income inequality.[40] To create an index of inequality they divided the income of those at the ninetieth percentile in a given county by the income of those at the median in that county. What they found is that people who live in counties with greater inequality are more likely to get divorced and more likely to file for bankruptcy, and they suffered through longer commutes to work.

This is hardly a recipe for happiness. The hedonic costs of marital discord and financial ruin are obvious. Less obvious is the fact that a long commute turns out to be one of the sources of dissatisfaction with everyday life to which people seem *not* to adapt. (So if you have any choice in the matter, finding a way to commute less, especially by automobile, will likely make you much happier).[41]

Frank and Levine argue that pronounced income inequality has a pernicious effect on what people feel they need for a happy, fulfilled life. A 2,000-square-foot home might seem perfectly ample until viewing the larger and more luxurious home of a wealthier relative (and that wealthy relative will experience similar feelings when viewing the tech billionaire's mansion featured in *Architectural Digest*). The ride in a Camry seems perfectly smooth unless it comes on the heels of a spin in the Lexus of a former classmate who cashed in during the dot-com frenzy. Dissatisfaction with one's own lot, brought on by comparisons with a well-heeled friend, neighbor, or coworker, makes people want more themselves—bigger houses, higher-performance cars, fancier clothes, and the latest electronic gadget with the newest features.

But keeping up with the Joneses is not cheap, and the costs go beyond dollars and cents. People work longer to afford what the competition requires, sacrificing time with their spouse and children. Divorce becomes more likely. Individuals may also take unwise financial risks to afford a more expensive lifestyle, increasing the likelihood of bankruptcy. And to afford a bigger house, many choose to move farther away from the expensive real estate near their jobs, resulting in punishingly long commutes and isolation from former friends, neighbors, and family members. All of these choices reduce individual and collective well-being.

The vicious cycle we are describing does not result from the poor comparing their lot with those who are fabulously wealthy. People tend to compare themselves to others at their own level or a bit above.* Nevertheless, these comparisons result in a cascade that carries all the way up and down the socioeconomic ladder. Professors do not compare their houses or cars with those of hedge fund managers. But when hedge fund managers get ever more opulent houses and more high-performance cars, their new acquisitions change the standards of what's desirable among those on the next rung of the economic ladder—successful lawyers, doctors, and real estate magnates. *Their* consumption patterns do influence what professors find acceptable, and the altered buying habits of professors alter the wants and perceived needs of those the next step down, and so forth. The habits of the very wealthy can thus have a negative impact on the well-being of those far down the economic ladder, even if the poor or middle class never directly compare themselves to the rich.

---

* This is true for virtually all dimensions of comparisons, not just wealth—whether it be intelligence, attractiveness, the ability to hit a crisp cross-court backhand, or the elaborateness of the decorations one puts up to welcome the holiday season.

Income inequality may also play a role in the ultimate threat to well-being. Figure 6.1 plots the homicide rate against income inequality in the fifty U.S. states (measured somewhat differently than in the Frank and Levine study).[42] The relationship is striking: States such as California and Louisiana with higher inequality have much higher homicide rates than states with low income inequality, such as Wisconsin and Utah. It is worth emphasizing that it is income *inequality* rather than wealth that predicts homicide rates. In fact, when the homicide rate across states is plotted against median income instead of income inequality, there is no discernible pattern. Living in a relatively poor versus a relatively wealthy state doesn't seem to matter; living in a state in which the gap between rich and poor is large matters a lot.

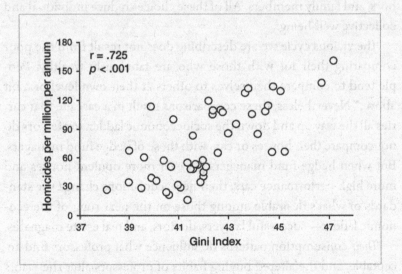

Figure 6.1 The relationship between homicide rates in the fifty U.S. states and the Gini index of income inequality in those states. (From Daly, Wilson, & Vasdev, 2001.)

This relationship also holds for homicide rates across Canada's ten provinces. When you plot the relationship between inequality and homicide in Canada and the United States on the same graph, the result is sobering. As figure 6.2 shows, the Canadian provinces are much lower on both income inequality and homicide rates than the fifty states. Of course, the relevant data are correlational, and Canada and the United States differ in a number of important respects. However, the two countries are similar enough to add further weight to the claim that heightened income inequality creates an environment that is conducive to the ultimate in antisocial behavior.

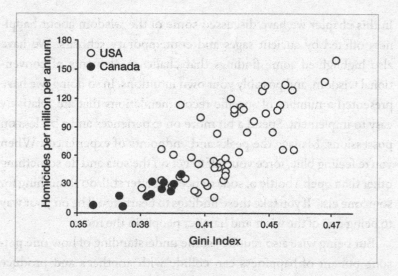

Figure 6.2 The relationship between homicide rates and the Gini index of income inequality in the fifty U.S. states and ten Canadian provinces. (From Daly, Wilson, & Vasdev, 2001.)

Is this a proscription for a liberal political agenda? It needn't be; recall that *both* conservatives and liberals want a world in which wealth is more evenly distributed than it currently is in the United States. What they disagree about is how to get closer to that mutually-agreed-upon ideal. What no one can dispute is that the modern global economy has tended to concentrate wealth, putting vastly higher sums in the hands of the few at the top of the pyramid—CEOs and financiers and their ilk—while eroding the economic power of the far greater number at the bottom and the lower reaches of the middle class. A wise economic policy, then, would be one that attends to these broader economic forces.[43] If the goal is a happier, less violent society, then decisions and policies that exacerbate globalism's effect on income inequality should be discouraged, and initiatives that would dampen the growth of inequality should be pursued.

In this chapter we have discussed some of the wisdom about happiness offered by ancient sages and contemporary scholars. We have also highlighted some findings that challenge elements of conventional wisdom, and possibly your own intuitions. In so doing, we have presented a number of specific recommendations that are relatively easy to implement. Spend a bit more on experiences and a bit less on possessions. Manage the peaks and endpoints of experiences. When you're feeling blue, force yourself to get off the sofa and do something other than open a bottle of soda or beer—better still, do something for someone else. If you take these findings to heart, you'll be on your way to being one of the wiser and happier people in the room.

But being wise also requires some understanding of how one person's pursuit of happiness can collide with another's and produce conflict. Such conflicts are an inevitable part of life. The key is to understand how to manage and defuse them. We therefore discuss the challenge of being wiser about conflict and conflict resolution in the next chapter.

7

Why We Don't "Just Get Along"

revered rabbi and an equally revered imam climb to the top
of Mount Sinai, where they are given the privilege of asking
God one question. The question they agree to ask is the obvious one:
"Will there ever be peace between Jews and Arabs?" God pauses,
sighs, and finally answers: "Yes, but not in my lifetime."

For most Americans, the Israeli-Palestinian conflict is the most
familiar and frustrating of the many seemingly intractable conflicts
that we read about and hear discussed on television news shows.
Well-meaning third parties and sensible moderates on both sides propose possible agreements that would improve the everyday lives of
the people in both societies. Majorities on both sides consistently say
they favor a "two-state solution." Yet the stalemate continues.

In the midst of a meeting between prominent Palestinians and Israelis at Stanford, one of the Palestinians said wistfully, "Imagine the
appeal to tourists of an itinerary that allowed them to ride in a luxurious air-conditioned bus, crossing borders at will, seeing the Church
of the Holy Sepulchre and the Al Aqsa Mosque and other holy sites in
Jerusalem and Bethlehem, then the archaeological treasures of Petra.
They could then go on to the pyramids and the Sphinx, sampling

the diverse cuisines, stopping to visit ancient cities, experiencing the natural beauty of the lush valleys on the way, then back to Tel Aviv's great beaches and bustling nightlife." Tourism, of course, is only one of the possibilities for mutual benefit that would present itself with a peaceful end to the conflict. Robert Kennedy famously said, "There are those who look at things the way they are and ask why. I dream of things that never were, and ask why not?" Nowhere are those sentiments more apt than in the Middle East.

The failure to achieve this inspirational vision of peace in the Middle East seems especially tragic because the basic formula for achieving it—peace, security, and greater prosperity for all, tolerance for minorities, ready access to sites that have cultural and religious significance for all three religions in the area, compensation for those who have borne the greatest costs of the struggle—has long been clear. But the prize remains elusive. One or both parties say the proposed trade of concessions put forward by would-be peacemakers fails to meet their minimum needs and demands. The ranks of the moderates grow thinner and thinner. Pessimism and distrust become more widespread. The hardliners assume an ever more dominant role in their respective societies. The status quo continues to impose a heavy burden on the Palestinians, and Israelis continue to feel insecure about the future. And periodic spasms of violent actions and reactions take place with tragic consequences for many families.

We are under no illusion that we have the answer to how to end this or other seemingly intractable conflicts. But we can offer a perspective that will make you a wiser and more sophisticated consumer of news reports about these conflicts and a calmer and saner voice when those around you engage in heated debates about who is at fault and who must do what to achieve a just and lasting peace in troubled areas of the world. We also think we can help you to deal more effectively with the more mundane conflicts that are an inevitable part of living with other people.

Disagreement and conflict between individuals, groups, and societies have always been an inescapable fact of human existence. Couples disagree about how to divide the responsibilities of child rearing, how to spend (or save) their money, and where to go on vacation (to say nothing about more intimate matters). Office-holders and their various constituencies disagree about how to allocate tax revenues and how those revenues should be raised. They also disagree about what should or should not be done to ensure the health, education, and welfare of our citizens. Citizen advocacy groups and business leaders disagree about laws and regulations that would affect profit margins, shareholder wealth, working conditions, and the quality of neighborhoods. The United States and other long-established economic powers disagree with newly emerging powers about who should bear the costs of combating global warming—a topic we discuss in chapter 9.

Some of the causes of disagreement and conflict are obvious and have already been touched on earlier in this book. Parties to a dispute have different motives and interests, different goals and priorities, and often different information and expectations as well. They see the issues through very different keyholes, filters, and lenses. When they disagree and thwart each other's ability to achieve their objectives, frustration and resentment build up, and accusations of unreasonableness, irrationality, and bad faith fill the air.

Yet resolutions of even the most tenacious conflicts do take place. They come about, at least in theory, once both parties see the costs of continued conflict as being no longer justified by the odds and potential benefits of prevailing. At that point, the parties consider what they are willing to give up to get what they want, and they strike a deal whereby each party gives up things it values less than the other side does in return for getting things it values more than the other side. (Again, this is in theory. We will get to what happens in practice a bit later.)

Teachers in a school district may care more about job security and keeping their current pension plans than they do about where they will be assigned to teach. They may be reasonably satisfied with their wages, but mindful that the cost of living has edged up since their last pay raise. The school board may care a great deal about having the flexibility to meet next year's staffing needs and may know that it can offer only small pay raises because of current budget constraints. They may recognize that future pension obligations are underfunded, but be willing to shift that burden to future school boards and taxpayers. Although a strike is possible if neither side is willing to compromise, the deal there for the taking is clear: There will be no teacher layoffs, but the board will be free to move teachers around as it wishes, the salary increase will be modest, and current pension provisions will be retained.

Economists would call such an exchange "efficient" because it exploits differences in the parties' priorities in a way that leaves them both better off than before. Efficient exchange is the formula for success not only in ending disagreements but in all forms of human commerce—from routine exchanges of cash for goods and services to negotiated trade agreements between countries.[1] So why don't parties more consistently reach agreements that serve their mutual interests and avoid overt conflict? Why do individuals, groups, and nations with different needs and goals sometimes come to hate each other and exchange insults and accusations of bad faith that make future negotiation more difficult? Most important, why do they pay the continuing costs of overt conflict when it would be to their mutual benefit to settle their dispute? Why don't they seize the "efficient" deal and devote more of their energies and resources to addressing other needs and goals?

Typically each side's answer is that the other side is being unreasonable and the solution therefore is for the other party to become more reasonable. But the wisest one in the room, and anyone else who appreciates the phenomenon of naïve realism discussed in chapter 1, has a more sophisticated, accurate, and useful account of the parties' failure to reach agreement, and also of the enmity that arises as the conflict continues. We trust that you can now provide such an account.

Parties who disagree about matters that are important to them inevitably feel that the disagreement is the result of the other party not seeing things objectively and reasonably. Each party thinks the other is either blinded by self-interest or ideology or, worse, that they are merely pretending to see things the way they claim to see them and that they are offering arguments they know to be false. Each party thinks that in light of the realities of the situation and the history of the conflict, it is the *other* side that should offer the compromises necessary to reach agreement. Each side is likely to feel that its own proposed exchanges of compromises are generous, while those offered by the other side are not generous at all and hence do not merit reciprocation. In a protracted conflict, these assessments become "essentialized." The failure to reach agreement is seen as something that reflects not the difficult realities of the conflict but the character of the other party. In short, naïve realism presents a potent psychological barrier to negotiated agreement. It also exacerbates the other barriers that we discuss in this chapter.

Zero-Sum versus Non-Zero Sum Negotiations

Negotiation theorists make a distinction between zero-sum and non-zero-sum negotiations. The distinction is intuitive. In a zero-sum conflict (such as that between a buyer and seller of a car), every dollar spent or saved by one party represents a dollar gained or lost by the other. In *non*-zero-sum conflicts, the total value of the agreement is not fixed. The parties can increase the total gains to be had in an agreement by making wise trades or concessions. For example, in making honeymoon plans, the bride may care more about the quality of the accommodations than the locale and the groom may care more about the locale than the view from the bridal suite or the softness of the sheets. But each has an obvious motive to make the other happy. Once they recognize who cares more about what, they will agree on their honeymoon plans. If they are wise, each may even indicate that they care *only* about making the other happy.

Negotiation mavens are quick to point out that even negotiations that may seem like zero-sum affairs have (or can be tweaked to have) integrative, win-win solutions that serve the interests of both parties, especially if the parties place value on fostering a rewarding future relationship. They are fond of offering examples of how apparent zero-sum problems can be turned into efficient win-win solutions in which everyone ends up happy and no one gives up anything they actually care about.

The classic examples in negotiation textbooks involve conflicts over the division of a dozen lemons, or a dozen eggs, or the use of a car by its two joint owners. In the first case, one person needs only the lemon peel to make lemon zest (or one of the other thirty-one things Google tells us we can do with the peel) and the other wants the juice for lemonade. In the second example, one of them needs only the egg whites to bake a cake and the other needs only the yolks to make a pudding. In the more realistic third case, one owner wants the car primarily for weekend excursions and late-night adventures and the other needs it to commute to and from work Monday through Friday.

In each case, if the parties are open and explicit about their needs, an agreement that leaves both parties satisfied is easily reached. More typical are cases in which both parties have to make concessions that involve real costs, concessions they are reluctant to make. What each side wants to do, therefore, is to minimize what it has to give up and maximize what it gets.

The Negotiators' Dilemma

In trying to formulate exchanges that take advantage of different needs and priorities in a way that benefits both parties, the negotiators face a mixed-motive dilemma. Such dilemmas are captured by the familiar metaphor of creating and dividing a pie. Each side benefits from enlarging the pie (i.e., its total value to the two sides), which is advanced by the candid sharing of information about priorities. But each side also seeks to claim as much of the pie as possible. Each thus has a motive to strategically withhold information, feign a lack of interest in aspects of the deal that would benefit them greatly, and pretend that they are reluctant to give up things they actually have little interest in retaining.

Such hardball tactics are designed to extract a larger slice of the pie, but their attendant secrecy, deception, and threats can create ill will, damage prospects of productive future relationships, and shrink the size of future pies. In particular, they damage the prospects for future log-rolling wherein one party makes a concession today that is much more valuable to the other party than it is costly to itself, with the understanding that the other party will do the same down the road when the costs and benefits are skewed in the opposite direction. Politicians frequently engage in this sort of log-rolling when it comes to gaining support for legislation that is crucial for one legislator but not to another from a different district. Both know that those priorities are likely to flip when it comes to future pieces of legislation and that their flexibility will be reciprocated.

There are also barriers to achieving maximally efficient agreements or, for that matter, any agreement at all, that arise from factors that limit the possibilities for such deal making.[2] There may simply be no channel open for communication because the parties won't accept each other's calls or because one or both are forbidden from having contact with the other. Or the representatives who could otherwise work out a mutually beneficial set of compromises may have tied their hands by prior promises. Politicians who pledge "no new taxes" or "no conversion of single-occupancy homes into condominiums" may be bound by their earlier vows and unable to make agreements that would otherwise benefit the majority of their constituents.

Rules and regulations can also pose barriers. The homeless shelter may not be able to pick up leftover food from restaurants and caterers, even though both parties would welcome such an arrangement, because the board of health forbids it. So-called principal-agent problems may also play a role. Lawyers may have an interest in continuing a legal struggle that is providing a welcome source of income for themselves while depleting the resources of their clients. Militia leaders may be reluctant to reach a truce if it would end the conflict and force them to find jobs outside the military—especially if they are well equipped to lead a militia but poorly equipped in terms of marketable civilian skills.

There are no magic-bullet solutions to offer when it comes to these sorts of barriers. But we urge you to keep them in mind when you are frustrated by the "other side's" failure to do its part in reaching an agreement. The all-too-human tendency is to be well aware of the strategic and situational constraints that prevent you or your side from moving quickly or taking the first step, but to commit the fundamental attribution error (chapter 2) when it comes to the other side's "foot dragging." Parties in conflict are particularly prone to overestimate the extent to which the other side's behavior is determined by character or personal flaws, and to underestimate the extent to which it reflects the same kinds of influences and considerations that are governing their own behavior.*

Beyond these impediments, another class of barriers can stand in the way of mutually advantageous agreements. We begin our discussion of these barriers with a quotation that captures an important moment in history, and an unusually acute bit of wisdom.

---

* This difference represents a special case of a more general actor-observer difference in attribution described by Ned Jones and Richard Nisbett.[3]

The Other Walls: Psychological Barriers

Yet, there remains another wall. This wall constitutes a psychological barrier between us, a barrier of suspicion, a barrier of rejection; a barrier of fear, of deception, a barrier of hallucination without any action, deed or decision. A barrier of distorted and eroded interpretation of every event and statement. It is this psychological barrier which I described in official statements as constituting 70 percent of the whole problem. Today, through my visit to you, I ask why don't we stretch out our hands with faith and sincerity so that together we might destroy this barrier?

—President Anwar al-Sadat of Egypt, statement before the Israeli Knesset, Jerusalem, November 29, 1977[4]

As President Sadat noted in his historic speech to the Israeli Knesset, the most important barriers to agreement, or at least the most difficult to overcome, are often psychological.* The study of such barriers has been a major project for Lee and his colleagues at the Stanford Center on International Conflict and Negotiation (SCICN).[5] The wisest in the room (including the boardrooms and the chambers where national leaders hammer out their policies) appreciate the importance of these barriers. In discussing them, we will share what we have learned from SCICN projects in Ireland, the Middle East, and other troubled areas of the world, from talking to seasoned negotiators who have represented their countries at the bargaining table or served as mediators, and from research we and others have conducted.

We believe that understanding these barriers is an important first

---

* The precision of Sadat's 70 percent estimate is noteworthy. He did not say two-thirds, or three-quarters, or 90 percent, which are used somewhat idiomatically. Given his use of such an exact percentage (somewhere between two-thirds and three-quarters), it seems that he had given careful thought to his estimate.

step for practitioners who seek to reduce conflict, improve relations, and pave the way for meaningful, mutually satisfactory solutions to bitter, long-running disputes. Understanding them should also help you get beyond shaking your head and blaming negotiation failures on stubbornness, greed, paranoia, or other human follies.

The Pursuit of Fairness, Justice, and Equity

Parties may turn down a deal that is an improvement over the status quo not because they think that intransigence will produce a better offer in the future and not because they want to establish a reputation for toughness. They may do so because they think the deal is unfair—that the other party is trying to take advantage of them. In a sense, they would prefer to give up the potential gains of the deal on the table and pay the costs of continued conflict rather than accept what they deem unfair, even humiliating.

Concerns about fairness, which can be present in any negotiation, are of particular importance in the context of protracted intergroup conflicts, especially those in which one party is much more powerful than the other. Both sides feel entitled to an agreement that is "just"—one that takes into account the comparative strength and legitimacy of their claims. Demands for a just settlement raise the bar for negotiators, especially when their individual notions about what would be fair differ enormously because they see the history and nature of their conflict so differently. The difficulties mount when both sides then view each other's claims and arguments through the prism of naïve realism.

This applies to the conflict President Sadat was hoping to end. Both sides feel that they are the ones who have acted more honorably in the past, that they have been more sinned against, and that they are now seeking no more than they are due. Both sides, furthermore, feel that it is their interests that most require protection in any negotiated agreement—for example, by avoiding ambiguities in language that could provide loopholes the other side could exploit.

The two sides are also likely to have divergent views about the future—about who will grow stronger with the passage of time and whose assurances can be taken at face value and trusted. These differences, in turn, can lead to disagreements about the balance of any proposal. Even when the two parties recognize what compromises each side will have to make if an agreement is to be reached, they both tend to feel that they will be the party who would be settling for less, and giving up more, than is equitable.

Each side, as our earlier discussion of naïve realism suggests, further believes that any observer of the conflict should agree with them and that the other party is being disingenuous when it defends its unreasonable demands. When a third party puts a deal on the table that calls on both sides to make wrenching concessions and accept a high degree of uncertainty about where the future will lead, each side is likely to respond tepidly. Each is also likely to be angry that the other did not quickly embrace the plan, since they were already being given more than they deserved, and now are demanding further concessions. This unhappy narrative captures a good deal of the history of the Israeli-Palestinian stalemate in the Middle East, the conflict that has served as a test case for much of the thinking that researchers have done on psychological barriers to dispute resolution.

Cognitive Dissonance and Rationalization

The history of sacrifice surrounding protracted disputes creates another barrier to reaching agreement: Previous actions taken and prices paid heighten the psychic costs of any compromises required for a successful resolution. The very rationalizations that allowed the parties to justify their past sacrifices and suffering—and their earlier rejection of potential agreements that would have put an end to such costs—constitute a barrier to now accepting a deal that is no better, and perhaps worse, than one that might have been available in the past.

The rallying cries of the rejectionists are all too familiar: *We can't break faith with the martyrs who fell in service of the cause; God (or his-*

tory) is on our side; The rest of the world is bound to wake up one day and recognize the justice of our aspirations; We can't deal with them because we can't trust them; We are more resolute than they are because right makes might. These calls, and the threats issued to anyone who doesn't heed them, increase the odds that the deadlock will continue—even when circumstances favoring agreement have changed for the better or the folly of continuing the struggle has become more apparent.

Although the implications of dissonance reduction may be bleak in the context of protracted stalemates, there is one optimistic note worth sounding. Once a settlement *has* been reached, the human penchant for rationalizing past behavior discussed in chapter 4 can play a constructive role. This is especially likely if the decision to settle was freely reached, if sacrifices were made in doing so, and if a public defense of the settlement was undertaken. In those circumstances, leaders and their constituencies may feel compelled to find and exaggerate positive features of the settlement and to minimize or disregard negative ones, even if (perhaps *especially* if) the settlement forced the two sides to make concessions they vowed they would never make.*

Reactive Devaluation, Loss Aversion, and the Reluctance to Trade Concessions

Those who recall the coldest days of the Cold War may remember it as a time when many Americans seemed to believe that if the Russians offered a proposal (say, about arms control) it must be good for them (a reasonable assumption) and bad for us (a much less reasonable as-

---

* There are numerous instances in which the public's support for an agreement increased markedly in the months and years after the agreement was reached. The détente with China that President Nixon reached in 1973 is but one example. However, in contrast to well-controlled laboratory experiments, it is impossible in these real-world cases to separate changes in attitudes that came about because of dissonance reduction from those that occurred when people simply saw how well (or how badly) the agreements worked out.

sumption). Decades later, when the optimism of the Arab Spring of 2008 gave way to chaos as different political factions competed for power, Moataz Abdel-Fattah, an Egyptian political scientist, summed up the problem of getting those factions to put aside their differences and coalesce around a set of shared principles for governing the country: "Everybody is trying to understand what the other side wants so that they can ask for the exact opposite."[6]

These examples illustrate a particularly frustrating barrier to reaching agreement: The evaluation of proposals often changes when they are no longer just hypothetical possibilities but are actually put on the table. This sort of devaluation is especially evident when the proposal is offered by a representative of the other side in a conflict. But it can also occur when the proposal comes from someone who is not really an enemy, just someone calling for mutual compromises.

A compelling demonstration of this sort of devaluation was provided by a study conducted at Stanford University in the early 1990s as the struggle against the apartheid regime in South Africa was reaching its climax. At the time, there were widespread student and faculty demands for the university to divest its holdings in companies doing business in that country. The university ultimately adopted a plan of "partial divestment" that fell short of those demands. Lee and his students measured campus attitudes about that plan on two occasions.[7] The first came before the university's adoption of the plan was made public—when the researchers knew what that plan would be, but for the students, it was merely one possibility among many. The second came shortly after the plan was announced. For comparison purposes, students' opinions about an alternative plan—one that called for an increase in the university's investment in companies that had *left* South Africa—were also measured.

The results were clear. Prior to the adoption of the plan in question, the students rated whichever plan they were led to believe the university was going to adopt less favorably than they rated the alternative. Moreover, when the university announced its partial divestment plan, students' evaluation of it plummeted, and their evaluations of the alternative plan (the one that called for increasing investment in companies that had left South Africa) became more positive.

A later study conducted in Israel with the cooperation of Lee's Israeli colleagues showed how this sort of devaluation plays out in the Israeli-Palestinian conflict.[8] The point of the study was to examine how responses to a given proposal can be influenced by the knowledge of which side had put it on the table. Participants in the study evaluated two proposals that had been put forward by the two sides four days apart in May 1993, shortly before the study. The proposals were intended to be the first stage in an ongoing peace process that had been jump-started by the Oslo Accords reached earlier that year.

These proposals did not deal with specific terms for ending the conflict (borders, degree of autonomy, and so on), but with general principles and less controversial issues such as the negotiation agenda, interim arrangements for security and policing, and coordination of activities and responsibilities. One proposal had been put forward by the Palestinian representatives and the other by the Israeli representatives. Half of the participants in the study were informed about the actual authorship of the two proposals while half were led to believe the authorship was reversed.

The results confirmed the worst fears of those hoping for peace in the Middle East. Israelis rated the actual Palestinian proposal, when it was attributed to their own side, more positively than they rated their own side's actual proposal, when it was attributed to the Palestinians.*

---

*We were also able to measure the response of Israeli Arabs to the Palestinian proposal. Not surprisingly, they thought it was better for Israel when it was attributed to the Israeli side than to its actual authors on their own side. But regardless of its putative authorship, and as a harbinger of the failed negotiations to come, these participants saw the proposal as being much better for Israel (again, regardless of putative authorship) than Israeli participants did.

The question that arises is sobering: If the proposal of one's *own* side seems unattractive when it is thought to come from the other side, how likely is it that something the other side put on the table will be deemed acceptable?

This sort of reactive devaluation can be traced to several psychological mechanisms that we discussed in previous chapters, some rational and some not so rational. These include subjective interpretation and labeling, the biasing effects of motivation and expectations, and the disproportionate focus on potential losses rather than potential gains.[9] Regardless of why it occurs, it is easy to understand how reactive devaluation can contribute to deadlocked negotiations and ensuing cycles of heightened enmity and mistrust. Not only are proposals likely to be received less positively than they ought to be in terms of the objective interests of the parties, but each side is likely to interpret the other side's actions and rhetoric as strategic ploys— dishonest, cynical, and dictated by animus rather than a sincere effort to end the conflict. It falls to the wisest in the room to offer a more charitable, more accurate, and certainly more constructive interpretation.

Overcoming Psychological Barriers to Resolution

The study of barriers and biases can do more than help us understand why negotiations sometimes fail when they should succeed and why the very act of negotiating can escalate rather than attenuate feelings of enmity and mistrust. It also provides insight into techniques for overcoming barriers and reducing misunderstanding. There is no shortage of books offering advice to would-be negotiators and peacemakers. But Lee's research and experience, and that of his colleagues at the SCICN, offer some particular insights about strategies for lowering some of the psychological barriers to conflict resolution.

Managing Attributions

Parties engaged in hard bargaining inevitably search for explanations of each other's behavior, especially for the content and timing of each other's concessions. The recipient of a unilateral concession or proposed trade of concessions is bound to wonder, "Why are they offering this *particular* proposal, and why *now*?" In the absence of other satisfactory answers, the likely conclusion is that the concession is probably less substantial than it might have seemed at first. Third-party mediators sometimes can help solve these attribution problems by explaining to each party, in caucus, the political realities compelling the other side to make or reject particular proposals. The knowledge that the other side is being *forced* to offer concessions, that it understands the status quo is unsustainable, reduces the tendency to think the offer is insincere or deceptive.

A simple acknowledgment that a concession is a response to the expressed desires and priorities of the other party can sometimes help with the attribution problem as well. To see how this can work, consider a negotiation that took place at Stanford between students who favored legalization of marijuana and a slightly older person said to be a representative of the university (but actually an experimental confederate following a prepared script).[10] The topic of the negotiation was the position the university should take on the issue.

In both conditions of the study, the confederate ultimately made the same "final offer" as time ran out in the negotiation (an offer to eliminate penalties for marijuana use but to increase penalties for harder drugs). In one condition, the offer was characterized by the confederate as one he had come to the negotiation intending to propose. In the other condition, the confederate conspicuously put aside a piece of paper containing what he said was his intended offer and instead made a "new offer"—one he claimed to be making in light of the specific goals and priorities expressed by his student counterpart.

Not only was the rate of acceptance of the confederate's proposal higher in the "acknowledgment" condition than in the "no acknowledgment" condition (63 percent versus 40 percent), but the confederate was seen as having made a greater concession and was liked better for having done so. Studies of procedural justice show that people tend to be more satisfied with agreements when their input has been sought and their voices have been heard.[11] This study makes clear that people are even more likely to be satisfied when they feel that their input has received real consideration and has had an impact.

This may seem obvious—people like to feel heard, and they tend to respond more positively when they feel their hopes and fears have received consideration. But it is worth noting that negotiators often neglect this important insight (as do administrators, politicians, parents, and romantic partners). Too often they boast, or reassure those whose interests they represent, that they "hung tough" and that any concessions they made were minor and inconsequential. But the wisest negotiators understand the value of acknowledging the needs and requests of those on the other side rather than insisting that no new concession is being offered. Most of all, whether in international negotiations, domestic political disputes, or personal quarrels, the wisest in the room appreciates the folly of publicly putting all the blame for the stalemate on the person on the other side.

Negotiator Expectations

Some negotiations succeed in the face of difficult obstacles. This is true for both exceptional events, such as the election of a pope, and for more ordinary events, such as passing a school budget or increasing the national debt ceiling. In many of these cases, the issues are complex, the differing views are deeply felt, and there is a real sense that no agreement could command an authentic majority (much less the two-thirds majority required to elect a pope or the 60 percent majority needed to avoid a Senate filibuster). Why then, do these difficult negotiations so often succeed? One factor may be the simple conviction on the part of the negotiators, sometimes buttressed by history and tradition and sometimes by a shared feeling of urgency, that an agreement *will* be reached: "We *must* have a pope." "We *have* to have a budget." "We *can't* shut down the government."

These real-world success stories suggest that when parties negotiate with the sense that they must and will succeed, the negotiation changes in a way that reduces reactive devaluation and facilitates agreement. The knowledge that a deal must be struck—and that the other side knows it—casts proposals (and the proposers) in a different light.

Lee and his Israeli colleagues tested this idea in a study conducted with Jewish students pursuing careers in business and government at an Israeli university.[12] The negotiation, although hypothetical, was highly absorbing and politically sensitive. It involved the allocation of funds to various West Bank construction projects, some of which were more valuable to Israelis and some more valuable to Palestinians. What the negotiators were not aware of was that their Arab counterpart in the negotiation was an experimental confederate following a carefully contrived script.

The negotiation proceeded in stages, with the Arab confederate making an initial offer, the Jewish student making a counteroffer, and the confederate making a "final offer" as time was expiring. The students assessed that offer on various dimensions and accepted or rejected it (in the latter case, knowing that the result would be a forfeiture of the funds in question until some later date). The experimental manipulation in this study was a simple one. Half the participants were informed at the outset of the negotiation that "virtually all" previous negotiation pairs had succeeded in reaching agreement. The other half were told nothing about prior negotiation outcomes. They were merely told to do their best to reach an agreement. The participants took their roles seriously, negotiating vigorously, and, in many cases, quite passionately.

The effect of this manipulation was remarkable: an 85 percent agreement rate when participants had reason to believe that an agreement was likely compared to 35 percent otherwise. Importantly, the manipulation changed more than the outcome; it also influenced how the participants felt about their Arab counterpart. Although she offered exactly the same terms in both conditions, she was better liked and her final proposal was seen as more generous and better for Israel in the positive expectation condition. Of course, there is no way to magically convince Israelis and Palestinians that their next negotiation session is bound to succeed. Giving them reason for even a little optimism that it will not be another exercise in futility is probably the most one could hope for. But the more general lesson is one that wise mediators take to heart and employ skillfully: They exude personal optimism and remind the parties of their record of earlier successes in the face of great obstacles.

When Experience Informs Theory: Four Lessons from Negotiations Around the World[13]

Researchers conduct laboratory and field investigations of real-world problems with the hope that their studies will provide useful ideas for application. But sometimes the reverse is also true: Applied research can reveal gaps in existing theory. It can also lead to the realization that certain factors are much more important (or much less so) than previously recognized. This has been especially true in the case of the experiences of Lee and his Stanford colleagues in undertaking various efforts at relationship building and second-track diplomacy* with

---

* Second-track diplomacy refers to the efforts of influential private citizens with ties to their governments or communities, or both, to forge agreements that are not official or binding on the parties in the dispute, but that reveal the bottom-line positions and potential compromises the parties might be willing to make and thus pave the way for official "first-track" agreements.

Israelis and Palestinians, Northern Ireland Unionists and Nationalists, and other adversaries.

A Shared Commitment to a Mutually Bearable Future

How was the remarkable nonviolent transition achieved in South Africa, a transition from the cruel apartheid regime to a system that offers opportunity for black and white citizens alike? Nelson Mandela's influence, it is widely agreed, was critical. But it was not just because he was revered and trusted by black South Africans, and it was not just because in the aftermath of his release from prison, he so clearly and consistently renounced violence. Nor was it because Mandela offered to make concessions that other black leaders had been unwilling to make. On the contrary, he was unyielding in his demands. What distinguished Mandela was that he was the man whose words and deeds made him the leader to whom white South Africans were willing to make the difficult concessions they had vowed they would never make.

Mandela accomplished this by communicating clearly and credibly a willingness to offer middle-class and working-class white Afrikaners the prospect of a bearable shared future.[14] In that future, the political power of their group would be greatly diminished, but the fabric of their own lives, and the everyday lives of their friends, families, and communities, would remain largely unchanged. They would live in the same homes, in most cases do the same jobs, and continue to enjoy the same pleasures and securities they had always enjoyed. In the face of worldwide pressure and with the recognition that the status quo could not be sustained much longer, they opted for that shared future.

We have found repeatedly in our own applied work that negotiators come to face-to-face encounters with members of the other side with a detailed proposal outlining what they want, why they are entitled to it, and what they are prepared to offer in return. We have found it useful to challenge them, in advance of these encounters, to come prepared to explain what life would be like for those on the other side if their proposal were accepted—specifically, how it would be better in that shared future than it is now, and why the other side's fears about that future are unwarranted. If they can't offer such a view of a shared future, we suggest, there is no point in meeting with the other side, because doing so would merely confirm its misgivings and strengthen its resolve.

In the Middle East, Israelis complain about the absence of a "Mandela on the other side," by which they mean a trustworthy, reasonable, moderate partner in negotiation. What they and others who seek such a Mandela fail to appreciate is that what they really need is not to *find* that "Mandela" but to learn from his example. They need to offer the other side a view of a shared future that is bearable, not humiliating, and not fraught with threatening uncertainty. In the epilogue to this book, we describe one dramatic example of how Mandela allayed the fears of white South Africans and why he was the black South African leader to whom they ultimately made the concessions that they had said they never would make.

Positive versus Poisonous Intergroup Sentiments

When diplomats or other third parties are called on to mediate long-standing disputes, they often believe that the key to finding a solution lies in crafting exactly the right agreement—in figuring out what trade of concessions would best satisfy the aspirations of the two parties and getting the specifics of that trade on paper for the two parties to sign. The hope is that agreement will lead to a normalization of relationships, to the building of trust required for continued cooperation, and ultimately to a fruitful and sustained peace. In our experience, this gets matters backward. It is the reduction of hatred, the building of some degree of empathy and understanding, and the creation of more trusting relationships that make it possible to get signatures on an acceptable agreement. Even more important, without trusting relationships, the parties are likely to stumble on the obstacles that inevitably arise as they proceed from signed documents to real peace.

Consider, for example, the problem of "spoilers" who will resort to violence to sabotage any agreement that would threaten their interests or diminish their future relevance. Political considerations prompt the leadership of both sides to insist that the other side take steps to curb such spoilers. At the same time, neither party is willing to pay the political price required to crack down effectively on the spoilers on their own side—especially those who enjoy public sympathy for their hardline demands.

In a sense, the solution to this problem is obvious: Each side must deal quietly but effectively with its own spoilers and avoid inflammatory rhetoric in the face of the actions of the spoilers on the other side. But such responses, rather than ones that are more politically expedient, require trust about the long-term willingness of the other side to implement the terms to which it has agreed. They also require a body politic that will accept patience and prudence rather than demand tit-for-tat retaliation.

The Futility of Trying to Convince People Who Can't "Afford" to Understand

Lee vividly remembers a Protestant militia leader in Northern Ireland who had come out of prison ready to renounce violence and begin earnest negotiations with the other side. But somehow no deal put on the table was ever good enough, no promise by the other side reliable enough, to get him to say, "Let's stop talking and close the deal!" Observing this charismatic man, who had devoted most of his life to the political struggle and had neither received the type of education nor achieved the type of work history that would offer him a future in a peaceful Ireland, one couldn't escape a discomforting thought. In the present situation, he was a respected leader with a place at the negotiating table. But in the aftermath of any agreement, he would be lucky to get a job driving a brewery truck. The issue of a "bearable future" pertains to large groups, as we noted in recounting the particular accomplishments of Nelson Mandela in South Africa. But it also pertains to particular individuals and small cliques, especially those with veto power over any agreement and the capacity to act as spoilers.

When the threat of change seems too great, disputants find reasons for continued intransigence. Rationalization and dissonance reduction, of the sort we described in chapter 4, kick in. Ambiguities are examined and resolved in ways that serve self-interest. Disputants who stand to lose too much in either material or psychic terms stubbornly refuse even to consider, much less understand, arguments put forward by the other side. They find ways to avoid the painful recognition that they have spent their lives in a fruitless endeavor and that the sacrifices of their group in terms of blood and treasure have been in vain. As in the case of the Protestant militia leader, those with the capacity to exercise a veto do so—often in the sincere belief that they are acting on principle and in accord with the best interests of their group. A wise negotiator understands that to win over potential spoilers, and get them to recognize the wisdom of reaching agreement, they must feel that their personal future in the aftermath of the agreement will be a bearable one.

Getting from 49 to 51 Percent

When those involved in a seemingly intractable conflict complain that they can't find a partner on the other side, or that the other side's leaders are incapable of compromise and lack common sense, we (sometimes) resist the urge to begin a windy lecture about the fundamental attribution error or naïve realism. Instead, we tell them a story about David Ervine, a Northern Ireland Loyalist and former combatant who was invited to give an address at Stanford University. At the conclusion of his engaging talk, he was asked the inevitable question: What had changed him from a militant relying on guns and bombs to a mainstream politician dedicated to finding a peaceful solution to the conflict that had waged for so long?

Ervine paused a bit, and then said it was a matter of "51 percent versus 49 percent." He went on to explain that his change was not a transformation of character. Rather, the struggle had reached a tipping point whereby the futility and costs of violence became marginally more obvious and the prospects of securing an acceptable agreement through normal politics marginally brighter. He then added the striking comment that when he was only 51 percent certain about his earlier stance, he was still "100 percent a bomber." And now, even though he is only 51 percent certain about the prospects for change through peaceful means, he is nevertheless 100 percent a politician and peace activist.

A wise negotiator takes heart from the knowledge that moving an antagonist from violent confrontation or steadfast intransigence to a willingness to explore nonviolent alternatives needn't involve a dramatic transformation. It can involve a mere change from "49 percent to 51 percent." Working hard to produce small changes can thus pay off with a big difference. Seemingly intransigent bombers can sometimes be tipped in a way that makes them open to nonviolent alternatives. A meeting with the other side that goes well or badly, a small concession that makes life for the other side more bearable, or a new regulation that makes it more unbearable can easily turn a bomber into a peacemaker, or vice versa.

Unfreezing Impasses by Violating Expectations

A remarkable event took place on the Stanford University campus during a talk about the Middle East conflict. The speaker had been a founding member of the militant Popular Front for the Liberation of Palestine. But by the time of his talk, he had become an outspoken advocate for negotiation and a two-state solution. The talk dealt with the broad outlines of the mutual compromises that would be required in any workable agreement between Israel and the Palestinians. His message went over well with the audience, which included students and faculty with a wide range of views about the conflict. But it is not the talk itself that those in attendance remember so vividly.

It was a response he gave during the question-and-answer period. An elderly psychiatrist who wanted to show his empathy for the Palestinian plight, if not for their specific goals, asked whether he thought Israelis and American Jews spent too much time obsessing about the Holocaust and not enough learning about and talking about the *Nakba*—the "catastrophe," a term that for Palestinians encompasses the founding of the state of Israel, the loss of the 1948 War, and the plight of the Palestinians who lost their homes, livelihoods, and, in many cases, their lives as a consequence.

The speaker paused, stepped down from the dais, and walked to within a few feet of the questioner. Then, looking the questioner directly in the eyes, he said, "Are you crazy? The *Nakba* was certainly a tragedy for Palestinians, and they continue to suffer from that injustice. But it was a tragedy of the sort that is all too common in the world and that many other peoples have suffered. The Holocaust was a *unique* and *unparalleled* tragedy—a defining event of the twentieth century." Then, wagging his finger at the questioner, he added, "Don't ever speak of them in the same breath again."

The effect on the room was profound. People stared at the speaker in hushed silence; many looked back and forth at each other to see if others shared their sense of the moment. Although his dramatic response did not speak to the ongoing stalemate, it was clear to all that a new type of discussion—at least among those in the room—would now be possible. And in the reception that followed the talk, it was that answer that was most on everyone's mind.

This incident illustrates how powerful a violation of expectations can be and how such violations might be used to get a negotiation moving when things seems stuck. Conflicts often become frozen, with neither party willing to be the first to offer a concession.[15] In such cases, both parties treat the other's intransigence as evidence of bad intentions, and both fear that if they make the first move, it will be seen as a sign of weakness that the other party will exploit. Actions big and small that violate entrenched expectations can help break the cycle of distrust and, in so doing, help to unfreeze the negotiation.*

This appears to be precisely what happened as a result of Egyptian president Anwar Sadat's 1977 visit to Jerusalem, where he delivered his speech before the Knesset. The content of the speech and its overall message of peace were important, although it is worth remembering that he offered no new material concessions. What was most important, however, was the clear signal his actions sent—a signal that something had changed, that Israel's doubts about what was possible might be unfounded. If an Egyptian president could not only come to Israel, but speak directly to the Israeli people from a platform in the disputed Israeli capital, then other important results might be possible—even long-term peace. Sadat's gesture changed the atmosphere in a way that ultimately led to the Camp David Accords and the peace treaty between Egypt and Israel. He understood the relational barriers that make agreements in the face of enduring conflict so difficult to achieve and he was wise enough, and brave enough, to do something dramatic to overcome it.

---

*Many seasoned negotiators can provide anecdotes about similar unexpected gestures, including ones that are more personal than political. Lee recalls the impact of an Israeli participant's request during a second-track session for the name of the recently deceased father of his Arab counterpart and also that of his grandfather—so that he could say Kaddish (the Hebrew ritual prayer for the dead).

8

A Tough Problem for America

At a 2010 track meet, Christophe Lemaitre recorded a 100-meter time just under 10 seconds—fast, but not a remarkable time for world-class sprinters of our era. In fact, seventy-one sprinters before him had broken the 10-second barrier. Usain Bolt's world record at the time was 9.58 seconds, four-tenths of a second faster. What made Lemaitre's performance noteworthy, and the subject of dozens of articles and interviews, was his race. Unlike seventy of the seventy-one other sprinters who had broken the 10-second barrier, he was white. Indeed, the dominance of black sprinters (more specifically those of West African ancestry) is apparent to any observer of top-level track meets.[1]

For obvious reasons, discussions of racial differences in ability and performance in any domain make people uncomfortable. But when it comes to athletic ability, such discussions have long been common.[2] Accounts of black domination in sprinting (and basketball and running back positions in football) usually focus on genetic factors—on fast-twitch muscle fibers and anaerobic enzymes, plasma testosterone, and various features of human musculature that translate into an advantage on the playing field. But in a 2011 interview, Lemaitre suggested that something beyond physiology plays a role in black athletes' domination of his event. He cited a "psychological barrier" faced by aspiring white athletes and insisted that skin color was less of a factor than desire and hard work. Other athletes and coaches have echoed similar sentiments—that white kids think that black kids are naturally more talented at certain sports, and rather than risk frustration and failure, the white kids who feel that way withdraw from competition.

Baylor's track coach put it bluntly in a *Sports Illustrated* interview a few years before Lemaitre's stereotype-defying performance: "There are plenty of white kids with fast-twitch fibers, but they've got to get off their rumps. Too many of them would rather go fast on their computers in a fantasy world. It's not [only] about genes. . . . It's about do you want it enough?"[3]

Everyone agrees that world-class athletic performance requires some combination of natural talent, incredible ambition, and hard work, as well as good coaching and encouragement. We'll leave it to the geneticists to figure out exactly what role genes play in various types of athletic performance. But the effects of stereotypes on how athletes are seen and the way they perform merit more discussion before we turn to the main concern of this chapter: the effect of stereotypes on the performances we see in America's classrooms.

Who Gets By on Sheer Talent versus Hustle and Smarts on the Basketball Court?

In a 1997 study, students listened to an edited broadcast of a college basketball game and were then asked to evaluate the athletic ability and performance of a particular player.[4] Before listening to the broadcast, they were shown a photo of the player. The photo was varied so sometimes the students thought the player was white and sometimes that he was black. The students' ratings at the end of the game revealed the impact of stereotype-based expectations. When the player was thought to be black, he was judged to have exhibited more athletic ability and to have played a better game. When he was thought to be white, he was rated as having shown more hustle and "basketball intelligence." Do coaches, scouts, and general managers employ the same filters and lenses when they evaluate players' performances and decide which players are the best prospects for the next level of competition? Anecdotal evidence suggests they do.* Furthermore, it is easy to imagine how the treatment aspiring athletes receive from scouts and coaches influences the players' own beliefs about their abilities and limitations.

Putting under the Pressure of Stereotypes

Until Tiger Woods began his remarkable career, golf was seen largely as a white man's game. It didn't require fast-twitch muscles, anaerobic stamina, or a particularly muscular physique. What golf mastery appeared to require beyond coordination and a naturally "sweet swing" were coolness under pressure, intelligent decision making, and thousands of hours of disciplined practice. That was why, most fans agreed, the leaders' board at the Masters tournament looked so different from the NBA all-star team.

Might these presumptions about success in golf, along with stereotyped notions about the strengths and weaknesses of black versus white athletes, have something to do with the composition of the PGA? Before answering, consider the results of a provocative study in which a number of black and white Princeton students (none of

---

*Consider the case of Jeremy Lin, who starred on the Harvard basketball team and now plays professionally in the National Basketball Association. Despite his strong grades and stellar career in leading Palo Alto High School (which is literally across the road from the Stanford campus) to the state championship, Lin was not offered an athletic scholarship to play for Stanford. It is hard to believe that Lin's Asian-American ancestry played no role in Stanford's decision to look elsewhere for talent.

whom played golf regularly) were given a task that involved both sinking putts and deciding which putts to try—difficult ones for lots of points or easier ones for fewer points.[5] Before undertaking this task, some of the students were told it was a test of "natural athletic ability": that is, hand-eye coordination of the sort involved in "shooting, throwing, or hitting a ball." Others were told the task was a test of "athletic intelligence" or the "ability to think strategically during an athletic performance."

These descriptions had a significant effect on the number of putts sunk and points earned. Black participants performed better when they thought the task tapped natural sports ability rather than athletic intelligence, while the reverse was true (although not as dramatically) for white participants. In other words, stereotype-based presumptions about race and athletic strengths and weaknesses proved to be self-fulfilling. This may have resulted in part from how hard the students tried and whether they attempted high-risk, high-reward or low-risk, low-reward putts. It may also have been due to differences in concentration and the extent to which the fear of failure impaired the students' performance. Teasing apart these influences in the broader world of sports is a task we leave to athletic performance gurus. But there is a domain where related questions about the effects of stereotypes on performance are of much greater concern to many more people. That domain is education.

Self-Fulfilling Expectations in the Classroom

It's no secret that many Americans, including educators, expect some groups to do better in the classroom than others, expectations that are largely consistent with statistics regarding test scores, grade point averages, college attendance, and graduation rates. Might these stereotypes influence not just expectations about student performance but actual performance as well—an example of what the great sociologist Robert Merton called self-fulfilling prophecies?[6] In particular, might stereotypes and the expectations they embody create barriers to success for certain minority groups and for women considering careers in STEM fields (science, technology, engineering, and math)?

Discussions of the impact of expectations in the classroom usually begin with an account of the famous study done in the 1960s by Robert Rosenthal and Eleanor Jacobson.[7] The idea of self-fulfilling prophecies in teacher-student interactions was not new. No one doubted that teachers often have different expectations about kids of different races, ethnicities, and social classes, and it was reasonable to assume that those expectations get translated into differential treatment. The notion that these differences in treatment could result in differences in student performance was an obvious inferential leap.

Two features of Rosenthal and Jacobson's study made it particularly provocative. First, it dealt with the effects of teacher expectations on IQ test performance, not on grades assigned by a teacher whose assessments might be biased. IQ performance was something that educators of that era thought was largely determined by some combination of heredity and home environment rather than anything that took place in the classroom or was otherwise under the teacher's control. Second, the researchers didn't compare the performance of students belonging to stereotyped and nonstereotyped groups. Instead, they gave teachers a list of students (20 percent of the class) who they said were likely to "bloom"—to show a learning spurt in the next eight months. What the teachers didn't know was that these students had been chosen at random, and their initial test scores did not differ from those of students not on the list.

When the same students were retested a year later, the seven first graders who had been labeled as likely spurters scored a mean 27-point gain in IQ compared to a 12-point gain among nonspurters, and the twelve second-grade spurters registered a mean 16.5-point gain compared to a 7-point gain for nonspurters. Almost half of the spurters in these two grades made gains of 20 points or more, while only a fifth of nonspurters achieved gains that large. Furthermore, months later, the teachers rated the students they had been led to believe would spurt as more intellectually curious, happier, and in less need of social approval.

The encouraging implication of this study was that if teachers expected *all* of their students to show rapid progress in their early school years, the performance of everyone might be lifted. That is, all might benefit from whatever positive cycle of higher standards and greater attentiveness on the part of teachers had boosted students' self-confidence, effort, and IQ scores in that study.

But an ominous implication was also apparent: *Negative* expectations, including those based not on lists of names but on stereotypes or troublesome first impressions, might prove similarly self-fulfilling. They might initiate a vicious cycle of teacher and student actions, reactions, and negative attributions that would result in academic underachievement and failure.

Attempts to replicate Rosenthal and Jacobson's study with larger and more diverse samples and more sophisticated research designs have not succeeded in producing such dramatic effects. As a consequence, the merits of their study and the legitimacy of their claims—especially about the size of the expectancy effects obtained—continue to be debated.[8] But the body of later work it inspired leaves little doubt about the importance of expectations—those of students even more than those of teachers. Any wise attempt to implement changes in the classroom to deal with underachievement by particular groups of students has to take these expectations into account.

Mind-Sets

For more than four decades, Stanford psychologist Carol Dweck has been focused on (her admiring colleagues might say obsessed with) two related questions: First, why do some students achieve better grades and make more year-to-year progress than others who score equally well on IQ or ability tests? Second, what can we do to help the underachievers do better? Dweck's initial idea was simple. Perhaps overachievers try harder and persist in the face of initial failure because they believe that success depends on effort and persistence, whereas underachievers feel that their efforts won't make much difference and that some kids are just smarter than others.

To test this idea, Dweck and her assistants ran a series of experiments with elementary school children identified by school personnel as showing a pattern of beliefs about success and failure that Dweck termed "helplessness." When these kids were given difficult math problems or anagrams they couldn't solve, they soon gave up. To make matters worse, they then failed to solve new problems that were no more difficult than ones they had solved earlier. But these experiments also offered a ray of hope. When the experimenters trained these students to attribute their errors to insufficient effort and to persist in the face of failure and frustration, they took the message to heart, and their performance improved markedly.[9]

Dweck went on to refine her theory and adopt the language of "mind-sets."[10] Students with a "fixed ability" mind-set, she argued, see ability as something static. Accordingly, they are willing to test their mettle only as long as success seems within easy reach. When the going gets tough, they shy away rather than risk failure. By contrast, students with a "growth" mind-set see ability as dynamic and something that can be enhanced through effort. They set high goals, see initial difficulties not as failures but as challenges to be overcome, and seek out new challenges that stretch their abilities.

Logically, of course, one can believe that hardwired differences in ability play a role and still recognize that effort can boost achievement. But many people with fixed mind-sets also think that if you have real ability, you shouldn't need to work hard to do well. Some also think that working hard on a task, even a very difficult one, implies a lack of ability, and so they are reluctant to take on tasks in which easy success is not guaranteed.

In a pair of related studies in a New York City middle school, Dweck and her colleagues provided evidence that mind-sets predict the trajectory of students' academic performance. Students with a growth mind-set showed an upward trajectory in grades over the course of middle school, while those with a fixed mind-set showed a flat trajectory. Further analysis provided evidence for the sequence of intervening processes that Dweck had postulated. The more students endorsed the view that intelligence is a malleable quality that can be enhanced with effort, the less undone they were by setbacks and the greater the gains they achieved in their math skills and course grades.

The investigators then showed that these mind-sets could be changed with some simple tweaks to existing instructional practices. Seventh graders attending a school with a 97 percent black and Latino enrollment participated in an eight-week program in which, during one twenty-five-minute session per week, they received instruction from specially trained research assistants about study skills and some information about the physiology of the brain. They even saw a film offering vivid depictions of neurons growing connections as individuals learned and were taught simple analogies suggesting that intelligence, like a muscle, grows stronger through exercise. Students in a control condition received just the normal classroom instruction.

The results were just what Dweck and her colleagues had hoped. The decline that both groups had been showing previously was reversed among students who received the growth mind-set intervention. In fact, their grades climbed a bit, while the grades of students who received only the standard information continued to fall.[11] Furthermore, three times as many mind-set intervention students were cited by their classroom teachers for improvements in performance, and in motivation and effort as well.

Scaling Up Growth Mind-Sets and Sense-of-Purpose Interventions

Skeptics question how practical such interventions are for large-scale use. But in one study, students of widely varying economic status from thirteen high schools in the East and Southwest participated in two forty-five-minute sessions late in their senior year (eight were public schools, four were charter schools, and one was a private school).[12] One-third received a growth mind-set intervention that included vivid video information about changes in the brain that occur with learning and effortful practice. This information was reinforced with writing exercises that required students to convey what they had learned in their own words. Another third received a "sense of purpose" intervention that prompted them to think about how their education could help them achieve meaningful "beyond the self" goals (e.g., making the world a better place, setting an example for others, or making their families proud). The remaining third, the control group, read and completed material about different parts of the brain and the different functions they performed, but no material about how the brain changes in response to learning.

Both the mind-set and sense-of-purpose interventions were successful in raising grades overall and, notably, at raising grades and reducing course failures among the at-risk students. These were the more than five hundred students in the study who had failed at least one core class the preceding semester or carried a 2.0 or lower GPA—two criteria that are highly predictive of dropping out before high school graduation. For these students, the two forty-five-minute interventions reduced the course failure rate from 48 percent to 40 percent. No reduction occurred in the control group. This effect may not seem large, but it translated into students failing eighty-three fewer courses than expected on the basis of the failure rate among control participants.

How much greater might the gains be if this message were provided consistently and thoughtfully throughout a student's entire educational experience? That is a question well worth pursuing. Ideally, wise educators would convey the message not just through the feedback they provide when students succeed and fail, but also through the materials students are exposed to in their writing, reading, and spelling exercises when they are young and the biographies they read when they are older. Exposure to tasks in which initial confusion and difficulty diminish with effort and experience would be another part of the recipe for producing a growth mind-set. As we discuss a bit later, so would some reassurance from older students that initial doubts and fears are normal and that success and a sense of belonging will come as they advance from one year to the next.

The message of the existing research should be clear to parents as well as educators. Psych-wise parents do not tell their children how smart or accomplished they are. Instead, they praise hard work and the willingness to tackle difficult challenges. When children are having difficulty, they reassure them that the task will get easier with practice and experience, and convey the message that it is satisfying and even fun to overcome obstacles along the way. They encourage their kids to read books or watch videos not about superheroes with amazing powers but ordinary men and women of all ages who struggled and failed before succeeding, and found satisfaction in the journey as much as the destination. In this way, they will help their children succeed not only in school but in meeting other challenges that life throws their way.

Stereotype Threat in the Classroom

In the 1980s, Claude Steele began to think about a problem closely related to the one that had long preoccupied his Stanford colleague Carol Dweck: Why do African American kids and those from a number of other ethnic groups who excel on the athletic field and in the arts and music so often underachieve in the classroom? Why do so many drop out before graduating from high school, and why do so few earn the college degree that jobs in today's world increasingly demand? Furthermore, why do women, who generally do at least as well in school as men, so often avoid math and the hard sciences? And why do the motivated and talented young women who initially elect to major in math, computer science, and engineering drop those pursuits and change majors more often than their male classmates?

Steele's work led him to introduce the concept of *stereotype threat*—the threat that one's actions will confirm negative stereotypes held about one's group.[13] This threat, he suggested, can be especially harmful when it becomes internalized and produces self-doubt, setting in motion the type of vicious cycle and self-fulfilling prophecy we have discussed throughout this chapter.

Three related problems can be linked to stereotype threat—the same ones faced by white sprinters like Christophe Lemaitre. The first is *disidentification*. People who believe they are likely to fail in a given domain may protect themselves by not investing their self-esteem or identity in that area and looking elsewhere for satisfaction and recognition. The second problem is *self-handicapping*. Too often, students who feel anxious or lack confidence when facing a challenge remove the sting of failure by arranging a good excuse for falling short.[14] Not studying very hard and disparaging academic pursuits are two of the most common self-handicapping tactics.

But it was a third problem that most captured Steele's attention: the anxiety and distraction arising from stereotype threat that can make students perform worse in test situations. To demonstrate this phenomenon and show that it could be overcome, Steele and his students employed a clever trick—the same trick the researchers used in the study of golf performance by black and white Princeton students (who, in fact, had borrowed the idea from Steele). The black and the white college students in their study were given a difficult set of questions from the verbal portion of the Graduate Record Exam.[15] Some were told the questions were a test of their intellectual ability, whereas others were told they had nothing to do with intellectual ability. Instead, they were told, the questions were from a new and as yet unproven test of problem-solving ability.

For the white students, the different descriptions made relatively little difference. When it was described as measuring something about them that they thought was important, they did a little better than when it was described as measuring something they deemed relatively unimportant. For the black students, in contrast, it was those who were told that the test was *not* diagnostic of their intellectual ability who did better on the test—presumably because it freed them from worrying about stereotype-based expectations and allowed them to devote all their energy and attention to the task at hand.

Dozens of studies now attest to the impact of lessening stereotype threat for black, Hispanic, and low-socioeconomic-status children taking standard tests of intellectual ability, and for women taking tests of math or reasoning ability.[16] In some cases, the experimental manipulation involved simply varying the description of what the test measured. But other methods have also been used. For example, researchers have shown that women are less likely to perform poorly when taking a math test in the presence of other women than when surrounded by men.[17] However, the real challenge for educators was to examine whether this research could be used to help students. Could it be used to assist students from groups that often have difficulty in school succeed in getting better grades and prevent them from quitting when they experience academic difficulties?

Characterizing tests as irrelevant to ability is a clever way to illustrate the impact of stereotype threat in the context of a laboratory experiment. But it is hardly a feasible technique in academic situations where students know all too well what the tests are designed to measure and also know that many people doubt their ability to succeed.

Nor can women in advanced math or science classes fail to notice their minority status. As with interventions designed to promote a growth mind-set, the question has been whether efforts to deal with stereotype threat can improve day-to-day and year-to-year academic performance.

There has been no shortage of skeptics. Some have claimed that differences in native ability and cultural values cannot be overcome. Others have insisted that nothing short of massive social change could compensate for the economic and other barriers responsible for the gaps in achievement on the part of disadvantaged groups. Concerned educators and politicians who have been more optimistic maintain that extensive (and expensive) educational interventions that provide expert instruction and sufficiently incentivize student (and teacher) effort could overcome the disadvantages these students face.

But a small band of social psychologists and educators have been even more optimistic. In fact, they have amassed a body of evidence demonstrating that relatively modest psych-wise interventions could reduce the "tough problem" that these performance gaps represent.

The goal of these researchers was not to show that the quality of instruction, the skill and dedication of teachers, or the adequacy of facilities were irrelevant to student success. These investigators knew all too well how much these factors matter. Nevertheless, they set out to show that the interventions they had designed could make a difference, even when they did not rely on handpicked faculty and students, or lavish facilities.

Although these interventions differ in their specifics, all of them were developed in light of theory and research that dealt specifically with stereotype threat. At the same time, these interventions employed the more general insights that were presented in the first five chapters of this book. They incorporate lessons about the powerful impact of social contexts (and the misattributions that result when that impact is underestimated) and the role of subjective interpretations of those situations. They also reflect insights about the ways in which actions influence thoughts and feelings and about the particular lenses and filters that determine, and potentially distort, judgment and decision making. We think you'll agree that these success stories are essential reading for anyone who wants to participate wisely in discussions about contemporary education and what can be done to deal with the tough problem of helping all students reach their full potential.

Magic? No, Just Psych-Wise Intervention

There are two kinds of success stories worth noting. The first involves the success of KIPP (Knowledge Is Power Programs) schools where impressive rates of high school completion (95 percent) and college entry (89 percent) have been achieved for minority and low-income students through a combination of a rigorous college-preparatory curriculum, effective leadership, dedicated teachers, motivated parents, and the availability of considerable outside financial support.

These resource-intensive programs and others like them confirm the lessons about the power of situational forces and constraints, the importance of the way individuals interpret efforts to shape their actions, and the value of behavioral commitment that we have heralded throughout this book. But a cautionary note is in order: The percentage of KIPP students who go on to complete a four-year college degree has proven to be disappointingly low (only 33 percent)—although that figure is still four times greater than for students with similar backgrounds who attended high schools without such programs.[18]

The other success stories involve relatively modest, highly cost-effective interventions that have been shown to provide a significant educational payoff for students whose social and economic backgrounds place them at a disadvantage. Both types of success stories challenge those on the political left who decry "band-aid solutions" and insist that we can't improve the academic success of disadvantaged students until we address problems of poverty, health, nutrition, societal racism, and other "root causes." Both types of interventions, of course, also challenge those on the political right who attribute the pervasive academic failure among particular disadvantaged groups to some combination of genetics, poor parenting, and other harmful cultural factors that cannot be addressed by "throwing money at the problem," much less by any intervention designed by liberal social scientists.

The interventions we describe next do not teach students all-purpose study skills or specific academic content. Yet all have produced not just short-term gains but sustained improvement in academic performance. In many cases they have done so with large enough numbers of students to demand the serious attention of administrators and politicians. These results are surprising in light of the modesty of the interventions—so surprising that they can seem like magic. But a deeper understanding of the underlying psychology we have been discussing throughout this book makes it clear that the interventions to be described are not magical at all. The effects are bigger than one might expect because the interventions are bigger than they seem—bigger in the sense that they change the very meaning students attach to their day-to-day experiences and thus how they respond to those experiences. In so doing, they transform what might otherwise be a vicious downward cycle into a virtuous upward cycle.

The Positive Impact of Self-Affirmation

Claude Steele and his collaborators have done more than document the negative effects of stereotype threat; they have shown the benefits of helping students cope with that threat. One of the most promising techniques they have explored involves "self-affirmation"—bolstering students' feelings of self-worth with regard to dimensions irrelevant to the threat itself. Students are induced to get in touch with specific values that are personally important to them (such as friendship and family, or religion, or making a difference in the world) by stipulating what those values are and writing essays about the role they play in their lives.[19]

In a seminal study, Geoffrey Cohen and his colleagues tested the effectiveness of self-affirmation interventions in three classrooms in a suburban northeastern middle school.[20] Students in these classes wrote a series of essays over the course of the year affirming the personal values they regarded as most important to them (most often the importance of family, but sometimes particular personal interests, such as music). This intervention improved the grades of black students (who faced stereotype threat) but not those of white students (who did not face it), with the result that the black-white gap in the targeted course was reduced by 40 percent. Even more impressive, the gap in overall GPA was reduced over the two years of middle school by 30 percent, and the number of black students who had to repeat a grade or who were assigned to a remedial program dropped from 9 percent to 3 percent.

In the wake of this pioneering study by Cohen and colleagues, there have now been many studies with similarly positive results for different types of groups facing stereotype threat. The theory is that these interventions succeed through recursive processes that bring about a virtuous cycle. Students who benefit from these interventions come to have a greater sense of self-worth and a little less fear about the implications of trying and failing. These changes make them more willing to persevere in the face of initial difficulties and more willing to ask questions and seek help. Teachers, including those unaware of the intervention, take note of that heightened effort and engagement and see the students first as more motivated and then, when the extra effort begins to produce positive results, as more able and worthy of further attention and mentoring. This in turn produces further improvement and makes the students more willing to take on greater challenges and to persist when success does not come easily, and so forth.[21] The results of some of these interventions have been truly impressive. Among one sample of low-achieving African American students in the seventh and eighth grades, self-affirmation exercises reduced the percentage of students having to repeat the same grade or be assigned to remediation classes from 18 to 5 percent.[22]

Solving the "Mentor's Dilemma" with Wise Feedback

Constructive feedback, including attention to shortcomings in performance and suggestions for improvement, can be a powerful tool to help students develop their skills. But when students have doubts about their ability to meet new academic challenges and concerns about how they are viewed by the person offering the criticism, such feedback can undermine their motivation and self-confidence. So what should a concerned and compassionate mentor do when confronted with mediocre efforts?

Too often, especially when providing feedback across racial or socioeconomic divides, the default answer is to withhold criticism and offer bland praise (perhaps for choice of topic, evidence of even mild interest, or diligence in some relatively unimportant aspect of the task). But in so doing, the mentor deprives the student of the type of pointed feedback that could challenge the student to do better, as well as the type of specific instruction that's needed for the student to improve. The mentor is spared the risk of being accused of bias, but the student either labors under the illusion that a mediocre effort is fully acceptable or, worse, concludes that the mentor doubts his or her capacity to do better.

A more appropriate answer to this dilemma, research suggests, is to provide a particular type of wise feedback. Ideally, the instructor should accompany honest assessments of the student's work (including identification of shortcomings and suggestions for improvement) with a clear signal that the mentor is judging the work against high standards and an assurance that the mentor fully believes that the student can meet those tough standards.

In the first of a series of studies, the percentage of seventh graders who accepted an invitation to revise and resubmit their essays after receiving such feedback jumped from 7 to 71 percent.[23] In a second study that required all students to submit a second draft, those receiving the wise feedback went on to hand in better essays. Both of these findings were more pronounced among African American students than white students. The effect of this type of wise feedback was particularly evident among students who had expressed the most distrust about the treatment they and members of their race typically receive. In fact, the further decline in trust over the next two years that is typical for this highly vulnerable group of students did not take place.

The researchers further showed that the power of this type of attribution training could be enhanced by having peers reinforce the core message. In a third study, conducted in a New York City high school with a predominantly low-income student body, the intervention featured testimonials from students that drove home the message that critical feedback reflected high standards and confidence in a student's ability to meet those standards. The result was a significant improvement in the grades of African American students (but, again, not those of white students) in the next grading period. Best of all, that improvement continued as time went on. A virtuous cycle was initiated whereby the training changed the way the students felt about their school and motivated them to exert additional effort toward their studies. That extra effort produced improved grades and other signs of success and approval, which further enhanced their motivation.

The Value of a Little Reassurance about Belonging

Many college freshmen, especially those facing stereotype threat or those from disadvantaged backgrounds, arrive on campus and experience a kind of culture shock and a feeling of not belonging. This is true even for students with a record of academic success and who are more than capable of meeting the academic demands of college. As one gifted African American woman who was admitted to Princeton University (and later to Harvard Law School before joining a prestigious Chicago law firm) wrote, "My experiences at Princeton have made me far more aware of my 'Blackness' than ever before. . . . No matter how liberal and open-minded some of my White professors and classmates try to be toward me, I sometimes feel like a visitor on campus; as if I really don't belong."[24] That student was Michelle Robinson Obama.

A similarly gifted Hispanic woman admitted to Princeton described feeling "like a visitor landing in an alien land. . . . I have spent my years since Princeton, while at law school, and in my various professional jobs, not feeling completely a part of the worlds I inhabit." That student was Sonia Sotomayor. As a justice on the U.S. Supreme Court, she later wrote in dissent on an affirmative action case that "race matters, because of the slights, the snickers, the silent judgments that reinforce that most crippling of thoughts: 'I do not belong here.' "[25]

This feeling of not belonging, accompanied by fears of being out of one's depth and not having what it takes to succeed (especially when those fears are reinforced by some initial academic struggles), can lead to a downward spiral of self-doubt and disengagement. To address this aspect of stereotype threat, Stanford psychologists Gregory Walton and Geoffrey Cohen had African American and white students read the results of a survey suggesting that it was common for new arrivals on campus, regardless of race, to feel that they don't belong, but that such feelings ease with time. The students also wrote an essay and gave a speech (ostensibly for the next year's class) about how their own worries about belonging and their early academic struggles had eased since their arrival.

Over the study's three-year observation period, this intervention, which Walton and Cohen call "stealthy," enabled the minority students to cope better with periods of adversity, disappointment, and stress.[26] It also prevented the semester-to-semester decline in grades that otherwise is common.* The result was that the achievement gap normally seen between African American and white students by the time of graduation was cut in half.

The authors of this provocative study again pointed to the importance of a virtuous cycle of recursive processes and cumulative consequences. They suggested that the intervention changed the way the students interpreted the negative events that are a normal part of the college experience and, in so doing, protected them from their adverse effects. It also set in motion changes in behavior—more time in the library, more clubs joined, less stress while studying—that cascaded to yield the long-term improvement in GPA. Consideration of such cascading effects has become an increasingly important theme in intervention research. Wise practitioners in education and other domains of achievement know that it is important not only to offer some assurance to those experiencing doubts about their ability to succeed but also to provide some convincing basis for that reassurance.

It's worth noting that, once again, the belonging intervention did not provide any consistent benefit for nonminority students, with the result that the gap in achievement between the minority and nonminority students was cut in half. It appears that white students, and those from other ethnic groups who do not face stereotype threat, tend to assume they belong and can succeed. They further tend to assume that any initial difficulties they do experience will pass, and that they eventually will become as self-assured and successful as the more senior students they observe (most of whom share their backgrounds).

---

* The intervention in this study (and others we describe here) was called "stealthy" by the investigators because it was not presented to the students as something intended to boost their grades or influence whether they stayed in school. Hearing that an intervention is designed to remedy a problem sends a message to the students that they need, or are thought to need, extra attention, a stigma that can become self-fulfilling. The stealthiness of the procedure, the investigators argue, thus contributes to its success.

The implication of the Cohen and Walton findings is that the benefits of their intervention are largely restricted to students whose backgrounds do not already provide that reassuring presumption. For those students, the messages of reassurance—that any current doubts and difficulties they are experiencing are likely to be transitory and if they persevere they too can make the grade—need to be made explicitly and delivered early in the students' college careers.

The Road Ahead

The optimistic message of these pioneering "wise intervention" efforts has now been reinforced by the findings of a great many follow-up studies. Again and again researchers find evidence of improvements in the academic performance of targeted groups and decreases in performance gaps that so often put members of those groups at a disadvantage as they progress through their schooling.[27] For example, when African American students graduating with high grades from charter high schools received a brief precollege reassurance about their "belonging" at the next rung in the academic ladder, the percentage who successfully completed their first year of college increased from 32 percent to 43 percent.[28] How impressed should we be by that increase? Consider this: It is roughly the same as the increase achieved by a program offering $3,500 scholarships to students who achieved that goal.

Wise interventions have also been shown to reduce the negative effects of stereotype threat faced by women pursuing degrees in STEM fields. In an important study, three consecutive cohorts of incoming engineering students at a Canadian university received either a brief "social belonging" intervention or a similarly brief "affirmation training" intervention. As in the studies we described earlier, the belonging intervention included descriptions by more senior students of the early travails they had experienced, along with reassuring words about the commonness and transient nature of their early self-doubts. It also included a request that the fledgling engineering students write essays endorsing, in their own words, the messages they had heard. The self-affirmation intervention, as in earlier studies, asked the students to affirm in writing some important personal value. The students in this study also completed diaries for twelve days after the interventions and, later in the year, additional questionnaires that dealt with their social lives, personal adjustment, and well-being.

Both of these interventions resulted in higher GPAs over the next year—especially for women who opted for the most male-dominated majors. In fact, the gender gap so often seen in science and engineering fields (and present in no-treatment groups) was completely eliminated. Analyses of the students' diary and questionnaire responses further indicated that the women in the treatment conditions were more resilient in the face of negative experiences and had more positive attitudes about themselves and their chosen field of study. The women who had received the social belonging intervention also formed more friendships with male engineering students.[29]

Further work will be required to see how well these results hold up when these types of psych-wise interventions are employed in large numbers of different schools with different personnel under different circumstances. But there is reason for optimism. Not only are there a growing number of reports of successful interventions, there is now increasing evidence that they reduce stereotype threat and promote adaptive mind-sets. As a consequence, students become more confident that they have what it takes to succeed, that inevitable setbacks and disappointments are transitory, and that effort and persistence will bear fruit. That increased confidence in turn makes students more willing to associate with peers pursuing similar goals and to engage with teachers and mentors who can help them reach those goals.

In the case of younger students, the chain of recursive processes that translate into better academic performance have yet to be fully explored. But we do know that interventions of the sort we have described influence not only the students' performance, but also the decisions that others make about them—notably, whether they are promoted at the end of the year rather than held back or tracked into classes for low-performing students. We also know that students' beliefs about their own abilities and the possibility of improving them influence their willingness to persevere in the face of difficulty and to take on new challenges. So it is not hard to imagine the other links in the chain whereby these younger students and their teachers respond to each other's efforts in a way that changes vicious cycles of mutual failure and frustration into virtuous cycles of mutual success and satisfaction.[30]

It is important to note once again that the psych-wise interventions we have been describing are not designed to be substitutes for skilled teachers, supportive administrators, or adequate resources. What they do is allow students to take full advantage of these vital components of an effective education. For some students, the interventions will not be sufficient to initiate such virtuous cycles even under the best of circumstances. For many others, the long-term gains will be modest. But for some, they will be life changing.

A metaphor offered by two of the most active researchers in this area is apt: A small but wise intervention is akin to a small change in the shape of an airplane wing that provides more lift. It doesn't eliminate the need for a powerful engine, but it does result in an easier and safer takeoff, and a better journey.[31]

The wisest one in the room, armed with a nuanced appreciation of this research, can contribute productively to any debate about how to improve the academic performance, and later contributions to society, of students and schools that are currently failing. The evidence we have reviewed also offers some broader lessons for anyone who wants to help the people they care about meet new and difficult challenges. Don't just intervene; intervene wisely. That means offering realistic feedback rather than empty praise. It means linking academic goals to personal values and broader aspirations that have real meaning for the individual and providing reassurance in the face of expressions of doubt. It also means accompanying that reassurance with the message that ability is not fixed. It is not a matter of having it or not having it. Abilities grow with effort, and failures are a part of that growth process. Persistence and confidence that continued effort will pay off, and the willingness to seek help when required, are the keys to success.

The wisest in the room will take those same messages to heart when *they* are the ones facing new and difficult challenges and coping with self-doubt. They will remember that their own capacities are malleable—for example, in the case of aging baby boomers, that coping with new information technologies is akin to learning to swim or learning to type (both of which most of us readily accompished in earlier days) rather than a test of intelligence. They will seek reassurance from friends and colleagues who can recount tales of their own faltering first steps, but they also ask for tips to ease their task. And they won't be afraid to ask questions when stymied. The wisest in the room recognize that asking for help does not reveal a person's limitations; rather, it demonstrates an openness to feedback and a confidence that success is obtainable.

9

An Even Tougher Problem
for the World

For decades, energy conservation advocates have urged Americans to turn off lights, turn down thermostats in winter and air conditioners in summer, unplug idle appliances, drive less and walk or bicycle more, install solar panels, and do whatever they could to reduce their energy use. The good news is that some very simple and inexpensive psych-wise initiatives can facilitate these kinds of modest (and dollar-wise) changes in individual behavior. The bad news is that the real challenge our planet faces—that of averting the serious consequences of climate change that our children, our grandchildren, and future generations will face on a warmer and stormier planet—is far more daunting.

Let's discuss the good news first and then consider what makes the global challenge so difficult. We should warn you that we don't have a simple psych-wise prescription to offer. But an understanding of some features of human psychology can help you appreciate the barriers that need to be overcome. That appreciation can in turn make you a more informed contributor to any discussion on the topic, and a wiser voter when candidates state their positions.

The Good News: Reducing Energy Use
for the Price of a Postage Stamp

Robert Cialdini, author of the 1984 classic *Influence*, has spent his career figuring out psych-wise ways to change people's behavior. In his years as a leading researcher at Arizona State University (ASU), Cialdini showed us that people will follow a well-dressed jaywalker across the street more often than a poorly dressed one, and they will say a cookie tastes better when it comes from a nearly empty cookie jar than one that's nearly full. He also showed that people's willingness to put their litter in a receptacle rather than throw it on the ground depends on how much litter they see already lying around. Employing the same social influence principle, he showed that one way to get hotel guests to reuse their towels rather than having them replaced every day is to let them know that most other guests (or, even better, most previous guests occupying *this very room*) have done so.[1]

Upon his retirement from ASU, Cialdini took up the challenge of energy conservation in earnest. He became chief scientist at OPOWER, a firm that advises utility companies on how to get their customers to cut down on how much energy they use. Convinced that the same principles of influence he had identified in his academic research would be helpful in this effort, Cialdini went to work. His goal was to devise techniques that worked better than mass media educational campaigns and better than the small financial incentives or penalties championed by conventional economic theorists. His techniques simply gave energy users a tiny nudge to take actions they already endorsed. They were attractive to power companies because they spared the companies the costs of upgrading their power plants.

One technique involved the same "social proof" principle that Cialdini had used to get hotel guests to reuse their towels. His team

went door to door in one San Diego suburb, attaching energy conservation messages to doorknobs. Four different messages were used.
One urged the homeowner to conserve energy for "the sake of the environment," another for "the sake of future generations," and a third to
help the homeowner "save money." The fourth message, the one employing Cialdini's social proof principle, read, "The majority of your
neighbors are undertaking energy saving actions every day" (which
was true; most residents were taking at least some small actions of
this kind). At the end of the month, when the meters were read, it
turned out that only one message made a difference: As Cialdini had
anticipated, energy use decreased significantly only in those households informed that their neighbors were trying to do the same.[2]

Cialdini and his OPOWER team went on to show that a more
precise message about energy consumption in the neighborhood
can have even more impact. They sent residents a monthly letter
with two pieces of information: the average energy use of their
neighbors and the extent to which their own household's use was
worse, or better, than that average. The result was that homeowners
who discovered they had been doing less well than their neighbors
at saving energy (and at reducing their electric bills) quickly began
to conserve more.

But there was a problem; homeowners who discovered they had
been doing better than their neighbors at conserving energy became
more wasteful. To address that problem, Cialdini added something to
the message these customers were given—a smiley face next to their
energy use figure (conveying the message, "Well done; you are acting
in accord with our community's shared values"). The result was that
the energy wasters, as before, tried harder to match their neighbors;
but now the energy conservers took satisfaction from the smiley faces
signaling their success and continued their energy-saving ways. Overall energy use in the neighborhood went down.[3] The energy savings
that resulted from letting people know where they stood in compari-

son to their neighbors, and congratulating those who were doing especially well, were modest. But the energy companies could hardly complain about the cost (that of a second-class postage stamp) or the cost-effectiveness of the effort.

The Larger Problem

Targeting individual energy users with information about norms is certainly a tactic worth employing. As Harvard social psychologist Joshua Greene put it, "The best way to get people to do something is to tell them that their neighbors are already doing it."[4] Other influence techniques discussed in the first four chapters of this book could also prove useful for communities and societies that have committed themselves to the goal of energy conservation. It would be especially helpful to attend to the channel factors that link good intentions more closely to actions and to default options that oblige individuals to opt out of socially desirable practices rather than obliging them to opt in.

But experts in climate science are quick to point out that intervention efforts like these that focus on changes in individual behavior cannot come close to meeting the global climate challenge we face. They tell us that more than 90 percent of the countries in the world have recently logged the warmest decade in their histories and that globally, nine of the ten hottest years on record have occurred since 2000. If you want a more dramatic number to indicate how this is affecting us, try this: From 2001 to 2010, there were 136,000 deaths from heat-related causes globally—more than twenty times as many as in the previous decade.[5] Looming climate disruption darkens the future with the prospect of agricultural disaster, widespread food shortages, and other threats to the stability of civilization as we know it.

We face enormous future costs because of our failure to address the causes of climate change—a double whammy whereby we will be paying both the costs of curtailing greenhouse gas emissions and the costs of mitigating the inevitable damages to our property, our food supply, and our health. If you are not convinced that the climate change crisis is real and that the threat is increasingly imminent, then you are very likely exercising the enormous human capacity for denial and rationalization we discussed earlier in this book. If you have followed coverage of global warming in the media, you are also aware of how little progress has been made in moving governments and industries to take the kinds of actions necessary to limit the costs and damages we face.

Many commentators would say there is no mystery about why it has proven so difficult to initiate major programs of the type and magnitude needed to address the climate change threat. The answer, they would say, is a combination of simple economics and the realities of domestic and international politics. National, to say nothing of global, regulation of greenhouse gases requires cooperative action of a kind that is fiercely resisted by entrenched, well-financed interest groups.

The hunger of corporations for short-term profits rather than long-term sustainability of the economy (to say nothing of the sustainability of our planet's ecosystems and our way of life) is a particular problem. Indeed, U.S. companies are virtually required to adopt a short-term outlook that discourages even fiscally prudent investments if they will pay off only in the long run. Transitioning to more efficient and renewable energy sources would hit immediate shareholder value hard, and our tax system offers few incentives for investors to focus on long-term concerns.

Closely related is the role of money in politics. Fossil fuel companies like ExxonMobil and conservative political foundations such as Americans for Prosperity give huge donations to political candidates and advocacy organizations that oppose restrictions on carbon emissions. They also fund media networks and "experts" who are enlisted to spread doubt about the need to reduce the extraction of coal, oil, and gas and to mislead people about the costs and benefits of converting to greener and more sustainable energy sources. Paid pundits actively encourage people to engage in the type of denial and rationalization to which they are already inclined, as do various interest groups, including trade unions whose members stand to lose their jobs if we transition to alternative energy sources.

The myth that global warming (or at least the role of human activity in producing it) is something about which experts disagree, can be seductive, and efforts to promote the myth have been highly successful.[6] Despite the near unanimity of the scientific community on anthropogenic climate change, a 2012 survey revealed that when asked, "Do scientists believe that the earth is getting warmer because of human activity?" almost as many Americans said no (43 percent) as yes (45 percent), with 12 percent saying that they didn't know. The right answer, of course, is that very few knowledgeable scientists (excluding those whose opinions are bought and paid for) have any doubts at all.[7]

Advocates for action to counter global warming can point out that the climate challenge also offers opportunities. Individuals and companies that develop clean energy technologies stand to reap large profits, especially if they become early leaders in this enterprise. New employment opportunities would be created as societies switch from carbon-based energy technologies to alternative energy supplies and as new products and services not yet envisioned become a part of our lives. But advocates of change have a hard time competing against entrenched interests that can use their enormous political and financial clout to forestall needed legislation and regulatory reform.

A particular problem is that most of those who might occupy the new jobs created by greener policies and practices do not know that they personally will get them. Neither potential employees, nor the investors, entrepreneurs, or others who stand to benefit from efforts to combat climate change (including ordinary citizens) constitute an organized group, much less possess the resources to lobby Congress or mount public information campaigns. And, of course, it is harder to marshal support for government programs that would subsidize the development of alternative energy sources than it is to fuel taxpayer (and voter) opposition to such expenditures. The costs that are already being paid for our failure to have acted earlier and the costs to be paid for our inaction today are, in marked contrast, not at all obvious to ordinary citizens.

There is no denying the importance of these political and economic factors. They help explain why confronting the climate change problem is different from securing the resources needed to build bridges, dams, or national railway and highway systems. But the United States and other nations have managed to meet previous challenges that called for some foresight and a willingness to invest significant resources when there was not an obvious immediate payoff for corporations and entrepreneurs motivated by the pursuit of profit.

Earlier societies built pyramids and great cathedrals designed to last for centuries and even millennia. America in the first half of the twentieth century managed to create national parks, provide universal education, and build great institutions of higher education and scientific research that became the envy of the world. In more recent decades, we managed to put men on the moon and make astonishing advances in medicine and public health. Why, then, have we found it so difficult to get off our collective posteriors, roll up our sleeves, and tackle the challenge of climate change and related problems such as resource depletion and loss of biodiversity?

To answer this vital question, it is necessary to consider certain features of human motivation and decision making. It is also important to examine the challenge of climate change through the lenses of evolutionary psychology and behavioral economics.

Time Frame, Beneficiary, and End-Point Problems

Meeting the challenge of climate change demands that people make personal sacrifices now to minimize harm that others will suffer in the future. That's a tough sell. Our species evolved as small-group animals with a focus on our own survival and short-term needs, along with those of our offspring and near kin. We are not programmed to worry much about the welfare of our great-grandchildren, much less the descendants of people living far away. You may be willing to resist some unhealthy snacks and find some time to exercise in order to be healthier and be around longer for your children. But how willing would you be to exercise more and eat a healthier diet—or save more of your disposable income—to increase the odds that your great-grandchildren will be a bit better off? It is that kind of sacrifice, one that requires us to protect the interests of generations we will never know, that is called for if we are to meet the challenge of climate change.

Moreover, what is called for are permanent changes, not temporary alterations in how we live our lives. The success of wartime mobilizations and calls for cooperation in the face of floods or economic crises show that people are willing to sacrifice for a period of time to achieve a victory that allows them to return to business as usual. The prospect of a new normal that is less free, less luxurious, and in some ways less enjoyable is not something likely to produce eager recruits for the campaign ahead.

The Free-Rider Problem

Even people who are willing to be good citizens and pay their share of the costs of combating global warming are not willing to be "suckers" or "saints" who pay the costs while others—free riders—share the benefits without footing their share of the bill. Individuals and nations that fail to curb energy consumption and carbon dioxide production will continue to reap most of the benefits that come from conducting their own "business as usual" while at the same time profiting from others' efforts to reduce greenhouse gas emissions.

This is a problem in any situation where people can benefit from the work and sacrifices of others without contributing themselves. But there is an additional problem when it comes to climate change. In many "commons dilemmas," selfish individuals may gain a temporary advantage over cooperative individuals, but *communities* of cooperators fare better than communities of noncooperators.* Companies that pay higher taxes to subsidize more livable communities may be at a disadvantage with respect to tight-fisted competitors in terms of their end-of-the-year balance sheets. But companies situated in more livable communities might find it easier to attract skilled workers who then stay around longer (and find that their homes appreciate faster). No such collective benefit will be forthcoming for cooperators in the struggle against climate change. Sun, wind, and water do not discriminate between cooperators and noncooperators. The virtuous who reduce energy use or adopt greener technologies will not endure any less degradation of their environments than the nonvirtuous who do nothing to change their ways.

The actions from which communities of cooperators (cooperative nations in particular) do stand to benefit are those that involve efforts to adapt to climate change and mitigate damages. Building higher sea walls and installing systems that provide earlier warnings of (increasingly common) severe storms will pay great dividends. Many climate scientists worry that discussions about such measures can easily become excuses for inaction and a source of undue confidence about the ability of engineers, inventors, entrepreneurs, and others to minimize future costs.

Later in this chapter, when we consider the reasons for at least some optimism, we explain why increased attention to issues of mitigation nevertheless would be highly desirable. For now, let us just say that recalling the key insight of chapter 4 on the primacy of behavior could make you the wisest in the room the next time the issue of preventing versus mitigating the effects of climate comes under discussion.

---

*The term comes from the dilemma posed by grazing areas (called "commons") wherein each herdsman entitled to use the commons has an incentive to graze as many animals as possible, even if it reduces the amount of feed for other herdsmen's animals. The individual would reap the full benefit of each animal added, but the costs of that animal in terms of reduced resources for feeding would be shared by all. Under such circumstances, the resource is soon exhausted so that none benefit, whereas restraint on the part of all would have allowed everyone to reap at least some benefit.[8]

The "Drop-in-the-Bucket" Problem

A powerful source of resistance to efforts to reduce carbon emissions is that people are all too aware that their own efforts, and the efforts of their communities, will not really make a difference. Even the efforts of our entire nation will not get the job done. "Why should I drive less and walk or bike more, or keep my thermostat higher in the summer and lower in the winter?" the average citizen may ask. "It will be inconvenient and sweaty, and keeping just a tiny bit of carbon dioxide out of the atmosphere won't make any difference to the health of the planet unless governments and industries change their ways." "Besides," this person might add to bolster the rationalization, "most people are not reducing their driving or enduring less comfortable temperatures in their homes," and "I bet China and India won't do anything to curb their energy consumption. I'd be a sucker to sacrifice for them when they won't do the same for me and my neighbors."

The Noisy Signal Problem

Climate change, even change that is already producing devastating effects on everyday life (floods and famines, rising tides and loss of shoreline, crises in food production, loss of animal habitat—the list goes on and on), is not leaving consistent footprints. None of these consequences, to say nothing of a gradual 1- or 2-degree change in temperature over two or three decades averaged over the entire globe, is easy to notice on a day-to-day basis. The biting winds and freezing temperatures of winter, and the weather's day-to-day and week-to week variability, can obscure the reality of gradual warming and give license, or at least vivid talking points, to climate change deniers. Conversely, those making the required changes in lifestyle will see no clear evidence of progress, especially when the "progress" is not a change for the better, just a slowing of the rate of deterioration.

Unless you happen to be a skier who notices that the snowpack isn't what it used to be or a farmer whose crops aren't doing as well as they used to, thoughts of global warming are likely to be the furthest thing from your mind. Only when news reporters call attention to the "once-a-century" storms that seem to be occurring more like once a decade, or to a shocking statistic like the twenty-fold increase in heat-related fatalities we noted earlier, or the image of a single polar bear marooned on a tiny piece of breakaway ice, does climate change become salient enough for most of us to feel that something needs to be done.

The Temptations of Denial and Rationalization

Perhaps the most difficult problem to overcome in mobilizing efforts to combat climate change is the most obvious one: the all-too-human inclination to engage in denial and rationalization, or what psychologists call dissonance reduction. When it comes to our failures and failings, to our sins of commission and omission, to threats to our well-being, security, and self-esteem, we humans are masters of these particular vices. We discussed some subtle and not-so-subtle instances of these processes in chapter 4. The climate change problem offers particularly tempting conditions for denial and rationalization.

In fact, when it comes to dealing with climate change, the line between rationalization and legitimate reasons for inaction can be very fine. The scientific models are not perfectly validated or precise. Is this a prudent reason to wait before acting, or is it just a rationalization? We do not demand to know the probability that we will suffer a car crash or a flood, or that we will die without leaving our family's finances secure, before buying insurance. What is it about the threat of climate change that justifies inaction and allows us to avoid thinking about the problem and instead just hope for the best?

As we already noted, our efforts alone, indeed the efforts of our whole community, will make virtually no difference in how much climate change takes place. Is this a legitimate reason not to at least do your part? Do you refrain from voting because your vote alone will not determine the outcome of the election? Do you excuse fellow citizens who offer that excuse? It is certainly true, and perhaps galling to you, that those who make no effort to conserve energy while you foot the bill for installing solar panels or driving a more fuel-efficient car will live in an environment no worse than yours. Is this a reason for not making these investments or a rationalization? Does the fact that some of your neighbors leave their sidewalks unshoveled after a snowstorm prompt you to shirk that responsibility? Or do you disregard the shirkers and continue to fulfill that community duty?

You get the point. Why then do so many people who resist the temptation to deny and rationalize when facing other problems yield to that temptation when it comes to climate change? In part, it is because the problem is so daunting and difficult, the looming consequences so dire, and the steps to be taken so costly and uncertain in their effectiveness that for many people, denial and rationalization simply provide more psychic comfort than any active steps available to them.

But in the case of climate change, denial and rationalization are especially potent because they are engaged in collectively. People don't independently arrive at their justifications for inaction. Nor do they independently evaluate the credibility of evidence, the reliability of statistics, or the flaws in the respective methodologies of those sounding the climate change alarm and those attacking them. Rather, they are encouraged to adopt their comfortable rationalizations by groups with powerful motivations and virtually limitless resources.

To be sure, those concerned about climate change also engage in collective action, and command considerable resources. But the contest is an unequal one. The voices warning of the immediacy of the problem and the dangers of inaction may be greater in number and more distinguished in their credentials, but the deniers are telling people what they prefer to believe rather than what they prefer not to believe.

Increasingly, the deniers are also telling people, sometimes explicitly and sometimes implicitly, that the issue is more about political identities than about who is right and who is wrong about the facts. The climate change issue, which elsewhere in the world involves questions of cost and benefits of potential policies, has to a disturbing degree in the United States become a question of which side you are on, Left or Right, and which side of the debate better represents your broader social and political values. Any concession to "their" side is thus seen as betrayal of "our" side.

We have made no secret of our personal beliefs that the climate change deniers are wrong and those advocating action are right. We also recognize that we are not immune to the human failings that can distort judgment and undermine sound decision making. But we nevertheless believe that any wise person in the room who looks at the climate change issue with an open mind will come away from that exercise asking the question we raise next.

So What's to Be Done?

Is the situation hopeless? Are our grandchildren doomed to face catastrophic changes in how they live? Are there any grounds for optimism? Perhaps. There is an outside chance that scientists and engineers will work some eleventh-hour miracles to cleanse the atmosphere of carbon dioxide, methane, and other greenhouse gases that are fueling climate change, or at least to slow the rate at which things get worse. There is probably a better chance that the lure of profits, if not more altruistic motives, will prompt private enterprise to develop better batteries for electrically powered cars, hasten the transition to (and reduce the cost of) cleaner energy sources, and create new "green" products we cannot even imagine today.

An examination of these possibilities and their likelihood lies outside our bailiwick. We know that experts can offer a long list of caveats, the principal one being that many things we might do to solve one problem would likely create or heighten others. Cleansing the atmosphere of greenhouse gases on a massive scale, for example, would itself almost certainly require enormous amounts of energy. Any scaling up of innovative programs would require a degree of international cooperation that does not seem likely in anything resembling the current political and economic climate.

Nevertheless, history offers at least some bases for cautious optimism. Although societies are slow to meet challenges, pessimistic experts characteristically underestimate humanity's capacity to make rapid progress once it gets to work in earnest. Necessity breeds invention and increases the willingness of governments and the general public to subsidize efforts to innovate. Success in solving problem X often provides new possibilities for addressing problems Y and Z. Moreover, solutions to particular problems often provide bonuses of obvious and immediate value to society.

The public might not be inspired by the prospect of slowing the rate of global warming from 0.2 degree centigrade to 0.1 degree per decade through an increase in the number of electrically powered cars or wind and solar power. But it might welcome cleaner lakes and rivers, fewer days of smoggy haze, and new jobs for a generation of new workers. Bonuses not anticipated at the time a program is launched may also be of social and economic value. Consider the space program and the dividends we have reaped from the discoveries and inventions made in getting us to the moon. In the field of medicine alone, the remote monitoring devices now used for intensive-care patients and cardiac patients with pacemakers were spinoffs of advances in telemetry systems first developed at NASA. Some of the portable medical equipment carried aboard ambulances today was also developed by NASA for its use in space.

As we noted at the outset of this chapter, what psychologists and behavioral economists have discovered can also help us meet the challenge of climate change. Psych-wise framing of choices (e.g., default rules so that individuals and communities have to opt out of voluntary and state-subsidized energy saving and emission-reducing

programs instead of opting in) could increase rates of participation.*
A clear implication of the research we described in chapter 4 is that
behavior change, especially when it is accomplished with gentle
nudges and modest incentives, can give rise to changes in attitudes
and values that in turn increase willingness to accept or even demand
additional changes in policies and priorities. Support for initiatives
to mitigate the effects of expected environmental changes, such as
building seawalls, may be easier to muster than support for draconian
measures to curb energy consumption. No powerful vested interests
are threatened by such projects, and entrepreneurs will emerge who
stand to benefit. Furthermore, the building of a new seawall reminds
people that their community has recognized the need to confront the
other challenges of climate change.

Some environmentalists fear that an emphasis on mitigation would
be a distraction and could lead people to minimize the real threats
posed by climate change. We think their fears are misplaced. Public
support for measures to reduce the likelihood and costs of potential
consequences of climate change can be a foot-in-the door tactic that
encourages support for other measures and discourages denial and
rationalization. As we noted in chapter 2, small actions that signal and
reinforce a willingness to act in accord with personal values can pave
the way for more difficult and consequential actions down the road.
Such actions in turn can influence what people expect and demand of
their neighbors.

This brings us to what is needed most, and also to the very heart
of social psychology. What is essential for the implementation of environmentally sound policies is a dramatic change in societal norms

---

* Such programs could include requiring or subsidizing the installation of usage meters that make it clear exactly how much energy is being used at a given time or over
a given period, and tell residents how their usage compares to that of their neighbors
or the standards adopted by their communities. Devices that automatically regulate
thermostats in response to input about what days and what times of day the home is
generally empty or occupied would also be useful.

and priorities. Our society, and ultimately the whole world, needs a major shift in what people think is good and virtuous, in what they deem worth sacrificing for, and what they believe is worth subsidizing with tax dollars. A shift is also needed in what is regarded as indefensible rather than merely regrettable, and in what is considered as not only wrong but beyond the pale. It is not necessary to convince everyone to become a fervent advocate of wiser environmental policies. It would be sufficient to create a social environment wherein even those who would prefer to put off changes that might be burdensome nevertheless tolerate those changes because they are seen as something that is normative—something that good citizens "just do."

Communities, states, and nations will be better off in the future if all concerned shoulder their share of the burden rather than leave the costs and sacrifices to others. In a sense, we would all benefit if we all treated the climate change problem as if it were something akin to a Community game rather than a Wall Street game (as described in chapter 3), and if everyone assumes that others will fulfill the obligations of the community rather than pursue individual self-interest. *That sounds fine,* you may be thinking, *but how do we achieve such a change in outlook and norms?* There is no magic bullet here. If one were at hand, the problem would not be the tougher one we allude to in our chapter title. But we can offer some suggestions.

Overcoming Barriers by Shifting Norms

Some strategies for accomplishing the required shift in norms, such as celebrating individuals, industries, communities, and nations that take leading roles in the struggle against climate change, are obvious. A related but less obvious strategy would be to employ highly visible and memorable ways to stigmatize the worst offenders and foot draggers. A "wall of shame" in every major city, or even virtual walls on the internet, might be a start in this direction. Engraved for posterity on these walls could be the unreasonable and bound-to-be discredited assurances of the best-known and most influential climate change deniers. Such an initiative would discourage politicians and other public figures, particularly those whose public words are not in accord with their private beliefs, from pronouncements that could tarnish their reputation for generations.

Educators at the K–12 level can play an important role here (as, of course, can universities). Denial and rationalization are less likely when we receive unwelcome information when we are young, before we form political allegiances and before we develop economic interests and entrenched habits that make us feel the need to rationalize. Bringing about a change in norms will be a tough slog at first because of the power of entrenched economic and political stakeholders we noted earlier. But such shifts in norms do take place, and once the ball gets rolling, momentum builds and remarkable change can occur quite quickly.

In the second half of the twentieth century, for example, wars between Western European powers that had been going on for centuries ended abruptly and now seem unthinkable. In the lifetimes of the two of us, the United States has changed from a country in which it was regarded as a major step forward to have a single African American actress play a regular, nonstereotypical TV role (a nurse in a doctor's office) in a network situation comedy,* to a country that twice elected an African American president. During the lives of our children, we have seen the rights of same-sex couples to marry go from something that even many gay rights activists were reluctant to advocate lest it scare off tepid supporters, to something that the most conservative U.S. Supreme Court in living memory has endorsed in recognition of a huge change in public opinion.

The change in norms regulating reproductive behavior around

---

* The show, *Julia*, starring Diahann Carroll, ran for eighty-six episodes from September 1968 to March 1971.

the globe offers another hopeful example. In 1970, no countries in Europe had an overall fertility rate under 1.7. By 2000, more than twenty-five European countries had a rate that low. Similar drops in fertility rates have taken place in the developing world as well—India from almost 6.0 in the 1950s to a near-replacement level of 2.6 today and Brazil from 6.3 in 1960 to 2.3 just four decades later.[9]

The striking change in social norms surrounding smoking in the United States may be particularly instructive not only with regard to the speed with which the norms themselves changed, but with respect to the widespread associations to smoking and smokers that accompanied those changes. Within the span of a few decades, smoking changed from something associated with being grown-up, cool, sophisticated, and even sexy to a behavior that, at least in middle-class circles and among the young and the educated, is stigmatized as something dirty and a sign of weakness and poor judgment. This took place despite a campaign by the tobacco industry that was even better organized and more richly funded than the current climate change denial effort.

The existence of a salient "evil" enemy like the tobacco industry (which played the part of villain particularly well) no doubt made it easier to enact restrictions, introduce punitive taxes on smokers, and ban cigarette advertising on television. Education in the schools about health risks also played a role. Yet it seems that the real driving force, much as it has been with changing attitudes and behavior regarding racism and the acceptance of same-sex couples, was the influence of the younger generation on the older one rather than vice versa.

A similar intergenerational process could bring about rapid change in views about the legitimacy of unwise energy use, indiscriminate carbon dioxide emissions, and other environmentally damaging behavior. In other words, if you want to be the wisest person in the room when it comes to discussions of climate change, it may be best to listen to what the youngest in the room has to say.

Virtuous Cycles of Behavior
and Belief Change

The two problems we've discussed in this and the previous chapter are very different, but they have one important thing in common: Vicious cycles in both cases need to be broken and replaced by virtuous ones. In the previous chapter, we described how this can work for education—how feelings of inclusion or self-affirmation can change a student's expectations, which makes studying seem a more promising enterprise, which leads in turn to improved performance and to further change in the student's (and teachers') expectations, and so on.

In the case of climate change, this means that the vicious cycle of inertia, rationalization, and despair engendered by economic pressures and the efforts of powerful industries needs to be broken. Educational efforts are required to make it difficult for the public, especially the young, to engage in denial when confronted with the scientific facts. At the same time, it is important to instill in the public a sense of personal and collective efficacy about the ability to produce change. Beyond confronting denial, it will be increasingly important to discourage rationalizations that justify inaction and to refute claims that it is impossible to take steps great enough to make a real difference. Most important, if we are to meet the challenge of climate change, we must alter what is thought to be the duty of solid members of the community, whether it be the community of individuals, the corporate community, or the global community.

When it comes to replacing vicious cycles with virtuous ones, the lessons offered in the earlier chapters of this book should be kept in mind. Gentle nudges like those discussed in chapters 2, 3, and 4 (e.g., changes in situational pressures and constraints, well-chosen default options, highly visible signals of community norms, strategic priming

of positive versus negative associations) are more likely to be fruitful than more heavy-handed tactics. These psych-wise measures, and
the changes in perceived norms they can bring about, could lead to
political activism by the few, and a willingness to accept reasonable
changes in daily life by the many who simply (even if sometimes re-
luctantly) accept the burdens of good citizenship. An appreciation of
naïve realism (chapter 1) and the biases that distort our judgments
and decisions (chapter 5) can make us more tolerant of those who fail
to see the light on climate change and spur us to craft change efforts
that are more sophisticated and psych-wise.

   What may ultimately be necessary is the creation of a social movement of the sort that has on past occasions transformed the world—
a movement like the ones that launched both Christianity and Islam,
or the one that transformed monarchies to democracies, or the one
that ended slavery, or the one that is now empowering women across
the globe. There is no set formula for creating such a movement,
but both history and research tell us how rapid and decisive change
can be once a tipping point is reached.[10] In the meantime, our more
modest hope is that this chapter will make you a more informed and
more persuasive participant in the inevitable social debates to come.
In short, we hope we have given you a start toward joining the wisest
environmentalists in the room.

Epilogue

When Nelson Mandela became president of South Africa on May 10, 1994, his new government faced countless challenges. He and many of his African National Congress colleagues had spent considerable time in prison thinking about how to govern a post-apartheid South Africa. But all the planning in the world is no substitute for the experience of actually running a government. Among the challenges were how to deal with the resentments and aspirations of the newly liberated black majority as well as the fears and potential for violent action on the part of the deposed white minority.

Indeed, the biggest threat facing Mandela and his new government was that of Afrikaner counterrevolution. In the run-up to the elections, white extremists detonated several bombs in public areas, killing twenty-one people and injuring many more. There was talk of a coup in the armed forces. White resistance parties of all sorts had formed. The Afrikaner Resistance Movement was the most prominent, but there was also the Boer Republican Army, Boere Kommando, the White Resistance Movement, the White Wolves, and the Order of Death. The membership of these groups consisted of the same sort of individuals who greeted Mandela's release from prison with banners reading, "Mandela Go Home, to Prison" and "Hang Mandela."

It took all of Mandela's considerable stock of wisdom to head off the very real threat of a catastrophic civil war. One of the many tactics he used to defuse the tension and division in the country sounds like the stuff of Hollywood. Indeed, it *was* the stuff of Hollywood. It was the tactic depicted (with much more fidelity to what actually happened than in most Hollywood fare) in the film *Invictus*.

To assuage the fears of the white minority, Mandela decided to embrace the national rugby team, the Springboks.[1] Widely popular with Afrikaners, to most blacks the Springboks were a reminder of the oppressive apartheid system, a reminder as resonant as the old South African flag that had recently been replaced. As one ANC member put it, "I was a loyal member of the ANC, a believer in the philosophy of nonracialism, and an admirer of Mandela. . . . But the Springboks, that Springbok emblem those people took such pride in: I hated it. It remained for me a potent and loathsome symbol of apartheid."

Nevertheless, Mandela pressed on. He lobbied for South Africa to host rugby's World Cup the following year. To drum up support for the event, a canny public relations person came up with a slogan for South Africa's mission in the tournament: "One team, one country." But as the games began, the slogan felt hollow to many. It seemed, instead, more like two countries—one that passionately wanted the Springboks to win and one that even rooted for the other team.

But slowly, as the Springboks continued to win, beating first Australia, then Romania, then Canada, and then squeaking by France in the semifinals, something had changed. When the Springbok players, all but one of them white, appeared anywhere in public, they were enthusiastically cheered on not just by Afrikaners and other white South Africans, but by blacks as well. Then it was on to the finals and a confrontation with the New Zealand All-Blacks, universally regarded as one of the best rugby squads ever put together (this being the stuff of Hollywood, after all).

On the day of the championship game, the two teams gathered in Johannesburg's Ellis Park stadium in front of sixty-five thousand fans who were beside themselves with excitement. Five minutes before game time, after all sixty-five thousand had been led in a rousing version of an old Zulu song, "Shosholoza," Mandela walked into the stadium. He was wearing a Springboks jersey, the very symbol of apartheid that so many in the country had hated. The crowd, over-whelmingly Afrikaner, went wild. A deafening chant of "Nel-son! Nel-son!" arose from the stands. The whole country, those in the stadium and those at home or in bars watching on TV or listening to the radio, were united by a common cause. As the Springboks manager, Morne du Plessis, described it, "This crowd of white people, of Afrikaners, as one man, as one nation, they were chanting, 'Nel-son! Nel-son! Nel-son!' over and over, and well, it was just . . . a moment of magic, a moment of wonder. It was the moment I realized that there really was a chance this country could work. This man was showing that he could forgive, totally, and now they—white South Africa, rugby white South Africa—they showed in that response to him that they too wanted to give back."

Completing the Hollywood script, the Springboks went on to win the thrilling, hard-fought game—the first time in the history of the World Cup that the final game went into overtime—to capture the trophy for the newly democratic, unified country.

Mandela's stance toward the Springboks reflected all five elements of wisdom we identified in the first half of this book.

First and foremost, Mandela was able to take a broad view of the challenges before him, somehow avoiding the tunnel vision that would have influenced the actions of almost anyone else elected to lead a truly democratic South Africa. After decades of the cruelties of apartheid and after twenty-seven years in prison, it would hardly have been shocking if he had focused on redressing economic and political imbalances, giving little attention to the hopes and fears of the white minority and how those hopes and fears might influence the future success of the country. Time and again in the aftermath of political revolutions, the world has witnessed new leaders focused on their own sect's interests at the expense of the broader interests of the country—Iraq's Nouri Al-Maliki, Egypt's Mohamed Morsi, and

Mandela's nearby counterpart, Zimbabwe's Robert Mugabe, are but a few examples. Somehow Mandela was able to maintain a wider view.

Mandela's treatment of the Springboks also reflected a savvy understanding of the primacy of behavior. He didn't spend a great deal of time cajoling his ANC comrades to support the Springboks. He didn't try terribly hard to convince black South Africans that they should embrace the sport of rugby. Instead, he leveraged his credibility: He cheered for the Springboks in the World Cup, and others followed. He knew that what might start out as tepid, even resentful, attention to the games would become something else entirely as the Springboks competed under the new South African flag. Although the Springboks might initially be seen by black South Africans as *their* team, they would come to be seen, especially if the team began to win, as *our* team. This is what Mandela meant when he said, "Sport has the power to change the world. It has the power to inspire, the power to unite people that little else has."

This calculated transformation of *their* team into *our* team also speaks to Mandela's intuitive understanding that the significance of any action lies not in its objective consequences, but in how the action and its consequences are interpreted and understood. Mandela's stance toward the Springboks served as a powerful symbol to his countrymen of what the new South Africa was all about. It wasn't about score settling. It was about moving forward as a unified country. But his audience was not just the black South Africans, who had every right to be looking to redress past injustice. His actions spoke to Afrikaners as well. By allowing them to maintain their link to their beloved Springboks and creating an environment in which they acted as they normally did on game days, he fostered the sense that there might be less to fear about what the future held for them in the new South Africa.

A situationist perspective on Mandela's approach to the Springboks is intertwined, as it so often is, with construal and the primacy of behavior. Again, Mandela did not argue or plead or try terribly hard to convince. But his stature was such that it would be very difficult for anyone to rail against the team after he embraced it. His very actions created a powerful barrier to rejection and dissent. Then, having taken a few steps in his direction, however begrudgingly, the meaning of those steps changed from movement away from the aspirations of their community to movement toward a promising future. That in turn made it easier and easier to take additional steps toward that future. And being in a stadium with thousands standing and cheering when the flag is raised—or sitting around a radio or television as your neighbors cheer—exerts a powerful force that's hard to resist. It is a force powerful enough to give truth to Springbok captain François Pienaar's comment, when asked what it was like to have the support of sixty-three thousand fans: "We didn't have the support of 63,000 South Africans today. We had the support of 42 million."

Finally, and perhaps most important, Mandela's actions reflected an ability to shake off the limitations of naïve realism. Mandela was able to look at the situation facing the new South Africa not just from the perspective of the ANC and the black majority in the country who had every reason to hate what the Springboks represented. He was also able to see what the new South Africa looked like to the white minority—not just the former political elites, but ordinary Afrikaners who enjoyed their weekends off, their barbecues, and, yes, their country's rugby team.

The actions he took, large and small, offered the Afrikaners a reassuring vision of what the new world they were entering might be like. By creating an environment in which they acted as they normally did, which included going to the stadium, watching the game on television, talking about the game the next week at work—he offered white South Africans a vision of the future that was bearable and even quite normal in terms of the quality of their personal lives (even if not in how the state would be run). Mandela's actions, in other words, reflected a wise understanding of how others—other people very different from himself—would react to events unfolding around them.

Few of us can hope to be as wise, or as brave, as Nelson Mandela, no matter what we do, what books we read, or what lessons we learn. Mandela, furthermore, drew on many more components of wisdom—many of them hard earned—than the five we have included in this book.

But psychology has a lot to teach all of us about wisdom. The five components discussed here represent a lot of what psychology has to offer. If they are taken to heart and applied to daily life, we are confident they will make you wiser and more effective as a parent, an employee or employer, a compassionate friend and trusted advisor, and perhaps most important, a global citizen who must deal with the inevitability of conflict and the possibility of reconciliation.

Acknowledgments

T om would like to thank Karen Dashiff Gilovich for nearly always being the wisest one in any room she's in. He would also like to acknowledge, gratefully, that living with Karen, Ilana, and Rebecca Dashiff Gilovich has given him the lion's share of whatever measure of wisdom—and happiness—he can claim.

Lee would like to thank his wife of fifty years, Judy, and his children, Josh, Tim, Becca, and Katie. Through both good and challenging times, their loving-kindness and patience have made possible and enriched the privileged life he leads. He also wants to acknowledge the very useful feedback provided by Sarah Spinks (Judy's sister) in the early stages of this book.

Together, we owe a great debt to Dick Nisbett, for his continuing friendship and for the example he has set in showing how passionate involvement with ideas can enrich our work and our lives. It is unlikely that we would have written *The Wisest One in the Room* without his inspiration, and it is to Dick that we dedicate this book. We owe a similar lifetime debt to Mark Lepper. He consistently is the wisest psychologist in the room, and also the kindest and most generous.

We would like to thank Katinka Matson of Brockman, Inc., for her steady hand in getting us connected to Free Press and Emily Graff for her skilled and equally steady hand in seeing the book through the publication process. We are grateful to Gary Belsky, Jesse Reynolds, and Tim Ross for commenting on drafts of several chapters. We are also indebted to Byron Bland, Lee's good friend and long-time partner in real-world conflict resolution and relationship building efforts in

Northern Ireland and the Middle East. His insight and efforts played a large role in providing whatever wisdom is to be found in chapter 7. We are similarly indebted to Geoff Cohen and Greg Walton for their generosity and patience as we tried to do justice to their work in chapter 8. We also are pleased to acknowledge the efforts of Rebecca Dashiff Gilovich, who brought fresh eyes and very useful input in the comments she offered on a draft of the whole book.

Finally, we acknowledge with thanks the insights we've gained over the years from working with and/or talking to the following valued friends and colleagues: Ted Alper, Elliot Aronson, Ken Arrow, Daryl and Sandy Bem, Paul Brest, Allen Calvin, Laura Carstensen, Herb Clark, Neil Docherty, David Dunning, Carol Dweck, Jennifer Eberhardt, Paul Ehrlich, Melissa Ferguson, Bob Frank, Dale Griffin, Al Hastorf, David Holloway, Danny Kahneman, Dacher Keltner, Varda Liberman, Sonja Lyubomirsky, Avishai Margalit, Hazel Markus, Bob Mnookin, Benoit Monin, David Pizarro, Brenna Powell, Emily Pronin, Don Redelmeir, Dennis Regan, Claude Steele, Richard Thaler, Ewart Thomas, Jeanne Tsai, Amos Tversky, Bob Vallone, Andrew Ward, Alan Weiner, David Wenner, Vivian Zayas, and Phil Zimbardo.

Notes

PART ONE: PILLARS OF WISDOM

Preface

1. Eisenhower and the lead-up to D-Day. Smith, J. E. (2012). *Eisenhower in War and Peace*. New York: Random House.

1: The Objectivity Illusion

1. Phonemic restoration effect. Samuel, A. G. (1991). A further examination of attentional effect in the phonemic restoration illusion, *Quarterly Journal of Experimental Psychology, 43*, 679–99. Warren, R. (1970). Perceptual restoration of missing speech sounds. *Science, 167*, 392–93. Warren, R. (1984). Perceptual restoration of obliterated sounds. *Psychological Bulletin, 96*, 371–83.
2. They saw a protest. Kahan, D.M., Hoffman, D.A., Braman, D., Evans, D., & Rachlinski, J.J. (2012). They saw a protest: Cognitive illiberalism and the speech-conduct distinction. *Stanford Law Review, 64*, 851–906.
3. They saw a game. Hastorf, A. H., & Cantril, H. (1954). They saw a game: A case study. *Journal of Abnormal and Social Psychology, 49(1)*, 129–34.
4. Mark McGwire quote. Brown, D. (2010, January 12). A tearful deconstruction of the Mark McGwire interview. Yahoo! Sports. Retrieved from http://sports.yahoo.com/mlb/blog/big_league_stew/post/A-tearful -deconstruction-of-the-Mark-McGwire-int?urn=mlb,213019.
5. False consensus. Ross, L., Greene, D., & House, P. (1977). The false consensus effect: An egocentric bias in social perception and attribution processes. *Journal of Experimental Social Psychology, 13*, 279–301.
6. Italian versus French cinema. Ross, Greene, & House. (1977).
7. Perceived commonness of transgressions. Alicke, M. D. (1993). Egocentric standards of conduct evaluation. *Basic and Applied Social Psychology, 14*, 171–92.
8. Bias in assumed political consensus. Granberg, D., & Brent, E. (1983). When prophecy bends: The preference-expectation link in U.S. presidential elections, 1952–80. *Journal of Personality and Social Psychology, 45*, 477–91.

273

9. Perceptions of nonvoters' leanings: Koudenburg, N., Postmes, T., & Gordijn, E. H. (2011). If they were to vote, they would vote for us. *Psychological Science, 22,* 1506–10.
10. Object of judgment: Asch, S. E. (1948). The doctrine of suggestion, prestige and imitation in social psychology. *Psychological Review, 55,* 250–76.
11. Construal and the false consensus effect: Gilovich, T. (1990). Differential construal and the false consensus effect. *Journal of Personality and Social Psychology, 59,* 623–34.
12. Cheney quote. Cited in Danner, M. (2015, February 8). No exit. *New York Times Book Review,* p. 1.
13. "I do not know a single person . . ." Stone, G. R. (2001). From: Equal Protection? The Supreme Court's Decision in *Bush v. Gore.* A version of this article was delivered at the Federal Bar Association in Chicago on May 23, 2001. Copyright 2001. The University of Chicago.
14. Thomas's view of the matter. Balkin, J. M. (2001). *Bush v. Gore* and the boundary between law and politics. *Yale Law Journal, 110,* 1407.
15. Scalia quote. Scalia: "Get over it." (2012). *The Daily Beast.* Retrieved from http://www.thedailybeast.com/cheats/2012/07/18/scalia-get-over-it.html.
16. Bias blindspot. Pronin, E., Lin, D. Y., & Ross, L. (2002). The bias blind spot: Perceptions of bias in self versus others. *Personality and Social Psychology Bulletin, 28,* 369–81.
17. Rational vs. biasing influences. Pronin, E., Gilovich, T., & Ross, L. (2004). Objectivity in the Eye of the Beholder: Divergent Perceptions of Bias in Self versus Others. *Psychological Review, 111,* 781–99.
18. Franklin quote. *The Founders' Constitution,* Vol. 4, Art. 7, Document 3. Retrieved from http://press-pubs.uchicago.edu/founders/documents/a7s3.html. Farrand, M. (Ed.). (1937). *The records of the Federal Convention of 1787* (Rev. ed.). New Haven, CT: Yale University Press.
19. Berlin quote. Berlin, I. (1981). Notes on prejudice. http://www.nybooks.com/articles/archives/2001/oct/18/notes-on-prejudice/.
20. Bias versus special insight. Ehrlinger, J., Gilovich, T., & Ross, L. (2005). Peering into the bias blindspot: People's assessments of bias in themselves and others. *Personality and Social Psychology Bulletin, 31,* 680–92.
21. Buck on World Series criticism. People think I'm biased no matter who's in the World Series (2011, October 18). Groller's Corner. Retrieved from http://blogs.mcall.com/groller/2011/10/buck-on-world-series-criticism-people-think-im-biased-no-matter-whos-in-the-world-series.html.
22. More from Joe Buck. Burns, A. (2012). Joe Buck knows that people think he is biased for the Cardinals, doesn't care. Retrieved from http://withleather.uproxx.com/2012/10/joe-buck-knows-that-people-think-he-is-biased-for-the-cardinals-doesnt-care#ixzz2Fe4fDNbE.

23. Perceptions of media bias. Vallone, R. P., Ross, L., & Lepper, M. R. (1985). The hostile media phenomenon: Biased perception and perceptions of media bias in coverage of the "Beirut Massacre." *Journal of Personality and Social Psychology, 49,* 577–85.
24. Their tastes may not be the same. Shaw, G. B. (1948). *Man and superman.* New York: Dodd, Mead.
25. Wisdom of crowds. Lorge, I., Fox, D., Davitz, J., & Brenner, M. (1958). A survey of studies contrasting the quality of group performance and individual performance, 1920–1957. *Psychological Bulletin, 55*(6), 337–72.
26. Wisdom of dyads. Liberman, V., Minson, J. A., Bryan, C. J., & Ross, L. (2011). Naïve realism and capturing the "wisdom of dyads." *Journal of Experimental Social Psychology, 48,* 507–12. Minson, J., Liberman, V., & Ross, L. (2011). Two to tango: The effect of collaborative experience and disagreement on dyadic judgment. *Personality and Social Psychology Bulletin, 37,* 1325–38. Jacobson, J., Dobbs-Marsh, J., Liberman, V., & Minson, J. A. (2011). Predicting civil jury verdicts: How attorneys use (and mis-use) a second opinion. *Journal of Empirical Legal Studies, 8,* 99–119. See also Soll, J. B., & Larrick, R. P. (2009). Strategies for revising judgment. *Journal of Experimental Psychology: Learning, Memory and Cognition, 35,* 780–805. Yaniv, I. (2004). The benefit of additional opinions. *Current Directions in Psychological Science, 13*(2), 75–78.

2: The Push and Pull of Situations

1. "Drive Safely" study. Freedman, J. L., & Fraser, S. C. (1966). Compliance without pressure: The foot-in-the-door technique. *Journal of Personality and Social Psychology, 4,* 196–202.
2. Seminarians. Darley, J. M., & Batson, C. D. (1973). From Jerusalem to Jericho: A study of situational and dispositional variables in helping behavior. *Journal of Personality and Social Psychology, 27,* 100–119.
3. War Bonds. Cartwright, D. (1949). Some principles of mass persuasion: Selected findings of research on the sale of United States War Bonds. *Human Relations, 2,* 253–67.
4. Defaults and organ donation. Johnson, E. J., & Goldstein, D. Do defaults save lives? *Science, 302,* 1338–1339. Figure reprinted with permission from AAAS.
5. Defaults in 401k plans. Beshears, J., Choi, J. J., Laibson, D., & Madrian, B. (2008). The importance of default options for retirement saving outcomes: Evidence from the USA. In S. J. Kay & T. Sinha (eds.), *Lessons from Pension Reform in the Americas* (pp. 59–87). New York: Oxford University Press.
6. Lewin history. Marrow, A. F. (1969). *The Practical Theorist: The Life and Work of Kurt Lewin.* New York: Basic Books.

7. Tax evasion in Greece. Artavanis, N., Morse, A., & Tsoutsoura, M. (2012). *Tax evasion across industries: Soft credit evidence from Greece.* Unpublished manuscript. Lagarde quote: Greeks observe preelection ritual of tax dodging. (2012, June 6). *Los Angeles Times.*

8. Tax evasion in the United States. U.S. Department of Treasury. (2009). *Update on reducing the federal tax gap and improving voluntary compliance.* Washington, DC: Author. Retrieved from http://www.irs.gov/pub/newsroom/tax_gap_report_-final_version.pdf.

9. Signature location. Shu, L., Mazar, N., Gino, F., Ariely, D., & Bazerman, M. (2012). Signing at the beginning makes ethics salient and decreases dishonest self-reports in comparison to signing at the end. *Proceedings of the National Academy of Sciences, 109*(38), 15197–200.

10. Obesity statistics. Centers for Disease Control. (2010). *National obesity trends.* Retrieved from Shalikashvili, J. M. (2010, April 30). The new national security threat: Obesity. *Washington Post,* p. A19. http://www.washingtonpost.com/wp-dyn/content/article/2010/04/29/AR2010042903669.html.

11. Dieting stats. Dieting on a budget. Consumer Reports; Nibbles: Survey shows 41 percent of Americans are dieting. Calorielab, retrieved 2012-08-3. http://calorielab.com/news/2007/05/08/nibbles-survey-shows-41-percent-of-americans-are-dieting/.

12. Altering the eating environment. Wansink, B. (2006). *Mindless eating: Why we eat more than we think.* New York: Bantam.

13. Plate sizes. Van Ittersum, K., & Wansink, B. (2012). Plate size and color suggestibility: The Delboeuf illusion's bias on serving and eating behavior. *Journal of Consumer Research, 39,* 215–28.

14. Milgram's studies. Milgram, S. (1974). *Obedience to authority.* New York: Harper.

15. Quiz study with questioners and answerers. Ross, L., Amabile, T. M., & Steinmetz, J. L. (1977). Social roles, social control, and biases in social-perception processes. *Journal of Personality and Social Psychology, 35,* 485–94.

16. Essentialism. Cimpian, A., & Salomon, E. (2014 in press). The inherence heuristic: An intuitive means of making sense of the world, and a potential precursor to psychological essentialism. *Behavioral and Brain Sciences, 37,* 461–527.

17. Reflexive even. Gilbert, D. T. (1991). How mental systems believe. *American Psychologist, 46,* 107–19. Gilbert, D. T. (2006). *Stumbling on happiness.* New York: Knopf.

18. Hurricane Katrina. Stephens, N. M., Hamedani, M. G., Markus, H. R., Bergsieker, H. B., & Eloul, L. (2009). Why did they "choose" to stay? Perspectives of Hurricane Katrina observers and survivors. *Psychological Science, 20,*

878–86. Shapiro, I., & Sherman, A. (2005). *Essential facts about the victims of Hurricane Katrina.* Washington, DC: Center for Budget and Policy Priorities.

19. The poor. Mullainathan, S., & Shafir, E. (2013). *Scarcity: Why having too little means so much.* New York: Times Books.

20. Jefferson. Finkelman, P. (2012, November 30). The monster of Monticello. *New York Times.*

21. Walter Mischel's impact. Mischel, W. (1968). Personality and Assessment. New York: Wiley. Mischel, W. (2004). Toward an integrative science of the person. *Annual Review of Psychology, 55,* 1–22. Mischel, W. (2014). *The Marshmellow Test.* New York: Little-Brown.

3: The Name of the Game

1. Roosevelt signing. http://www.ssa.gov/history/.

2. Roosevelt on the Beveridge plan. Perkins, F. (1946). *The Roosevelt I Knew.* New York: Viking Press.

3. Wall Street or Community Game. Liberman, V., Samuels, S. M., & Ross, L. (2002). The name of the game: Predictive power of reputations vs. situational labels in determining prisoner's dilemma game moves. *Personality and Social Psychology Bulletin, 30,* 1175–85. See also Kay, A. C., & Ross, L. (2003). The perceptual push: The interplay of implicit cues and explicit situational construal in the prisoner's dilemma. *Journal of Experimental Social Psychology, 39,* 634–643.

4. Construal of organ donation. Davidai, S., Gilovich, T., & Ross, L. D. (2012). The meaning of defaults for potential organ donors. *Proceedings of the National Academy of Sciences, 109*(38), 15201–205.

5. Tuition price and number of applications. Glater, J. D., & Finder, A. (2006, December 12). In tuition game, popularity rises with price. *New York Times.*

6. Motivated perception. Balcetis, E., & Dunning, D. (2006). See what you want to see: The impact of motivational states on visual perception. *Journal of Personality and Social Psychology, 91,* 612–25.

7. Above average effects. Alicke, M. D., Klotz, M. L., Breitenbecher, D. L., Yurak, T.J., & Vredenburg, D. S. (1995). Personal contact, individuation, and the better-than-average effect. *Journal of Personality and Social Psychology, 68*(5), 804–25. Brown, J. D. (1986). Evaluations of self and others: Self-enhancement biases in social judgments. *Social Cognition, 4*(4), 353–76. Dunning, D., Meyerowitz, J. A., & Holzberg, A. D. (1989). Ambiguity and self-evaluation: The role of idiosyncratic trait definitions in self-serving assessments of ability. *Journal of Personality and Social Psychology, 57*(6), 1082–90. Svenson, O. (1981). Are we all less risky and more skillful than

our fellow drivers? *Acta Psychologica, 47*(2), 143–48. Suls, J., Lemos, K., & H. L. Stewart (2002). Self-esteem, construal, and comparisons with the self, friends and peers. *Journal of Personality and Social Psychology, 82*(2), 252–61.

8. Better than average drivers. Svenson, O. (1981). Are we all less risky and more skillful than our fellow drivers? *Acta Psychologica, 47*(2), 143–48.

9. Motivated self-enhancement. Brown, J. D. (2011). Understanding the better-than-average effect: Motives (still) matter. *Personality and Social Psychology Bulletin, 38,* 209–219. Beauregard, K. S., & Dunning, D. (2001). Defining self worth: Trait self-esteem moderates the use of self-serving trait definitions in social judgment. *Motivation and Emotion, 25,* 135–62.

10. Best dog on the block. Schelling, T. C. (1978). *Micromotives and macrobehavior.* New York: Norton, pp. 64–65.

11. Better than average effects on wide versus narrow traits. Dunning, D., Meyerowitz, J. A., & Holzberg, A. D. (1989). Ambiguity and self-evaluation: The role of idiosyncratic trait definitions in self-serving assessments of ability. *Journal of Personality and Social Psychology, 57*(6), 1082–90.

12. Distance from events. Trope, Y., & Liberman, N. (2003). Temporal construal. *Psychological Review 110,* 403–21. Trope, Y., & Liberman, N. (2010). Construal-level theory of psychological distance. *Psychological Review, 117,* 440–63.

13. Fat vs. lean. Levin, I. P., & Gaeth, G. J. (1988). Framing of attribute information before and after consuming the product. *Journal of Consumer Research, 15,* 374–78.

14. 95% success versus 5% failure. Linville, P. W., Fischer, G. W., & Fischhoff, B. (1993). AIDS risk perceptions and decision biases. In J. B. Pryor & G. D. Reeder (eds.), *The social psychology of HIV infection* (pp. 5–38). Mahwah, NJ: Erlbaum.

15. Framing income inequality. Chow, R. M., & Galak, J. (2012). The effect of income inequality frames on support for redistributive tax policies. *Psychological Science, 23,* 1467–69. See also Lowery, B. S., Chow, R. M., & Crosby, J. R. (2009). Taking from those that have more and giving to those that have less: How inequity frames affect corrections for inequity. *Journal of Experimental Social Psychology, 45,* 375–78.

16. Lives saved vs. lives lost. Tverksy, A., & Kahneman, D. (1986). Rational choice and the framing of decisions. *Journal of Business, 59,* 251–78.

17. Framing early or later retirement. Fetherstonhaugh, D., & Ross, L. (1999). Framing effects and income flow preferences in decisions about social security. In H. J. Aaron (ed.), *Behavioral dimensions of retirement economics* (pp. 187–209). Washington DC: Brookings Institution Press and Russell Sage Foundation.

18. Medical outcome statistics framed in terms of survival vs. mortality rates. McNeil, B. J., Pauker, S. G., Sox, H. C., & Tversky, A. (1982). On the elicitation of preferences for alternative therapies. *New England Journal of Medicine, 306,* 1259–62.

19. Buy more if stronger currency. Wertenbroch, K., Soman, D., & Chattopadhyay, A. (2007). On the perceived value of money: The reference dependence of currency numerosity effects. *Journal of Consumer Research, 34*, 1–10.
20. Skewed judgments of risk. Yamagishi, K. (1997). When a 12.86% mortality is more dangerous than 24.14%: Implications for risk communication. *Applied Cognitive Psychology, 11*, 495–506.
21. A&W's new burger. Green, E. (2014, July 23). Why do Americans stink at math? *New York Times Magazine*. Retrieved from http://www.nytimes.com/2014/07/27/magazine/why-do-americans-stink-at-math.html?_r=0.
22. Choosing vs. rejecting. Shafir, E. (1993). Choosing versus rejecting: Why some options are both better and worse than others. *Memory and Cognition, 21*, 546–56.

4: The Primacy of Behavior

1. Influence of behavior on feelings. Niedenthal, P. M., Barsalou, L., Winkielman, P., Krauth-Gruber, S., & Ric, F. (2005). Embodiment in attitudes, social perception, and emotion. *Personality and Social Psychology Review, 9*, 184–211. Winkielman, P., Niedenthal, P., & Oberman, L. (2008). The embodied emotional mind. In G. R. Semin & E. R. Smith (eds.) *Embodied grounding: Social, cognitive, affective, and neuroscientific approaches* (pp. 263–88). New York: Cambridge University Press.
2. James's view of emotion. James, W. (1890). *Principles of Psychology* (Vol. 2). New York: Holt.
3. Emotional labeling. Schachter, S., & Singer, J. E. (1962). Cognitive, social and psychological determinants of emotion. *Psychological Review, 69*, 379–99.
4. Pen and cartoon study. Strack, F., Martin, L. L., & Stepper, S. (1988). Inhibiting and facilitating conditions of the human smile: A nonobtrusive test of the facial feedback hypothesis. *Journal of Personality and Social Psychology, 54*, 768–77.
5. Misattribution at the gym. Zillmann, D. (1983). Transfer of excitation in emotional behavior. In J. T. Cacioppo & R. E. Petty (eds.), *Social psychophysiology: A sourcebook*. New York: Guilford Press.
6. Love on a bridge study. Dutton, D. G., & Aron, A. P. (1974). Some evidence for heightened sexual attraction under conditions of high anxiety. *Journal of Personality and Social Psychology, 30*, 510–17.
7. Effect of head nodding and shaking. Wells, G. L., & Petty, R. E. (1980). The effects of overt head movements on persuasion: Compatibility and incompatibility of responses. *Basic and Applied Social Psychology, 1*, 219–30.
8. Effect of pushing vs. pulling movement. Cacioppo, J. T., Priester, J. R., & Berntson, G. G. (1993). Rudimentary determinants of attitudes. II: Arm

flexion and extension have differential effects on attitudes. *Journal of Personality and Social Psychology, 65,* 5–17.

9. The "finger" study. Chandler, J., & Schwarz, N. (2009). How extending your middle finger affects your perception of others: Learned movements influence concept accessibility. *Journal of Experimental Social Psychology, 45,* 123–28.

10. Room temperature and belief in global warming. Risen, J. L., & Critcher, C. R. (2011). Visceral fit: While in a visceral state, associated states of the world seem more likely. *Journal of Personality and Social Psychology, 100,* 777–93.

11. Ambient temperature and belief in global warming. Li, Y., Johnson, E., & Zaval, L. (2011). Local warming: Daily temperature changes influences belief in global warming. *Psychological Science, 22,* 454–59.

12. Power posing. Carney, D. R., Cuddy, A. J. C., & Yap, A. J. (2010). Power posing: Brief nonverbal displays affect neuroendocrine levels and risk tolerance. *Psychological Science, 21,* 1363–68.

13. Link between attitudes and behavior. Glasman, L. R., & Albarracin, D. (2006). Forming attitudes that predict future behavior: A meta-analysis of the attitude-behavior relation. *Psychological Bulletin, 132,* 778–822. Lapiere, R. T. (1934). Attitudes versus actions. *Social Forces, 13,* 230–37. Wicker, A. W. (1969). Attitudes versus actions: The relationship of verbal and overt behavioral responses to attitude objects. *Journal of Social Issues, 25,* 41–78.

14. Self perception theory. Bem. (1972). Self-perception theory. In L. Berkowitz (ed.), *Advances in experimental social psychology* (Vol. 6, pp. 1–62). New York: Academic Press.

15. Changes in political affiliation. Niemi, G., Katz, R. S., & Newman, D. (1980). Reconstructing past partisanship: The failure of party identification recall questions. *American Journal of Political Science, 24,* 633–51.

16. Attitudes toward busing. Goethals, G. R., & Reckman, R. F. (1973). The perception of consistency in attitudes. *Journal of Experimental Social Psychology, 9,* 491–501.

17. Cognitive dissonance. Festinger, L. (1957). *The theory of cognitive dissonance.* Stanford, CA: Stanford University Press.

18. Post-decision dissonance reduction. Brehm, J. (1956). Post-decision changes in the desirability of alternatives. *Journal of Abnormal and Social Psychology, 52,* 384–89. Sharot, T., Velasquez, C. M., & Dolen, R. J. (2010). Do decisions shape preference? Evidence from blind choice. *Psychological Science, 21,* 1231–35.

19. Dissonance reduction at the race track. Knox, R. E., & Inkster, J. A. (1968). Postdecision dissonance at post-time. *Journal of Personality and Social Psychology, 8,* 319–23.

20. Dissonance reduction and voting. Regan, D. T., & Kilduff, M. (1988). Optimism about elections: Dissonance reduction at the ballot box. *Political Psychology, 9*, 101–7.

21. The downside of keeping your options open. Gilbert, D. T., & Ebert, J. E. J. (2002). Decisions and revisions: The affective forecasting of changeable outcomes. *Journal of Personality and Social Psychology, 82*, 503–14.

22. Lying, dissonance, and dissonance reduction. Festinger, L., & Carlsmith, J. M. (1959). Cognitive consequences of forced compliance. *Journal of Abnormal and Social Psychology, 47*, 382–89.

23. Child raising and dissonance. Eibach, R. P., & Mock, S. E. (2011). Idealizing parenthood to rationalize parental investments. *Psychological Science, 22*, 203–8.

24. The IKEA effect. Norton, M. I, Mochon, D., & Ariely, D. (2012). The IKEA effect: When labor leads to love. *Journal of Consumer Psychology, 22*, 453–60.

25. Sale vs. regular price. Doob, A. N., Carlsmith, J. M., Freedman , J. L., Landauer, T. K., & Tom, S., Jr. (1969). The effect of initial selling price on subsequent sales. *Journal of Personality and Social Psychology, 11*, 345–50.

26. Energy drinks. Shiv, B., Carmon, Z., & Ariely, D. (2005). Placebo effects of marketing actions: Consumers may get what they pay for. *Journal of Marketing Research, 42*, 383–93.

27. Wine tasting. Plassmann, H., O'Doherty, Shiv, B., & Rangel, A. (2008). Marketing actions can modulate neural representations of experienced pleasantness. *Proceedings of the National Academy of Sciences, 105*, 1050–54.

28. Talmud. Tractate Sanhedrin 105 B.

29. Rewards for playing math games. Greene, D., Sternberg, B., & Lepper, M. R. (1976). Overjustification in a token economy. *Journal of Personality and Social Psychology, 34*, 1219–34.

30. Marker study. Lepper, M. R., Greene, D., & Nisbett, R. E. (1973). Undermining children's intrinsic interest with extrinsic reward: A test of the overjustification hypothesis. *Journal of Personality and Social Psychology, 28*, 129–37.

31. Voting versus voter. Bryan, C. J., Walton, G. M., Rogers, T., & Dweck, C. S. (2011). Motivating voter turnout by invoking the self. *Proceedings of the National Academy of Sciences, 108*, 12653–56.

32. Eyes and honesty box contributions. Bateson, M., Nettle, D., & Roberts, G. (2006). Cues of being watched enhance cooperation in a real-world setting. *Biology Letters, 2*, 412–14.

33. Eyes and littering. Ernest-Jones, M., Nettle, D., & Bateson, M. (2011). Effects of eye images on everyday cooperative behavior: A field experiment. *Evolution and Human Behavior, 32*, 172–78.

34. Banality of Evil. Arendt, H. (1963). *Eichmann in Jerusalem: A report on the banality of evil.* New York: Viking Press.

35. Banality of evil thesis overdone? See Cesarani, D. (2006). *Becoming Eich-
    mann: Rethinking the life, crimes and trial of a "desk murderer."* Cambridge,
    MA: Da Capo Press. Goldhagen, D. J. (1996). *Hitler's willing executioners:
    Ordinary Germans and the Holocaust.* New York: Knopf.
36. Unexceptional lives of most low-level perpetrators of the Holocaust. Brown-
    ing, C. R. (1992). *Ordinary men: Reserve Police Battalion 101 and the final
    solution in Poland.* New York: Aaron Asher. Lifton, R. J. (1986). *The Nazi
    doctors: Medical killing and the psychology of genocide.* New York: Basic Books.
37. Quiet Heroes. Stein, A. (1991). *Quiet heroes: True stories of the rescue of the Jews
    by Christians in Nazi-occupied Holland.* New York: New York University Press.

5: Keyholes, Lenses, and Filters

1. Invasion quotes. Chandrasekaran, R. (2007). *Imperial life in the Emerald
   City.* New York: Vintage Books.
2. Occupation quotes. Chandrasekaran. (2007).
3. Seven +/- two. Miller, G. A. (1956). The magical number seven, plus or minus two: Some limits on our capacity for processing information. *Psychological Review, 63,* 81–97.
4. We first heard this way of conceptualizing common errors of judgment from
   University of California economist Matthew Rabin (now at Harvard).
5. "Linda" experiment. Tversky, A., & Kahneman, D. (1983). Extensional versus intuitive reasoning: The conjunction fallacy in probability judgment.
   Psychological Review, 90, 293–315.
6. Read the description. Gould, S. J. (1988). *The streak of streaks.* New York:
   McGraw-Hill.
7. Positive test strategy. Klayman, J., & Ha, Y. W. (1987). Confirmation, disconfir-
   mation, and information in hypothesis testing. *Psychological Review, 94,* 211–22.
8. Testing whether working out before a match helps or hurts tennis players.
   Crocker, J. (1982). Biased questions in judgment of covariation studies. *Personality and Social Psychology Bulletin, 8,* 214–20.
9. Mother of all biases. Lilienfeld, S. (2007). Presentation given at the Harriet
   Elliott Lecture Series, University of North Carolina, Greensboro, NC.
10. East vs. West Germany. Tversky, A. (1977). Features of similarity. *Psycholog-
    ical Review, 84,* 327–52.
11. Choosing vs. rejecting. Shafir, E. (1993). Choosing versus rejecting: Why
    some options are both better and worse than others. *Memory and Cognition,
    21,* 546–56.
12. Enzyme deficiency test: Ditto, P. H., & Lopez, D. F. (1992). Motivated skep-
    ticism: Use of differential decision criteria for preferred and nonpreferred
    conclusions. *Journal of Personality and Social Psychology, 63,* 568–84.

13. Bacon quote. Bacon, F. (1899). *Advancement of learning and the novum organum* (rev. ed.). New York: Colonial Press. (Original work published 1620).

14. Capital punishment study. Lord, C., Ross, L., & Lepper, M. R. (1979). Biased assimilation and attitude polarization: The effects of prior theories on subsequently considered evidence. *Journal of Personality and Social Psychology, 37,* 2098–2109.

15. Consider the opposite. Milkman, K. L., Chugh, D., & Bazerman, M. H. (2009). How can decision making be improved? *Perspectives on Psychological Science, 4,* 379–85.

16. Snapple decision. Finkelstein, S. (2003). *Why smart executives fail.* New York: Portfolio.

17. Rise in canonizations. Zaleski, P. (2006, March). The saints of John Paul II. *First Things.* Retrieved from http://www.firstthings.com/article/2007/01/the-saints-of-john-paul-ii-46.

18. Pre-mortem. Klein, G. (2009). *Streetlights and shadows: Searching for the keys to adaptive decision making.* Cambridge, MA: MIT Press.

19. Know where the exits are. Dawes, R. M. (1988). *Rational choice in an uncertain world.* San Diego: Harcourt.

20. How well do we know what others think of us? Kenny, D. A., & DePaulo, B. M. (1993). Do people know how others view them? An empirical and theoretical account. *Psychological Bulletin, 114,* 145–61. The quote can be found on p. 159 of Kenny, D. A. (1994). *Interpersonal perception: A social relations analysis.* New York: Guilford Press.

21. Knowing our status in a group. Anderson, C., Srivastava, S., Beer, J., Spataro, S. E., & Chatman, J. A. (2006). Knowing your place: Self-perceptions of status in social groups. *Journal of Personality and Social Psychology, 91,* 1094–110.

22. False beliefs and superstitions. Gilovich, T. (1991). *How we know what isn't so.* New York: Free Press. Shermer, M. (1997). *Why people believe weird things.* New York: Holt.

23. Tempting fate. Risen, J. L., & Gilovich, T. (2007). Another look at why people are reluctant to exchange lottery tickets. *Journal of Personality and Social Psychology, 93,* 12–22. Risen, J. L., & Gilovich, T. (2008). Why people are reluctant to tempt fate. *Journal of Personality and Social Psychology, 95,* 293–307. Tykocinski, O. E. (2008). Insurance, risk, and magical thinking. *Personality and Social Psychology Bulletin, 34,* 1346–56. Van Wolferen, J., Inbar, Y., & Zeelenberg, M. (2013). Magical thinking in predictions of negative events: Evidence for tempting fate but not for a protection effect. *Judgment and Decision Making, 8,* 44–53.

24. Seemingly-fulfilled prophecies. Gilovich, T. (1991). *How we know what isn't so.* New York: Free Press.

25. Pluralistic ignorance. Katz, D., & Allport, F. H. (1931). *Student attitudes.* Syracuse, NY: Craftsman. Kuran, T. (1995). *Private truths, public lies: The social consequences of preference falsification.* Cambridge, MA: Harvard University Press. Miller, D. T. (2006). *Social psychology: An invitation.* Belmont, CA: Thomson.

26. Pluralistic ignorance and alcohol on college campuses. Prentice, D. A., & Miller, D. T (1993). Pluralistic ignorance and alcohol use on campus: Some consequences of misperceiving the social norm. *Journal of Personality and Social Psychology, 64,* 243–256. Perkins, H. W., & Berkowitz, A. D. (1986). Perceiving the community norms of alcohol use among students: Some research implications for campus alcohol education programming. *Journal of Addictions, 21,* 15–31.

27. Eliminating pluralistic ignorance about alcohol consumption on college campuses. LaBrie, J. W., Hummen, J. F., Neighbors, C., & Pedersen, E. R. (2008). Live interactive group-specific normative feedback reduces misperceptions and drinking in college students: A randomized cluster trial. *Psychology of Addictive Behaviors, 22,* 141–48.

28. Burnout. Maslach, C. (1982). *Burnout: The cost of caring.* Englewood, Cliffs, NJ: Prentice Hall, p. 11–12. Quoted in Miller, D. T. (2006). *Social psychology: An invitation.* Belmont, CA: Thomson.

29. Groupthink. Janis, I. L. (1972). *Victims of groupthink.* Boston: Houghton Mifflin. Janis, I. L. (1982). *Groupthink: Psychological studies of policy decisions and fiascos* (2nd ed.). Boston: Houghton Mifflin.

30. Incestuous amplification. http://www.cybercollege.com/ia.htm (July 29, 2013).

31. The common knowledge effect. Stasser, G. (1999). The uncertain role of unshared information in collective choice. In L. L. Thompson, J. M. Levine, & D. M. Messick (eds.), *Shared cognition in organizations: The management of knowledge* (pp. 46–69). Mahwah, NJ: Erlbaum. Stasser, G., & Titus, W. (1985). Polling of unshared information in group decision making: Biased information sampling during discussion. *Journal of Personality and Social Psychology, 48,* 1467–18.

32. Overcoming the common knowledge effect. Thompson, L. L. (2000). *Making the team: A guide for managers.* Upper Saddle River, NJ: Prentice-Hall.

PART TWO: WISDOM APPLIED

6: The Happiest One in the Room

1. Zupan quote. Zupan, M. (2006). *Gimp: When life deals you a crappy hand, you can fold—or you can play.* New York: HarperCollins.

2. Well-being among spinal cord injury victims. Hall, K. M., Knudson, S. T., Wright, J., Charlifue, S. W., Graves, D. E., & Warner, P. (1999). Follow-up study of individuals with high tetraplegia (C1–C4) 14 to 24 years postinjury. *Archives of Physical Medicine and Rehabilitation, 80*, 1507–13.

3. Predicted well-being on the part of emergency care providers. Gerhart, K. A., Koziel-McLain, J., Lowenstein, S. R., & Whiteneck, G. G. (1994). Quality of life following spinal cord injury: Knowledge and attitudes of emergency care providers. *Annals of Emergency Medicine, 23*, 807–12.

4. Watching television and happiness. Kahneman, D., Krueger, A. B., Schkade, D. A., Schwarz, N., & Stone, A. A. (2004). A survey method for characterizing daily life experience: The day reconstruction method. *Science, 306*, 1776–1780. Killingsworth, M. A., & Gilbert, D. T. (2010). A wandering mind is an unhappy mind. *Science, 330*, 932.

5. Parenthood. Eibach, R. P., & Mock, S. E. (2011). Idealizing parenthood to rationalize parental investments. *Psychological Science, 22*, 203–08. Jones, R. K., & Brayfield, A. (1997). Life's greatest joy? European attitudes toward the centrality of children. *Social Forces, 75*, 1239–70.

6. Happier in California? Schkade, D., & Kahneman, D. (1998). Does living in California make people happy? A focusing illusion in judgments of life satisfaction. *Psychological Science, 9*, 340–46.

7. Money and happiness. Aknin, L. B., Norton, M. I., & Dunn, E. W. (2009). From wealth to well-being? Money matters, but less than people think. *Journal of Positive Psychology, 4*, 523–27. Cone, J., & Gilovich, T. (2010). Understanding money's limits: People's beliefs about the income–happiness correlation. *Journal of Positive Psychology, 5*, 294–301; Stevenson, B., & Wolfers, J. (2008). *Economic growth and subjective well-being: Reassessing the Easterlin paradox* (No. w14282). Cambridge, MA: National Bureau of Economic Research.

8. Lottery winners and happiness. Brickman, P., Coates, D., & Janoff-Bulman, R. (1978). Lottery winners and accident victims—is happiness relative? *Journal of Personality and Social Psychology, 36*, 917–27. Gardner, J., & Oswald, A. J. (2007). Money and mental well-being: A longitudinal study of medium-sized lottery wins. *Journal of Health Economics, 26*, 49–60.

9. Mencken quote. Mencken, H. L. (n.d.). BrainyQuote.com. Retrieved from http://www.brainyquote.com/quotes/quotes/h/hlmencke161801.html.

10. Social connection and happiness. Diener, E., & Seligman, M. E. P. (2004). Beyond money: Toward an economy of well-being. *Psychological Science in the Public Interest, 5*, 1–31. Dunn, E. W., Biesanz, J. C., Human, L. J., & Finn, S. (2007). Misunderstanding the affective consequences of everyday social interactions: The hidden benefits of putting one's best face forward. *Journal of Personality and Social Psychology, 92*, 990–1005. Fowler, J. H., &

Christakis, N. A. (2008). Dynamic spread of happiness in a large social network: Longitudinal analysis over 20 years in the Framingham Heart Study. *British Medical Journal, 337,* 1–9. Mogilner, C. (2010). The pursuit of happiness time, money, and social connection. *Psychological Science, 21,* 1348–54. House, J. S., Landis, K. R., & Umberson, D. (1988). Social relationships and health. *Science, 241*(4865), 540–45.

11. Giving to others and happiness. Aknin, L. B., Barrington-Leigh, C. P., Dunn, E. W., et al. (2013). Prosocial spending and well-being: Cross-cultural evidence for a psychological universal. *Journal of Personality and Social Psychology, 104,* 635–52. Dunn, E. W., Aknin, L. B., & Norton, M. I. (2009). Spending money on others promotes happiness. *Science, 319,* 1687–88. Lyubomirsky, S., Sheldon, K. M., & Schkade, D. (2005). Pursuing happiness: The architecture of sustainable change. *Review of General Psychology, 9,* 111–31. Myers, D. G., & Diener, E. (1995). Who is happy? *Psychological Science, 6,* 10–19.

12. Happiness and post-decision dissonance reduction. Lyubomirsky, S., & Ross, L. (1999). Changes in attractiveness of elected, rejected, and precluded alternatives: A comparison of happy and unhappy individuals. *Journal of Personality and Social Psychology, 76,* 988–1007.

13. Happiness and social comparison. Lyubomirsky, S., & Ross, L. (1997). Hedonic consequences of social comparison. A contrast of happy and unhappy people. *Journal of Personality and Social Psychology, 73,* 1141–57.

14. Happiness and reflecting on the past. Liberman, V., Boehm, J. K., Lyubomirsky, S., & Ross, L. (2009). Happiness and memory: Affective significance of endowment and contrast. *Emotion, 9,* 666–80.

15. Happiness trade books. Ed Diener's *Happiness: Unlocking the Mysteries of Psychological Wealth,* Dan Gilbert's *Stumbling on Happiness,* Jon Haidt's *The Happiness Hypothesis,* Sonja Lyubormirsky's *The How of Happiness,* and David Myers's *The Pursuit of Happiness* all have much to offer. So too do more journalistic accounts, such as Eric Weiner's *The Geography of Bliss* and Charles Montgomery's *Happy City.*

16. Peak-end rule. Fredrickson, B. L., & Kahneman, D. (1993). Duration neglect in retrospective evaluations of affective episodes. *Journal of Personality and Social Psychology, 65,* 45–55. Kahneman, D., Fredrickson, D. L., Schreiber, C. A., & Redelemeier, D. A. (1993). When more pain is preferred to less: Adding a better end. *Psychological Science, 4,* 401–05.

17. Colonoscopy. Redelmeier, D. A., & Kahneman, D. (1996). Patients' memories of painful medical treatments: Real-time and retrospective evaluations of two minimally invasive procedures. *Pain, 66,* 3–8.

18. Satisfaction with material vs. experiential purchases. Gilovich, T., & Kumar, A. (2015). We'll always have Paris: The hedonic payoff from experien-

tial and material investments. In M. P. Zanna & J. M. Olson (eds.), *Advances in experimental social psychology* (Vol. 51, pp. 147–87). Orlando, FL: Academic Press. Van Boven, L., & Gilovich, T. (2003). To do or to have: That is the question. *Journal of Personality and Social Psychology, 85,* 1193–1202.

19. Differential adaptation to material/experiential purchases. Carter, T. J., & Gilovich, T. (2010). The relative relativity of experiential and material purchases. *Journal of Personality and Social Psychology, 98,* 146–59. Mitchell, T. R., Thompson, L., Peterson, E., & Cronk, R. (1997). Temporal adjustments in the evaluation of events: The "rosy view." *Journal of Experimental Social Psychology, 33,* 421–88. Nicolao, L. Irwin, J. R., & Goodman, J. K. (2009). Happiness for sale: Do experiential purchases make consumers happier than material purchases? *Journal of Consumer Research, 36(2),* 188–98. Sutton, R. I. (1992). Feelings about a Disneyland visit: Photographs and reconstruction of bygone emotions. *Journal of Management Inquiry, 1,* 278–87.

20. Considering the same item in material or experiential terms. Carter & Gilovich. (2010). Rosenzweig, E., & Gilovich, T. (2012). Buyer's remorse or missed opportunity? Differential regrets for material and experiential purchases. *Journal of Personality and Social Psychology, 102,* 215–23.

21. Social comparison with material and experiential purchases. Carter & Gilovich. (2010).

22. Hedonic treadmill. Brickman, P., & Campbell, D. (1971). Hedonic relativism and planning the good society. In M. H. Appley (ed.), *Adaptation-level Theory: A Symposium* (pp. 287–302). New York: Academic Press.

23. No change in happiness over time. Easterlin, R. A. (1974). Does economic growth improve the human lot? Some empirical evidence. *Nations and Households in Economic Growth, 89,* 89–125. Easterlin, R. A., McVey, L. A., Switek, M., Sawangfa, O., & Zweig, J. S. (2010). The happiness–income paradox revisited. *Proceedings of the National Academy of Sciences, 107(52),* 22463–68.

24. Story telling. Kumar, A., & Gilovich, T. (in press). Some "thing" to talk about? Differential story utility from experiential and material purchases. *Personality and Social Psychology Bulletin.* Van Boven, L., Campbell, M. C., & Gilovich, T. (2010). The social costs of materialism: On people's assessments of materialistic and experiential consumers. *Personality and Social Psychology Bulletin, 36,* 551–63.

25. Identity from material and experiential purchases. Carter, T., & Gilovich, T. (2012). I am what I do, not what I have: The differential centrality of experiential and material purchases to the self. *Journal of Personality and Social Psychology, 102,* 1304–17.

26. Regrets. Gilovich, T., & Medvec, V. H. (1995). The experience of regret: What, when, and why. *Psychological Review, 102,* 379–395. Gilovich, T., Medvec, V. H., & Kahneman, D. (1998). Varieties of regret: A debate and

partial resolution. *Psychological Review, 105,* 602–5. Gilovich, T., Wang, R. F., Regan, D., & Nishina, S. (2003). Regrets of action and inaction across cultures. *Journal of Cross-Cultural Psychology, 34,* 61–71.

27. Henry James on regret. Henry James. (n.d.). BrainyQuote.com. Retrieved June 21, 2015, from BrainyQuote.com website: http://www.brainyquote .com/quotes/quotes/h/henryjames109178.html. Read more at http://www .brainyquote.com/citation/quotes/quotes/h/henryjames109178.html #DBlWgWk4PxOZQ65w.99.

28. Lykken quote. Lykken, D. T. The heritability of happiness. *Harvard Mental Health Letter* (no date). Downloadable from www.psych.umn.edu/psylabs /happiness/hapindex.htm.

29. Flow. Csikszentmihalyi, M. (1990). *Flow: The psychology of optimal experience.* New York: Harper.

30. Correlation between television viewing and well-being. Frey, B. S., Benesch, C., & Stutzer, A. (2007). Does watching TV make us happy? *Journal of Economic Psychology, 28,* 283–313.

31. Self-esteem and participation in sports. Jackson, S. A., & Marsh, H. W. (1986). Athletic or antisocial? The female sport experience. *Journal of Sport Psychology, 8,* 198–211. Waldron, J. J. (2009). Development of life skills and involvement in the Girls on Track program. *Women in Sport and Physical Activity Journal, 18,* 60–74. Yiğiter, K. (2013). Improving the university students' locus of control and self-esteem by participating in team sports program. *European Journal of Scientific Research, 107,* 64–70.

32. Edelman quote. Edelman, S. (2013). *The happiness of pursuit.* New York: Basic Books.

33. "Things won are done." *Troilus and Cressida,* Act I, Scene iii.

34. Cross-cultural differences. Tsai, J. L. (2007). Ideal affect: Cultural causes and behavioral consequences. *Perspectives on Psychological Science, 2,* 242–59. Tsai, J. L., Knutson, B., & Fung, H. H. (2006). Cultural variation in affect valuation. *Journal of Personality and Social Psychology, 90,* 288–307.

35. Age and happiness. Argyle, M. (1999). Causes and correlates of happiness. In D. Kahneman, E. Diener, & N. Schwarz (eds.), *Well-being: The foundations of hedonic psychology* (pp. 353–373). New York Russell Sage Foundation. Clark, A. E., & Oswald, A. J. (2006). *The curved relationship between subjective well-being and age* (Paris: PSE Working Paper 2006–29). Easterlin, R. A. (2006). Life cycle happiness and its sources: Intersections of psychology, economics and demography. *Journal of Economic Psychology, 27,* 463–82.

36. Different types of happiness for young and old. Mogilner, C., Kamvar, S. D., & Aaker, J. (2011). The shifting meaning of happiness. *Social Psychological and Personality Science, 2,* 395–402.

37. Spending money on others. Dunn, E. W., Aknin, L. B., & Norton, M. I.

(2009). Spending money on others promotes happiness. *Science, 319,* 1687–88. Aknin, L. B., Barrington-Leigh, C. P., Dunn, E. W., Helliwell, J. F., Burns, J., Biswas-Diener, R., . . . Norton, MI. (2013). Prosocial spending and well-being: Cross-cultural evidence for a psychological universal. *Journal of Personality and Social Psychology, 104,* 635–52.

38. John Wooden on doing for others. Tentmaker: John Wooden quotes. http://www.tentmaker.org/Quotes/john_r_wooden_quotes.html.

39. Preferred wealth distribution in the U.S. Norton, M. I., & Ariely, D. (2011). Building a better America—one wealth quintile at a time. *Perspectives on Psychological Science, 6,* 9–12.

40. County-by-county effects of income inequality. Frank, R. H., Levine, A. S., & Dijk, O. (2014). Expenditure cascades. *Review of Behavioral Economics, 1,* 55–73.

41. Commuting and happiness. St-Louis, E., Manaugh, K., van Lierop, D., & El-Geneidy, A. (2013). The happy commuter: A comparison of commuter satisfaction across modes. *Transportation Research Part F: Traffic Psychology and Behavior, 26,* 160–70.

42. Income inequality and homicide. Daly, M., Wilson, M., & Vasdev, S. (2001). Income inequality and homicide rates in Canada and the United States. *Canadian Journal of Criminology, 43,* 219–36.

43. Economic policies adapted to the modern global economy. Frank, R. H. (1999). *Luxury fever.* New York: Free Press. Frank, R. H., & Cook, P. J. (1995). *The winner-take-all society: Why the few at the top get so much more than the rest of us.* New York: Free Press.

7: Why We Don't "Just Get Along"

1. Efficient agreements and exchanges of concessions. Homans, G. (1961). *Social behaviour: Its elementary forms.* London: Routledge and Kegan Paul. Fisher, R., Ury, W., & Patton, B. (1991). *Getting to yes: Negotiating agreement without giving in* (2d ed.). Boston: Houghton Mifflin.

2. Barriers to agreement. Mnookin, R., & Ross, L. (1995). Strategic, psychological, and institutional barriers: An introduction. In K. Arrow, R. Mnookin, L. Ross, A. Tversky, & R. Wilson (eds.), *Barriers to conflict resolution.* New York: Norton.

3. Actors and observers. Jones, E. E., & Nisbett, R. E. (1972). The actor and the observer: Divergent perceptions of the causes of the behavior. In E. E. Jones, D. E. Kanouse, H. H. Kelley, R. E. Nisbett, S. Valins, & B. Weiner (eds.), *Attribution: Perceiving the causes of behavior* (pp. 79-94). Morristown, NJ: General Learning Press.

4. Sadat quotation. Cited in Sanders, H. S. (1999). *A public peace process: Sustained dialogue to transform racial and ethnic conflicts.* New York: St. Martin's Press.

5. SCICN. Arrow, K., Mnookin, R., Ross, L., Tversky, A., &. Wilson, R. (1995), *Barriers to conflict resolution.* New York: Norton.

6. Moataz Abdel-Fattah quote. (2012, December 22). As charter nears passage, Egyptians face new fights. *New York Times*, http://www.nytimes. com/2012/12/23/world/middleeast/egyptian-vote-on-constitution-sets -up-new-stage-of-factions-struggle.html.

7. Stanford divestment Study. Ross, L. (1995). The reactive devaluation barrier to dispute resolution. In K. Arrow, R. Mnookin, L. Ross, A. Tversky, & R. Wilson (eds.), *Barriers to conflict resolution*. New York: Norton.

8. Israeli-Palestinian study. Maoz, I., Ward. A., Katz, M., & Ross, L. (2002). Reactive devaluation of an "Israeli" vs. a "Palestinian" peace proposal. *Journal of Conflict Resolution, 46*, 515–46.

9. Reactions to potential losses and gains. Tversky, A., & Kahneman, D. (1995). Conflict resolution: A cognitive perspective. In K. Arrow, R. Mnookin, L. Ross, A. Tversky, & R. Wilson (eds.), *Barriers to conflict resolution* (pp. 44–61). New York: Norton.

10. Acknowledging the other side's priorities. Ward, A., Disston, L. G., Brenner, L., & Ross, L. (2008, July). Acknowledging the other side in negotiation. *Negotiation Journal, 24*, 269–85.

11. Procedural justice. Lind, E. A., & Tyler, T. (1988). *The social psychology of procedural justice*. New York: Springer. Lind, E. A., Kanfer, R., & Earley, P. C. (1990). Voice, control, and procedural justice: Instrumental and noninstrumental concerns in fairness judgment. *Journal of Personality and Social Psychology, 59*, 952–59.

12. Knowing that a deal may be struck. Liberman, V. Andersen, N., & Ross, L. (2010). Achieving difficult agreements: Effects of positive versus neutral expectations on negotiation processes and outcomes. *Journal of Experimental and Social Psychology, 46*, 494–504.

13. Fuller discussion of real world lessons. Ross, L. (2012). Perspectives on disagreement and dispute resolution: Lessons from the lab and the real world. In E. Shafir (ed.), *The behavioral foundations of public policy*. Princeton, NJ: Princeton University and Russell Sage Foundation Press.

14. Mandela and the promise of a shared future. Mandela, N. (1995). *Long walk to freedom*. Boston, MA: Little, Brown & Company. Sampson, A. (1999). *Mandela: The authorized biography*. London: HarperCollins.

15. Discussion of freezing and unfreezing to produce social change. Lewin, K. (1947). Group decisions and social change. In T. M. Newcomb & E. L. Hartley (eds.), *Readings in social psychology*. New York: Holt.

8: A Tough Problem for America

1. Lemaitre. Our account of Christophe Lemaitre, including our quotes, comes from Demirel, E. (2012, August 9). Lemaitre: Why it matters the fastest white man on earth is, well, white. *Bleacher Report*.

2. Racial differences in athletic performance. Johnson, B. (2000). *Why black athletes dominate sports and why we're afraid to talk about it.* New York: Perseus.

3. Baylor's track coach (Clyde Hart). (2004, December 6). *Sports Illustrated.*

4. Basketball study. Stone, J., Peny, Z. W., & Darley, J. M. (1997). "White men can't jump": Evidence for the perceptual confirmation of racial stereotypes following a basketball game. *Basic and Applied Social Psychology, 19,* 291–306.

5. Golf putting study. Stone, J., Lynch, C. I., Sjomeling, M., & Darley, J. M. (1999). Stereotype threat effects on black and white athletic performance. *Journal of Personality and Social Psychology, 77*(6), 1213–27.

6. Self-fulfilling prophesies. Merton, R. K. (1948). The self-fulfilling prophecy. *Antioch Review, 8,* 193–210.

7. Self-fulfilling prophecies in the classroom. Rosenthal, R., & Jacobson, L. (1966). Teachers' expectancies: Determinants of pupils' IQ gains. *Psychological Reports, 19,* 115–18. Rosenthal, R., & Jacobson, L. (1968). *Pygmalion in the classroom: Teacher expectations and student intellectual development.* New York: Holt.

8. Replicability of Rosenthal and Jacobson. Harris, M. J., & Rosenthal, R. (1985). Mediation of interpersonal expectancy effects: 31 meta-analyses. *Psychological Bulletin, 97,* 363–86. Jussim, L., Robustelli, S., & Cain, T. (2009). Teacher expectations and self-fulfilling prophecies. In A. Wigfield & K. Wentzel (eds.), *Handbook of motivation at school* (pp. 349–80). Mahwah, NJ: Erlbaum. Rosenthal, R. (1987). "Pygmalion" effects: Existence, magnitude, and social importance. *Educational Researcher, 16*(9), 37–41. Snow, R. E. (1995). Pygmalion and intelligence? *Current Directions in Psychological Science, 4,* 169–71.

9. Effect of training students to attribute success to effort and persistence. Dweck, C. S., & Repucci, N. D. (1973). Learned helplessness and reinforcement responsibility in children. *Journal of Personality and Social Psychology, 25,* 109–16.

10. Mind-sets. Dweck, C. S. (2006). *Mindset: The new psychology of success.* New York: Ballantine Books.

11. Mind-set studies. Blackwell, L., Trzesniewski, K., & Dweck, C. S. (2007). Implicit theories of intelligence predict achievement across an adolescent transition: A longitudinal study and intervention. *Child Development, 78,* 246–63.

12. Intervention in 13 high schools. Paunesku, D., Walton, G. M., Smith, E. N., Romero, C. L., Yeager, D. S., & Dweck, C. S. (in press). Mindset interventions are a scalable treatment for academic underachievement, *Psychological Science.*

13. Stereotype threat. Steele, C. M. (1995). A threat in the air: How stereotypes shape intellectual identity and performance. *American Psychologist, 52,* 613–29.

14. Self-handicapping. Jones, E. E., & Berglas, S. (1978). Control of attributions about the self through self-handicapping strategies: The appeal of alcohol and the role of underachievement. *Personality and Social Psychology Bulletin,* 4, 200–06. Deppe, R. K., & Harackiewicz, J. M. (1996). Self-handicapping and intrinsic motivation: Buffering intrinsic motivation from the threat of failure. *Journal of Personality and Social Psychology, 70,* 868–76.

15. Stereotype threat among African American students. Steele, C. M., & Aronson, J. (1995). Stereotype threat and the intellectual test performance of African Americans. *Journal of Personality and Social Psychology, 69,* 797–811.

16. Additional evidence of stereotype threat. Steele, C. M., Spencer, S. J., & Aronson, J. (2002). Contending with group image: The psychology of stereotype and social identity threat. In M. P. Zanna (ed.), *Advances in experimental social psychology* (Vol. 34, pp. 379–440). San Diego, CA: Academic Press. Schmader, T., Johns, M., & Forbes, C. (2008). An integrated process model of stereotype threat effects on performance. *Psychological Review, 115,* 336–56.

17. Stereotype threat for women in math. Spencer, S. J., Steele, C. M., & Quinn, D. M. (1999). Stereotype threat and women's math performance. *Journal of Experimental Social Psychology, 35,* 4–28. Maass, A., D'Ettole, C., & Cadinu, M. (2008). Checkmate? The role of gender stereotypes in the ultimate intellectual sport. *European Journal of Social Psychology, 38,* 231–45. Inzlicht, M., & Ben-Zeev, T. (2000). A threatening intellectual environment: Why females are susceptible to experiencing problem-solving deficits in the presence of males. *Psychological Science, 11,* 365–71.

18. KIPP benchmarks. College completion report. *PP Public Charter Schools, Knowledge Is Power Program.* KIPP: Knowledge Is Power Program. Retrieved from http://www.kipp.org/results/college-completion-report.

19. Self-affirmation. Cohen, G. L., & Sherman, D. K. (2014). The psychology of change: Self-affirmation and social psychological interventions. *Annual Review of Psychology, 65,* 331–71.

20. Seminal self affirmation study by Cohen et al. Cohen, G. L., Garcia, J., Apfel, N., & Master, A. (2006). Reducing the racial achievement gap: A social-psychological intervention. *Science, 313,* 1307–10.

21. The theory behind self-affirmation manipulations. Cohen, G. L., & Sherman, D. K. (2014). The psychology of change: Self-affirmation and social psychological interventions. *Annual Review of Psychology, 65,* 331–7.

22. Impressive effects self-affirmation intervention. Cohen, G. L., Garcia, J., Purdie-Vaugns, V., Apfel, N., & Brzustoski, P. (2009). Recursive processes in self-affirmation: Intervening to close the minority achievement gap. *Science,* 324, 400–403.

23. Mentor's dilemma. Yeager, D. S., Purdie-Vaughns, V., Garcia, J., Apfel, N., Brzustoski, P., Master, A., . . . Cohen, G. L. (2014). Breaking the cycle of

mistrust: Wise interventions to provide critical feedback across the racial divide. *Journal of Experimental Psychology: General, 143,* 804–24. See also an earlier study showing similar effects of wise feedback on minority students at Stanford University by Cohen, G. L., Steele, C. M., & Ross, L. (1999). The mentor's dilemma: Providing critical feedback across the racial divide. *Personality and Social Psychology Bulletin, 25,* 1302–18.

24. Michelle Obama quote. Michelle Obama. (n.d.). BrainyQuote.com. Retrieved April 14, 2015, from BrainyQuote.com Web site: http://www.brainyquote.com/quotes/quotes/m/michelleob452284.html.

25. Sotomayor quote. Warner, J. (2009). The outsiders are in. *New York Times,* May 28, 2009. http://opinionator.blogs.nytimes.com/2009/05/28/sotomayor/?_r=0.

26. Stealthy interventions. Yeager, D. S., & Walton, G. M. (2011). Social-psychological interventions in education: They're not magic. *Review of Educational Research, 81,* 267–301.

27. Evidence found again and again of improvements. Cohen, G. L., & Sherman, D. K. (2014). The psychology of change: Self-affirmation and social psychological intervention. *Annual Review of Psychology, 65,* 333–371. Garcia J., & Cohen G. L. (2012). A social psychological approach to educational intervention. In E. Shafir (ed.), *Behavioral Foundations of Policy* (pp. 329–350). Princeton, NJ: Princeton University Press.

28. Intervention with freshmen African American students. Walton, G. M., & Cohen, G. L. (2007). A question of belonging: Race, social fit, and achievement. *Journal of Personality and Social Psychology, 92,* 82–96.

29. Wise interventions to keep women in STEM fields. Walton, G. M., Logel, C., Peach, J. M., Spencer, S. J., & Zanna, M. P. (in press). Two brief interventions to mitigate a "chilly climate" transform women's experience, relationships, and achievement in engineering. *Journal of Educational Psychology.*

30. For a fuller discussion of these sorts of recursive processes: Yeager, D. S., & Walton, G. M. (2011). Social-psychological interventions in education: They're not magic. *Review of Educational Research, 81,* 267–301.

31. Like the changing the shape of an airplane wing. Yeager & Walton. (2011).

9: An Even Tougher Problem for the World

1. Customer re-use of hotel towels. Goldstein, N. J., Cialdini, R. B., & Griskevicius, V. (2008). A room with a viewpoint: Using social norms to motivate environmental conservation in hotels. *Journal of Consumer Research, 35,* 472–82.

2. Social proof and energy conservation. Cialdini, R., & Schultz, W. (2004). *Understanding and motivating energy conservation via social norms.* Project report prepared for the William and Flora Hewlett Foundation.

3. Learning you did better or worse than your neighbors. Schultz, P. W., Nolan, J., Cialdini, R., Goldstein, N., & Griskevicius, V. (2007). The constructive, destructive, and reconstructive power of social norms. *Psychological Science, 18*, 429–34.

4. Greene quote. Greene, J. (2013). *Moral tribes: Emotion, Reason, and the Gap Between Us and Them.* New York: Penguin.

5. Climate change evidence. United Nations World Meterological Organization (2013). The global climate 2001–2010: A decade of extremes. WMO-No. 1119. Retrieved from http://www.wmo.int/pages/index_en.html. Morales, A. (2013, July 13). UN charts "unprecedented" global warming since 2000. *Bloomberg News.* Retrieved from http://www.bloomberg.com/news/2013 -07-03/un-charts-unprecedented-global-warming-since-2000.html.

6. Efforts to confuse the climate change discussion. Brulle, R. J. (2013). Institutionalizing inaction: Foundation funding and the creation of U.S. climate change counter-movement organizations. Under review for publication in *Climatic Change.*

7. Belief in global warming. Pew Research Center October 2012 poll cited in Brulle. (2013).

8. Commons dilemmas. Axelrod, R. (1984). *The evolution of cooperation.* New York: Basic Books. Hardin, G. (1968). The tragedy of the commons. *Science, 162*, 1243–48.

9. Changes in reproduction rates. Frejka, T., & Tomas, S. (2008). Fertility in Europe: Diverse, delayed and below replacement. *Demographic Research, 19*, 15–46. Jones, G. (2007). Delayed marriage and very low fertility in Pacific Asia. *Population and Development Review, 33*, 453–78. La Ferrara, E., Chong, A., & Duryea, S. (2008). *Soap operas and fertility* (Research Department Publications 4573). Brazil Inter-American Development Bank. Office of the Registrar General and Census Commissioner. (2011). *Census 2011* (India), Ministry of Home Affairs I. Rele, J. R. (1987). Fertility levels and trends in India. *Population and Development Review, 19*, 513–30.

10. Tipping points. Gladwell, M. (2000). *The Tipping Point: How Little Things Can Make a Big Difference.* New York: Little, Brown.

Epilogue

1. Our account of Mandela's actions with respect to the Springboks draws heavily on Carlin, J. (2008). *Playing the Enemy: Nelson Mandela and the Game That Made a Nation.* New York: Penguin.

Index

Page numbers in *italics* refer to illustrations and tables.
An *n* following a page number refers to the notes section.

specific steps to achieve, 17, 18, 26,
28, 33, 36, 40–41, 45, 48, 50, 55–58,
62, 69–70, 79, 83, 99–100, 107, 109,
124–25, 127, 130, 136, 147–49,
155, 157, 159–64, 170, 173–74,
177, 184, 185, 187, 194, 230,
237–38, 243, 245, 253, 262, 270
three types of, 2–4
women:
academic gap and, 10, 225
in STEM fields, 225, 231, 232–33,
240–41

Wooden, John, 188
Woods, Tiger, 223
World Cup (rugby), 266–67
World War I, 50
World War II, 45–46, 74, 126–30, 141
"Would've Done the Same for Me," 21–22

Young, Robert, 65
youth, role in shifting norms, 262, 263

zero-sum negotiations, 199–200
Zupan, Mark, 165–66, 168–70

About the Authors

THOMAS GILOVICH is professor of psychology at Cornell University and codirector of the Cornell Center for Behavioral Economics and Decision Research. He is coauthor of *Social Psychology* and *Why Smart People Make Big Money Mistakes,* and author of *How We Know What Isn't So.*

LEE ROSS is professor of psychology at Stanford University and cofounder of the Stanford Center on Conflict and Negotiations. He is coauthor of *The Person and the Situation* and *Human Inference.*